Children and young people's worlds

Developing frameworks for integrated practice

This reader forms part of 'Children and young people's worlds: frameworks for integrated practice' (E807), a course belonging to The Open University Masters in Childhood and Youth.

The Open University Masters in Childhood and Youth

The Open University Masters in Childhood and Youth is a new, innovative interdisciplinary programme, which offers students the opportunity to explore aspects of both theory and practice, and the interplay between the two. It is aimed at practitioners from all disciplines, as well as researchers, and offers a range of critical perspectives on children's lives in the early 21st century. One of the defining features of the course is that it tackles both global and local issues and their impact on children's lives. Students are expected to undertake their own independent research and the range of topics that can be covered is very broad and all kinds of research, from ethnographic work in a classroom, to an extended literature review on a subject of the student's own choice, will be supported.

Details of this and other Open University courses can be obtained from the Student Registration and Enquiry Service,
The Open University, PO Box 197, Milton Keynes MK7 6BJ, United Kingdom.
Telephone: +44 (0) 845 300 6090.
Email: general-enquiries@open.ac.uk.

Alternatively, you may wish to visit the Open University website at http://www.open.ac.uk, where you can learn more about the wide range of courses and packs offered at all levels by The Open University.

Children and young people's worlds

Developing frameworks for integrated practice

Edited by Heather Montgomery and Mary Kellett

First published in 2009 by

The Policy Press • University of Bristol
Fourth Floor • Beacon House
Queen's Road • Bristol BS8 1QU, UK

Tel +44 (0)117 331 4054 • Fax +44 (0)117 331 4093
e-mail tpp-info@bristol.ac.uk • www.policypress.org.uk

North American office:
The Policy Press • c/o International Specialized Books Services (ISBS)
920 NE 58th Avenue, Suite 300 • Portland, OR 97213-3786, USA
Tel +1 503 287 3093 • Fax +1 503 280 8832
e-mail info@isbs.com

in association with

The Open University, Walton Hall, Milton Keynes, MK7 6AA, United Kingdom,
www.open.ac.uk

British Library Cataloguing in Publication data
A catalogue record for this book is available from the British Library

Library of Congress Cataloging-in-Publication Data
A catalog record for this book has been requested.

ISBN 978 1 84742 388 7 (hardback)
ISBN 978 1 84742 387 0 (paperback)

Typeset by The Policy Press
Cover design: Qube Associates, Bristol
Front cover: image kindly supplied by Paul Green
Printed and bound in Great Britain by TJ International, Padstow

Contents

Acknowledgements   vi

Notes on the contributors   vii

Introduction   1
Heather Montgomery and Mary Kellett

One   Children, young people and politics in the UK   7
           Nigel Thomas

Two   Children and international politics   23
           Karen Wells

Three   Children and young people's participation   43
           Mary Kellett

Four   Children, young people and their families in the UK   61
           Virginia Morrow

Five   Children and families in an international context   77
           Heather Montgomery

Six   Race, ethnicity and young people   91
           Anoop Nayak

Seven   International children's rights   109
           Afua Twum-Danso

Eight   Children, young people and the law   127
           Julia Fionda

Nine   Child protection   145
           Judith Masson

Ten   Children, young people and poverty   165
           Heather Montgomery

Eleven   Children and consumer culture   181
           David Buckingham and Sara Bragg

Twelve   Youth, religion and multiculture   199
           Anoop Nayak

Thirteen   Children, young people and sexuality   219
           Mary Jane Kehily

Fourteen   Children and young people's voice   237
           Mary Kellett

Index   253

Acknowledgements

This book was produced for the Open University course 'Children and young people's worlds: frameworks for integrated practice' (E807), which is part of the Masters course in Childhood and Youth. As is always the case with Open University books, many people contributed to its production and the collaborative nature of the book needs to be acknowledged. Not only are we appreciative of our contributors, all of whom provided their chapters promptly and were extremely patient with our editorial changes, but we would also like to thank those who put in a great deal of work and effort behind the scenes.

Janet Collins, Lesley Gallacher and John Oates were all members of the course team and contributed critical feedback and support while Maria Francis-Pitfield and Denise Raley, as course managers, ensured the smooth and efficient running of the course. Gill Gowans and Gary Nelmes were instrumental in this book's production and Emma Smith provided a great deal of editorial help in shaping the manuscript. We are indebted to them all.

Our external assessor, Phil Jones, read through many outlines and drafts and provided excellent feedback on them all, as did our critical readers and developmental testers, Grace Clifton, Rose Drury, Jim McKechnie and Rachel Thomson. All made important critical contributions and provided us with excellent, constructive feedback and we are very grateful to them for their time, effort and enthusiasm for the project.

Finally, we would like to thank the team at The Policy Press, in particular Karen Bowler and Kathryn King, for all their help.

Notes on the contributors

Sara Bragg is Academic Fellow in Child and Youth Studies at The Open University, UK. She has worked at the University of Sussex and at the Centre for the Study of Children, Youth and Media at the Institute of Education, London. Her research interests include young people as media audiences; media education; creative research methods; young people's participation rights in schools. Publications include *Young People, Sex and the Media: The Facts of Life?* (Palgrave Macmillan, 2004) with David Buckingham.

David Buckingham is Professor of Education at the Institute of Education, University of London, UK, where he directs the Centre for the Study of Children, Youth and Media. He is also Visiting Professor at the Norwegian Centre for Child Research, NTNU Trondheim. He has directed several major research projects on young people's relationships with the media and on media education. He is also currently leading an independent assessment of 'the impact of the commercial world on children's well-being' for two UK government departments. He is the author of numerous books, including *Children Talking Television* (Routledge, 1993), *Moving Images* (Manchester University Press, 1996), *After the Death of Childhood* (Polity Press, 2000), *The Making of Citizens* (Routledge, 2000), *Media Education: Literacy, Learning and Popular Culture* (Polity Press, 2003) and *Beyond Technology: Children's Learning in the Age of Digital Culture* (Polity Press, 2007).

Julia Fionda is a Senior Lecturer in Law and Director of the Institute of Criminal Justice at Southampton University, UK. Her teaching and research interests lie in criminal justice, youth justice and criminal law and her publications include *Public Prosecutors and Discretion: A Comparative Study* (Oxford University Press, 1995), *Legal Concepts of Childhood* (Hart Publishing, 2001) and *Devils and Angels: Youth, Policy and Crime* (Hart Publishing, 2005).

Mary Jane Kehily is Senior Lecturer in Childhood and Youth Studies at The Open University, UK. She has research interests in gender and sexuality, narrative and identity and popular culture and has published widely on these themes. Her books include *Sexuality, Gender and Schooling: Shifting Agendas in Social Learning* (Routledge, 2002) and, with Anoop Nayak, *Gender, Youth and Culture: Young Masculinities and Femininities* (Palgrave Macmillan, 2008).

Mary Kellett is Professor of Childhood and Youth, and Director of the Childhood and Youth Studies programme at The Open University, UK. Her main research interests are the empowerment of children and young people as researchers, disabilities, rights, participation and voice. She is the Founding Director of the Children's Research Centre, which facilitates and supports research *by* children and young people. Her book *How to Develop Children as Researchers* (Paul Chapman, 2005) has inspired several international projects and been culturally adapted into Greek and Arabic versions. She was an editor of the twin readers *The Reality of Research with Children and Young People* and *Doing Research with Children and Young People* (Sage Publications, 2003). More recent publications include *Rethinking Children and Research* (Continuum, 2009) and *Children's Integrated Services: Every Child Matters and Beyond* (Palgrave Macmillan, forthcoming).

Judith Masson is Professor of Socio-Legal Studies at Bristol University, UK, specialising in child law and socio-legal research. She has undertaken numerous studies on the application of child law, including a study of stepparent adoption – *Yours, Mine or Ours* (HMSO, 1983); representation of children in care proceedings – *Out of Hearing* (Wiley, 1999); the possibilities for and barriers to social work with parents of children looked after long term – *Lost and Found* (Ashgate, 1999); and emergency intervention in child protection – *Protecting Powers* (Wiley, 2007). In 2007–08, she co-directed a project examining 400 child protection cases that resulted in applications in care proceedings – *Care Profiling Study* (Ministry of Justice, 2008). She is co-author of *Cretney's Principles of Family Law* (Sweet and Maxwell, 8th edition, 2008), a leading text on family law, and is a member of the Family Justice Council.

Heather Montgomery is Senior Lecturer in Childhood and Youth Studies at The Open University, UK. Her research interests are in the anthropology of childhood, children's rights and gender and sexuality. She is the author of *Modern Babylon: Prostituting Children in Thailand* (Berghahn, 2001) and *An Introduction to Childhood: Anthropological Perspectives on Children's Lives* (Wiley-Blackwell, 2008).

Virginia Morrow is Reader in Childhood Studies at the Institute of Education, University of London, UK, where she is Course Leader of the Masters in the Sociology of Childhood and Children's Rights. Her main research interests are methods and ethics of social research with children; sociology of childhood and children's rights; social capital in relation to children and young people; child labour and children's work; and children's understandings of family and other social environments. She is an editor of *Childhood: A Global Journal of Child Research*. She is also the author of numerous papers and reports, including *Understanding Families: Children's Perspectives* (NCB/JRF, 1998).

Anoop Nayak is Reader in Social and Cultural Geography at Newcastle University, UK. His research interests are in the fields of race, migration and asylum; youth cultural studies; masculinities, education and labour; whiteness, nationalism and new theories of social class. He is author of the monograph *Race, Place and Globalization: Youth Cultures in a Changing World* (Berg, 2003) and has recently published a book with Mary Jane Kehily entitled *Gender, Youth and Culture: Young Masculinities and Femininities* (Palgrave Macmillan, 2008).

Nigel Thomas is Professor of Childhood and Youth Research at the University of Central Lancashire, UK, and Co-Director of The Centre for Childhood and Youth Research, which promotes and researches children and young people's participation, inclusion and empowerment. He is the author of *Children, Family and the State: Decision-Making and Child Participation* (The Policy Press, 2002) and *Social Work with Young People in Care* (Palgrave Macmillan, 2005). He is joint editor of *An Introduction to Early Childhood Studies* (Sage Publications, 2004 and 2009), *Children, Politics and Communication* (The Policy Press, 2009) and *A Handbook of Children's Participation* (Routledge, forthcoming). He is also co-editor of the journal *Children & Society* and an editorial board member of the *British Journal of Social Work*, the *International Journal of Children's Rights* and *Childhoods Today*.

Afua Twum-Danso is Lecturer in the Sociology of Childhood at the University of Sheffield, UK. Her recently completed PhD thesis from the University of Birmingham is entitled 'Searching for a middle ground in children's rights: the implementation of the Convention on the Rights of the Child in Ghana'. Her research interests relate to the universality and relativity of children's rights and how these engage with children's local realities. Her other publications include 'A cultural bridge, not an imposition: legitimising children's rights in the eyes of local communities', in the *Journal for the History of Childhood and Youth*, vol 1, no 3, 2008; 'The political child', in Angela McIntyre (ed) *Invisible Stakeholders: The Impact of Children on War* (The Institute of Security Studies, 2004); and *Africa's Young Soldiers: The Co-option of Childhood* (The Institute of Security Studies, 2003).

Karen Wells is Programme Director of International Childhood Studies at Birkbeck College, University of London, UK, where she teaches on the political economy of childhood and material and visual cultures of development. She is the author of *Childhood in a Global Perspective* (Polity Press, 2009). Her research interests are in the impact of globalisation on childhood and the material and visual cultures of childhood with a particular interest in 'race'. She has published widely on these issues including in the *Journal of Visual Communication, Visual Studies* and the *Journal of Children and Media*. She is currently researching the social networks of young refugees in London.

Introduction

Heather Montgomery and Mary Kellett

The worlds of children and young people are more visible than ever. The first decade of the 21st century has seen unprecedented levels of interest, anxiety and governance in their lives. From education to health, law to academia, every aspect of children and young people's experiences has been analysed. There is a strong impetus to change policy and practice to ensure that all children reach their potential and fulfil their role as future citizens. This book puts these concerns into context by looking at ways that new frameworks can be developed for studying and understanding the lives of children and young people; frameworks created by academic theory, international legislation, government policy, local practice and, most importantly, children and young people themselves. It is concerned with dialogue and integration: between different academic disciplines, between individuals and agencies, between the local and the global and between theory and practice.

The overarching framework for anyone working with, or having an interest in, children and young people, is that of children's rights. Although children's rights were first formally codified internationally in 1924, the 1989 United Nations Convention on the Rights of the Child (referred to throughout this book as UNCRC; UN, 1989) represents a watershed in international and national policy on children. In signing the Convention, governments agreed to guarantee the rights of children and young people and to bring its provisions into their own national laws through ratification. Furthermore, they agreed to hold themselves accountable in international law for the ways in which children are treated.

The universal ratification of the UNCRC was never intended as an end in itself and, in the decades following its adoption, the focus has shifted from persuading nation states to sign up to ensuring that the rights it enshrines are properly integrated, not just into local statutes but also into the very fabric of society. It is here that policy makers and practitioners, whether they are law makers, civil servants, teachers, health and social care professionals, prison officers or academics, come to the fore. It is through their practice and in their interface with children and young people that the realities of children's rights are realised. It is in these interactions that we become aware of the complexities and challenges of a rights-based approach.

The UNCRC, despite its limitations, remains the blueprint and overall standard to which all governments aspire. The idea that children have rights to protection and provision and that the 'best interests of the child' should always be paramount are universally accepted in theory, if not always enforced in practice. Whatever the failings and obstacles, it is clear that policy makers and practitioners are attempting to integrate children's rights into their work. In the UK, there is a new willingness to respect children's rights, evidenced in the legislation finally announced on Armistice Day 2008 – after a decade of campaigning – to place a duty on all maintained schools in England and Wales to consider the views of children and young people. The notion that adults always know best is slowly being eroded and children's own agency recognised and supported. Nevertheless, some rights have been implemented more enthusiastically than others and children's right to participation continues to be problematic. Successive reports of the UNCRC have criticised the UK government for its failure to implement many of its promises.

Even the most cursory glance at UNICEF's compilation of statistics on global childhoods, *The State of the World's Children* (UNICEF, 2008), shows a gap between rhetoric and reality. Up to three quarters of the world's children exist without adequate food, clothing, shelter or education, so there is no room for complacency. In the UK, integrated practice has been identified as a key driver in the improvement of children's services and the transformation of their lives. Tragic cases such as Maria Colwell, Victoria Climbié and Baby 'P' document the catastrophic outcomes when interagency working breaks down and deficiencies in knowledge are exposed. The aim of this book is for theory to inform quality, integrated practice and vice versa. *Every Child Matters* and the subsequent *Children's Plan* are central tenets in the implementation of joined-up children's services and feature significantly in many of the chapters.

This book underlines the principle of integrated practice as a holistic approach where children and young people are not simply seen as having a series of needs – to education, protection, healthcare and so on but also in need of as good a childhood as is possible. Too often, policies for children focus on long-term outcomes; much more rarely are policies put in place that benefit children immediately and improve their lives in the present.

Such a vision involves a shift in perspective to acknowledge children as stakeholders in their lives who must be consulted about decisions made about them. It also means recognising the ways in which children and young people negotiate their own experiences and meanings. Issues such as multiculturalism, religion or sexuality can be theorised on many levels, legislated for and initiatives drawn up, but young people themselves, away from the gaze of the authorities, may have different views and different ways of integrating these issues into their daily lives and worldviews. Even supposedly straightforward questions to children about family relationships may reveal very different meanings for adults and children and very different ways of understanding the world.

The chapters

The chapters in this book draw on different disciplinary perspectives and there is not, nor is there designed to be, a consistent authorial voice throughout the reader. Academics working in the fields of education, cultural studies, sociology, anthropology and the law draw on different bodies of knowledge and theories and the volume is designed to introduce readers to the complexity of the debates and the ways in which different professionals tackle the same problems from very different perspectives, bringing new insights, but also sometimes difficult challenges, to established working practices. The key point is that there are multiple practices and multiple frameworks and integrating them is never easy. The chapters therefore provide debate and controversy rather than offering simple solutions. Different authors in the book use the terms 'children' and 'young people' in different ways. The terms are, of course, highly contested and this is reflected in the ways they are discussed. A child, in international legalisation, is anyone under the age of 18, and yet this is culturally specific and does not always take into account the different stages and levels of responsibility that young people begin to take on as they make the transition to adulthood. It also fails to acknowledge the especial vulnerability of some young people as they pass their cut-off birthday of 18. Young people leaving care, for example, may technically be adults at 18 but still need longer-term care and protection. Their vulnerabilities have to be recognised and acknowledged. Throughout this book, therefore, there is no formal definition of 'childhood' or the term 'young people'. In some cases, the word 'childhood' is used for brevity when discussing all young people under the age of 18, while in others it is used to refer only to younger children. This is made clear in the context of the chapters.

The importance of an integrated approach to children and young people is one that is stressed throughout this book, particularly in settings where practitioners are making decisions about children's lives and well-being. One of the aims of this book is to provide opportunities for readers from different backgrounds to engage with different ways of thinking in different academic disciplines and, in doing so, make the first steps towards developing frameworks for integrated practice. There is little point knowing only the academic work done within sociology or anthropology if it is not related to how the child is conceptualised by other disciplines. Within each chapter, therefore, the interplay between theory, lived experience and practice is emphasised but the chapters are designed as a way to start developing a framework for integrated practice; they are not frameworks in themselves.

Each of the authors has also interpreted the word 'practice' very differently. For some, the term is rooted in service provision and relates to practice around working with, and supporting, children and young people. Others, however, especially those who deal with racism, multiculturalism or sexuality, understand practice much more broadly and examine particular aspects of children and young people's lives, such as music, or youth subcultures.

One way in which the issues of theory and practice are integrated throughout this volume is in the use of case studies. Each chapter has a contemporary case study, illustrating the complexities of children and young people's lived experiences in the UK and worldwide. In some cases this is a specific concept while, in others, it is a description of a small-scale example that highlights aspects of good or bad practice and shows the challenges, as well as the benefits, of integrating different approaches. A distinctive feature of this book is its emphasis on the links between the global and the local, the national and the transnational. While some chapters use the UK as a case study, others look at children's lives in a cross-cultural context, asking questions about how global circumstances have an impact on the daily lives of children and young people.

The book starts with two chapters by Nigel Thomas and Karen Wells, who consider the notion of the political child. In Chapter One, Thomas analyses the ways in which the idea of the child has been deployed in political discourse and the reasoning behind political interventions to improve children's lives, while in Chapter Two, Wells looks at the child in international politics, particularly how the child is politicised and brought into movements for social change. The concept of participation is central to both chapters and Mary Kellett examines this idea in more detail in Chapter Three, where she discusses the history of the concept, how it relates to issues in practice and its multiple meanings. In Chapters Four and Five, Virginia Morrow and Heather Montgomery examine children's experiences of family life in the UK and elsewhere. Based on sociological and anthropological approaches, they look at how family structures and relationships change over time and how children understand their own families and their roles and responsibilities within them.

The focus shifts in Chapter Six, by Anoop Nayak, to issues of race and ethnicity in contemporary Britain and how children and young people experience and negotiate their identities. The impact of the global on the local is further explored by Afua Twum-Danso in Chapter Seven, where she looks at the history of children's rights legislation and some of the philosophical and practical problems that have proved to be obstacles to the universal implementation of the UNCRC. Using Ghana and other African countries as examples, she discusses the often dangerous lack of dialectic between local experience and global expectation. Leading on from this, in Chapter Eight, Julia Fionda examines UK law; one of the most important arenas in which childhood is contested. She assesses the different ways in which the child is constructed by different areas of the law and the impact this has on the rights and responsibilities accorded to them. Different branches of the law conceptualise the child in different ways but the right to protection is enshrined in both national and international law and is, on one level, relatively uncontroversial. In Chapter Nine, Judith Masson examines child protection policies in the UK and discusses the different problems and needs of vulnerable children and youth and the state's responses to them.

Despite laws in place to safeguard children's well-being, many children in the UK still fail to reach their potential. The impact of policy on children's lives is taken up in Chapter Ten by Heather Montgomery, who analyses rates of child poverty in the UK, which, despite many years of government interventions and prioritisation, remain among the highest in the industrialised world. One key area that poor children are excluded from is the world of consumption and Chapter Eleven, by David Buckingham and Sara Bragg, examines the role of young people as consumers and evaluates the ways in which marketing is aimed at children and young people, and how they understand and adapt to these economic forces. Alongside, and interchangeable with, their material circumstances, it is obvious that children and young people's lives are further shaped by a variety of factors, including their gender, their ethnicity, their religion and their age and the next two chapters look at two of these issues. In Chapter Twelve, Anoop Nayak analyses different theoretical perspectives on multiculturalism and looks at the way religion has become politicised, is understood and is deployed, by children and young people in the UK. In Chapter Thirteen, Mary Jane Kehily focuses on theories of young people's sexuality, on their sexual socialisation and on new ways of understanding and thinking about teenage motherhood. Finally, the book concludes with Chapter Fourteen by Mary Kellett, who explores the rhetoric, realities and constraints of child voice, an emerging theme in childhood studies in its own right and a pertinent note on which to end a book about children's worlds.

References

UN (United Nations) (1989) 'Convention on the Rights of the Child', UN General Assembly, Document A/RES/44/25, available online at www.hrweb.org/legal/child.html (accessed 18/02/05).

UNICEF (United Nations Children's Fund) (2008) *The State of the World's Children*, New York, NY: UNICEF.

One

Children, young people and politics in the UK

Nigel Thomas

Introduction

'The child' is one of the most potent political images of our times. Since the middle to late 19th century, concern with the welfare and education of children has been a marked feature of public life. In the 20th century, this concern grew into a preoccupation, in parallel with the development of services to nurture and improve children's minds and bodies, and with the growth of industries and commercial enterprises catering to children's needs and wishes – or at least, what were thought to be their needs and wishes (see Hendrick, 1994; Cunningham, 2006).

This concern, or preoccupation, can be attributed to several different factors:

- a recognition that children, particularly younger children, are vulnerable and in need of care and protection;

- a concern that children and young people should acquire the skills and values necessary for their role in adult life;

- the symbolic value of children and what they represent to society.

In a society characterised by rapid change and uncertainty about the future, children come to occupy a crucial position. Because they are taken to represent the future, they become containers for both hopes and fears. If our children are growing up wrong, then society is going to hell in a handcart.

In contemporary Britain, children are at the centre of public attention as never before. Every issue of every newspaper contains items about schooling, about children's health, diet and exercise, about juvenile crime, about the effects of television, computer games or the internet on children's minds and bodies. The New Labour government has made children and young people a central part of its project to 'modernise' Britain, with initiative after initiative to promote their education and assess their progress, to promote good parenting, to manage and supervise their lives in increasing detail. At the same time, it has energetically pursued policies to deal with the perceived threat from children who are 'out of control' – including prosecutions, Antisocial Behaviour Orders (ASBOs), curfews and detention.

In this chapter I want to look at three particular aspects of the politics of childhood in contemporary Britain: the relationship between children, their families and the state; the progress of policies to improve children's lives; and the scope for children to be political actors themselves. In what follows I use 'children' and 'children and young people' to a degree interchangeably. Excessive precision about age can obscure the extent to which the 'child' is a social and cultural construct: as Denzin (1975: 2) put it so vividly, 'Children must be viewed as historical, cultural, political, economic, and social productions. There is nothing intrinsic to the object called "child" that makes that object more or less "childlike".'

For a baby of one, a child of six or a young person aged 14, what they are is a product not just of biology and their own immediate environment, but also of all the attitudes, habits and expectations built into the culture, the law and the politics of the society in which they are doing their work of 'growing up'. In particular, the degree of their dependence or independence is determined not only by their physical and mental development, but also by the space and opportunity that the law, and prevailing social attitudes, allow them. Although these factors play out differently for children and young people at different ages, they can never be escaped entirely.

Children, parents and the state[1]

Do children belong to their parents, or to society as a whole, as represented by the state? In the past it was a common view that children were the *property* of their parents, and in practice they often were. A more acceptable view now is perhaps that children are in *trust*, and that parents hold rights only to enable them to carry out their responsibilities. However, having children is still largely a private undertaking, and it is generally accepted that parents have the right to bring up their children in the way that seems right to them, while at the same time we all have a collective interest in the upbringing of future citizens and in ensuring that children are treated decently (Barton and Douglas, 1995). A stronger argument is that parents are 'agents' or 'trustees' who exercise their parental rights on an implied licence from the community, which entitles them to help and support and also makes them subject to control. Underlying this is a view that 'all children have an equal *prima facie* claim against the present adult world, for optimal conditions of upbringing compatible with society's fundamental economic and ideological structure' (Dingwall and Eekelaar, 1984: 25).

How the state exercises support for, and control over, families is something that varies from country to country. In 1978, Kamerman and Kahn distinguished between:

- countries with explicit and comprehensive family policies, with clear overarching goals;

- states that accept the existence of family policy as a field and evaluate policies to some extent in terms of their impact on families; and

- a third group that only have 'implicit and reluctant' family policies.

In this last group they included the UK and the US. Thirty years later, it is arguable that the UK has moved into the second group, if not the first.

There is an assumption that the state has a legitimate interest in the welfare of all children, and that they do not simply belong to their parents. In the past, destitute children were sometimes regarded as 'children of the state' and a potential asset, as Pinchbeck and Hewitt (1969) show for Tudor England, but this did not apply to children in families. The modern concern with the welfare of *all* children may be linked to the twin developments of political democracy and mass armies at the end of the 19th and beginning of the 20th century. Political democracy produced concern with the development of children's minds; the demands of warfare with their bodies. As a result, it became important for the state to concern itself with what went into both: with education on the one hand, and health and nutrition on the other.

The culmination of this concern with the welfare of all 'the nation's children' was the period just after the Second World War, when the experience of 'pulling together' to defeat Nazism meant that optimism about democracy and social solidarity were high. Steedman (1986: 122) has written movingly of how state welfare provision in the 1950s was able to give a sense of being valued and having 'a right to exist' to a child whose own family failed to give them that message, 'I think I would be a very different person now if orange juice and milk and dinners at school hadn't told me, in a covert way, that I had a right to exist, was worth something'.

In modern societies, the autonomy of all parents is significantly reduced by compulsory education and universal health surveillance. In contemporary Britain, the state decrees when children can leave school, when they can work, marry, have sex, drink and smoke. It provides financial support through the tax and benefit system. It maintains records of all children and shares this information between different state agencies.

In some circumstances it is considered legitimate for the state to intrude further than this into individual families to regulate, or even to substitute, their parenting. What is the ideological justification for this? Donzelot (1980) argues that it is at bottom no more than a concern with maintaining order. He identifies the 'tutelary complex' – experts representing the state, who make alliance with mothers through which the family is brought under surveillance – as the state's response to the challenge of controlling the working-class family and dealing with poverty without challenging existing power structures. However, this is to discount the much more varied motivation of the philanthropists, trade unionists, doctors, teachers and social workers who struggle to improve child welfare services. Parton (1991: 12) puts the question differently, 'How can the state establish the rights of individual children while promoting the family as the natural sphere for raising children and hence not intervening in all families and thus reducing its autonomy?'

Of course the extent of state intrusion into parental autonomy is not the same for all social groups. Others besides Donzelot have argued that surveillance and intervention fall more extensively and heavily on the working class or the poor (Holman, 1988; Frost and Stein, 1989; Jordan, 1990; also Stedman Jones, 1971). There are different views about the proper boundary between the authority of parents and the power of the state – about the circumstances in which the state may intervene, and about whether the state's primary duty is to children and their best interests, or to families as social units that include children. Fox Harding (1991) analyses this in terms of four value positions: 'laissez–faire', state paternalism, parents' rights and children's rights.

■   The 'laissez-faire' position believes in the benefits for society of a minimum state and also in the value to all, including children, of undisturbed family life.

■   State paternalism sees the child as dependent, vulnerable and with needs that are different from those of the adult. Parents' duties rather than rights are emphasised, and the state has the duty to intervene where there is inadequate care, and the capacity to provide something better for the child.

■   The parents' rights perspective favours supportive, rather than coercive, state intervention. Birth families should be supported, and children who need substitute care should be kept in touch with their original family and return if possible.

■   The children's rights perspective emphasises the child's own wishes and choices, rather than adults deciding what is 'best' for the child.

Fox Harding (1991) suggested that all four strands were significant in British policy making in the 1980s, but that the dominant elements were parental rights and state paternalism. The children's rights perspective at that time appeared marginal, although it may be more influential now.

An extreme version of the laissez-faire position is that taken by Goldstein et al (1973), who argue strongly that parental autonomy is good for children. To focus on children's 'best interests' as perceived by outsiders is to encourage over-interference, and in reality it is not possible to do the job of parenting well without having full authority. Goldstein et al even propose that courts should not make orders governing contact between a child and a separated parent, because the custodial parent should have complete discretion as to whether to allow such contact. They base their argument on a concept of the 'psychological parent', asserting that a child is incapable of forming attachments to more than one set of parent figures. Although their argument has been discredited academically (Richards, 1986), it still represents a significant strand in thinking about the state and the family. Rather than parenthood as ownership, this is parenthood as sovereignty. As Owen (1992: 128) puts it, 'the sovereignty argument allows the family to be treated as a benevolent dictatorship, which can be justifiably swept away and replaced by another dictatorship if it becomes corrupt'.

The web of powers and responsibilities that extends between children, their parents and the state is complex, ambiguous and contested. There is no dominant view of the relationship that is officially prescribed or generally supported, and there are contradictions in most of the positions taken. The central tensions come from the state's wish to support families without undermining their 'independence', and the desire to ensure that children are brought up 'properly' without interfering officiously in family life or parental autonomy; delegating responsibility to welfare professionals is one way to distance the state from head-on collision with families. To the extent that children's rights to participation and autonomy have become part of official policy, the same ambiguities apply. If it is difficult for the state to overcome its reluctance to intrude in order to protect children from physical or sexual abuse, it is even harder to do so in order to defend a child's right to an opinion. Article 12 of the UNCRC (UN, 1989) does not apply to decision making within families, and few countries have begun to establish the right for children to be consulted in such decisions; one example being Scotland, where in law parents now have a duty to consider children's wishes. Frequently the assumption continues to be made that parents represent their children's wishes and interests, for instance in decisions about education.

All these ambiguities are contained within the 1989 Children Act, which still provides the framework governing state intervention in the upbringing of children in England and Wales; the 1995 Children (Scotland) Act and the corresponding Northern Ireland Order are similar in crucial respects. The Act locates parental rights within parental responsibility. It provides that other family members, and children themselves, may intervene in matters of children's upbringing. It defines the duty of local authorities to provide services in terms of children's need to achieve a reasonable level of health and development, but it sets a criterion for compulsory intervention based on significant harm to the child caused by inadequate parental care. It provides that the law should intervene in private disputes only if it is in the child's interest to do so, and on the presumption that it will normally be in the child's interests to remain in contact with parents and other significant figures. Finally, it provides for children to be consulted and to have a voice in decisions about their lives, taking account of their age and understanding.

Policies to improve children's lives

As I noted in the introduction, since 1997, children and young people have been central to the New Labour project. Three areas of policy have been of particular significance: education, poverty and crime. The promise, made before entering government, to prioritise 'education, education, education' presaged a series of reforms to curriculum and assessment, initiatives to monitor and improve teaching and pupil achievement, changes to governance and a substantial programme of investment in school infrastructure. The commitment, made after entering government, to halve child poverty by 2010 and eliminate it by 2020 has attracted less attention but has driven much fiscal policy over the past decade (see Chapter Ten). The undertaking to be 'tough on crime, tough on the causes of crime' has provided a backdrop for a series of controversial interventions in the youth justice system and also into parenting.

In a sense, these three key areas of policy correspond to the three aspects of concern with children outlined in the introduction. The education reform programme is driven primarily by the imperative to make the UK a highly skilled and competitive knowledge-based economy. Children in this instance are important principally because they are the workers of the future. The child poverty target, on the other hand, is based on a perception of children as having present as well as future needs that deserve to be met, and on the belief that all children should enjoy the benefits of prosperity (even if not to the same extent). In this sense, it may be linked to the initiatives to improve conditions in the care system. In contrast, the strategy to tackle youth crime is focused on children as a threat to the social order and to conventional values. It is instructive to look at each of these three areas of policy in a little more depth, in order to get an idea of the underlying purposes behind the programmes, the different impacts they have had on children's lives and the often conflicting views as to their desirability.

'Education, education, education'

The education reforms were fuelled by a sense that the UK was losing its comparative advantage in terms of having a highly educated workforce, as other countries in Europe and Asia were beginning to catch up, and also by a view that too many children were being failed by the system and leaving school without qualifications – even without being able to read properly. Although part of the programme was a commitment to raising the proportion in higher education to 50%, the main focus was on the school system. The main changes introduced by the Conservatives – the national curriculum, league tables of school performance, a strict regime of inspection, and radical changes to school governance – were all retained and extended. All children were required to take Standard Assessment Tests (SATs) at each 'key stage' (at ages 7, 11, 14 and 16). The curriculum was extended to younger children (even to those in preschool), and further centralised components were added such as prescribed times for reading in class and prescribed methods of teaching. A massive programme of school building and investment was also introduced.

Tomlinson (2003: 196) summarises the approach succinctly:

> The New Labour government retained the Conservative faith in choice and competition, with education developing as a market commodity driven by consumer demand, fuelled by league tables of examination results, school 'choice' by parents, specialist schools and failing schools. There was a continued rhetoric of 'raising standards' and a weakening of the declared commitment to end academic selection. There was adherence to the belief that education institutions should be managed along the lines of private business, with enhanced business funding and influence, and headteachers trained in managerial techniques of leadership. There was a continued emphasis on government regulation and control of the curriculum and assessment, more inspection regimes, further control of teachers and their training, and curtailment of local authority influence.

Tomlinson also points out that while the curriculum was actually narrowed by the new requirements for literacy and numeracy, the increasing complexity resulted in children taking some 75 external tests and examinations between the ages of 7 and 16.

No doubt many children were being failed by the existing system, but many have questioned the benefits of the remedies being introduced, and indeed whether they were not adding to the problems they purported to tackle. The rhetoric of 'choice' often cloaked a reality of competition and disadvantage. The drive to weed out 'failing' schools and teachers appeared to result in demoralisation and sickness, with many teachers leaving the profession. Above all, there was increasing evidence that for many children the intensive regime of assessment led to increasing pressure and anxiety. Despite evidence of rising standards (although some of this is disputed), there were also many children who felt they were failing. Children with low achievement or exceptional difficulties were unattractive to schools seeking to improve their league table position, and the system appeared to become more socially divided as more schools began to select their pupils.

'Child-centred' education seemed to have become an expression of scorn, which may be surprising to those with knowledge of other school systems such as those in Finland and Sweden, where children start school later and are tested far less, with impressive results. The devolved governments of Wales, Scotland and Northern Ireland have begun to adopt different approaches, turning away from SATs and league tables, and in Wales introducing a more child-centred approach to early years, but in England the government remains wedded to a regime of testing, apparently seeing education as something done *to* children rather than as something that they are helped to do for themselves.

'The first generation to end child poverty forever'

The aim of reducing, then abolishing, child poverty was widely supported, although many have questioned the seriousness of the government's commitment to its stated goals. There is no doubt that child poverty in the UK was a scandal by 1997. As Bradshaw (2003) points out, the relative child poverty rate had more than trebled in the 1980s, and in the 1990s there had been no reduction. At the time of his review, evidence of a decline in child poverty was just beginning to emerge, and indicators appeared to be moving in the right direction. However, there was scepticism as to whether the government would achieve its targets without more radical policies, and this scepticism has grown over subsequent years. Although considerable progress was made in the early years of the policy, this has been characterised as 'picking the low-hanging fruit'; children just below the poverty line can be lifted over the threshold more easily than those in deeper need.

Bradshaw and Bennett (2007: 1), in a review for the European Commission, concluded that the government had only narrowly failed to meet its initial aim of reducing child poverty by a quarter by 2004/05, but that in 2005/06, child poverty had increased and trends in 2007 made it 'unlikely that the Government will succeed in its aim of halving child poverty by 2010 unless there are radical changes in policy'. The principal constraints they identified as 'structural inequalities in British society' and 'public attitudes towards people in poverty', tackling which would require 'significant political will and leadership'.

Detailed analysis by Evans and Scarborough (2006), carried out for the Joseph Rowntree Foundation, shows that the government's use of measures based on relative household income 'before housing costs' seriously distorts the actual numbers in poverty, raising the possibility that even if the targets were reached there could still be large numbers of children in real poverty. A more recent review for the Joseph Rowntree Foundation by Sutherland et al (2008) analysed uprating methods used in the tax and benefit system. This demonstrated that over the next 20 years there would be a 'steep and dramatic' rise in child poverty; from 18% to 33% if measured before housing costs, and from 27% to 39% after housing costs. Instead of eradicating child poverty, the effect would be almost to double it.

Given the continued increase in wealth of the richest groups in society, this may inspire cynicism about the commitment to reducing inequality, which many commentators regard as a sine qua non for eradicating poverty. Whether one concludes that the intentions are good but the task is simply too difficult, or that politicians are using children as a political tactic rather than prioritising their needs, may have to be a matter of opinion.

'Tough on crime, tough on the causes of crime'

Crime and antisocial behaviour were defined as a major social problem by the incoming New Labour administration – a view shared by leading Conservatives and by influential sections of the media. The 1998 Crime and Disorder Act created the Youth Justice Board and Youth Offending Teams in England and Wales, and also introduced ASBOs, Child Safety Orders and local child curfews among other measures. The last two applied to unsupervised children under 10, but were later extended to young people under 16. At the same time, the rule of *doli incapax*, under which a prosecutor had to prove that a child under 14 was able to understand the meaning of an offence, was abolished so that any child over 10 could be prosecuted in a youth court or, in certain circumstances, in an adult court (see Chapter Eight).

These reforms coincided with a sharp and continuing rise in the use of custody for young offenders. Other sentencing options and 'restorative justice' schemes offered alternatives, but the overall effect was to criminalise increasing numbers of young people, often for petty offences or no criminal offence at all. Moral panics about 'hoodies' and bans by shopkeepers on young people, plus the use of electronic devices such as CCTV and the 'Mosquito' ultrasound deterrent (which can only be heard by young people) contributed to a climate of 'demonisation'.

Recent research by the Centre for Crime and Justice Studies at King's College London (Solomon and Garside, 2008) appears to show that none of these measures has had any appreciable effect on youth crime; but it is arguable that the measures have had a deleterious impact on the quality of life for children and young people, most dramatically for those who have died in custody. This failed strategy is notable for many things, but perhaps most of all for its focus on young people as a menace to society. Despite the promise also to be 'tough on the causes of crime', the investment in resources for young people has not been forthcoming.

Political footballs?

The intention behind these three major policy initiatives has been varied, as have the outcomes, but none of them can be said to be an unmitigated success in promoting the well-being of children and young people, and to a significant degree at least two of them can be considered harmful. It is arguable that in part this is due to children and young people being regarded at best as the objects of policy rather than as political subjects, and at worst as political footballs. It must be acknowledged that this is a selective sample of policy initiatives directed at children and young people; a focus on other areas and initiatives (such as Sure Start, 'extended schools' or Quality Protects) might have led to different conclusions. It is perhaps ironic that at the same time New Labour has espoused the rhetoric, and to a significant degree the practice, of including young people in decision making (see Chapters Three and Fourteen).

Children as political actors – the players, not the ball?

Children are excluded from membership of the political community in a number of ways, which may be characterised as formal or informal. By 'formal' I mean a range of legal definitions and institutions, such as denial of children's legal competence, their disqualification from public office and their exclusion from so-called 'universal' suffrage. By 'informal' mechanisms I mean those expectations and dispositions embedded in individuals and social interaction, which may be understood in terms of *discourse* (Foucault, 2002) or in terms of *habitus* (as embodied history) and children's lack of 'capital' (Bourdieu, 1992). Children will only be fully included as political subjects if changes happen in both formal and informal dimensions, which are of course mutually reinforcing.

The informal bias against children's inclusion is often unstated, but is occasionally made explicit – for example when proposals to lower the voting age are countered with the objection that children cannot possibly understand what is at issue in political decision making (see Chapter Two). Stevens (1982) found that even young children seemed to have an ability to grasp political principles and that 11-year-olds had a depth of understanding comparable with many adults. She also found that children's understanding of democracy and authority came largely from their observation of the ways in which schools operated as institutions. This contrasts with the way in which 'citizenship' is now presented as something that children have to be taught through the formal curriculum.

Children have also shown their capacity to be political actors in a range of situations, especially situations of conflict and upheaval such as Palestine (Hart, 2009) or Mexico (Smith, 2007), or closer to home in Northern Ireland. Children cannot be kept isolated from politics, especially when their families or communities are under attack; and in many contexts it is better to be an active participant than a bystander. The horror expressed when children marched out of school in 2003 to protest against the invasion of Iraq perhaps shows a less confident age than the milder patronising comments that greeted the school strikes of 1911 (Marson, 1973).

Other objections to extending the right to vote to children and young people are that it would be ineffective because young voters are currently the least likely to participate in elections. This was possibly one reason why the Electoral Commission in 2004 rejected Tony Blair's suggestion to reduce the age of voting. Despite this, most British political parties have at one time or another supported the reduction of the voting age to 16. Although it might not result in a high proportion of them voting, widening the franchise would have substantial symbolic value in extending membership of the political community to younger people. Many of the objections to this are remarkably similar to those made in the past against votes for women or the working class. The political theorist, Young (2000), held that voting equality was a minimal condition of political equality. Allowing children to vote would give legitimacy to their participation, and to their perspectives.

Some of these issues come into sharper focus in the case study that concludes this chapter. This example shows children acting politically, and indeed in a way that brings them into conflict with the authorities and that might be dismissed as 'hooliganism'. It also shows children agitating, not just about their own personal interests, but also about wider issues of justice and fairness in relation to their teachers. Another interesting feature of this protest is that the pupils and teachers seem to have been working together, and also that (despite the conflict with the police) the local Conservative Assembly Member (AM) appears to have spoken in support of their action. Attitudes to children's rights do not always coincide neatly with other political divisions, and the reality of children's political action may be different from conventional understandings of 'participation'.

Case study: pupil protests in Wales

In 2008 150 pupils from Pontllanfraith Comprehensive in Caerphilly, Wales staged a walkout from their school to protest against proposed teacher redundancies. They blocked the road outside the school and two 15-year-old girls and a 13-year-old boy were arrested for obstructing the highway. Ten police officers from the Gwent force were sent to control the protest.

The school was inspected in November 2006 when it was classified as failing. Thirty-five teachers had been on strike in a dispute about extra responsibility, and the school was judged as not having reached the required standards. The school was put into special measures in January 2007 but by March 2008 there had been a significant improvement and the school was deemed not to need constant monitoring. The head teacher was reported to a have a 'clear vision' with 'high expectations', and the report noted:

> There is a positive learning ethos in most classrooms and little evidence of the low-level disruption evident at the time of the inspection in 2006. The number of recorded incidents of misbehaviour has reduced over a quarter compared with the same period a year ago. There has also been a reduction in fixed-term exclusions over the same period, with significantly fewer days lost from school (cited in BBC News Online, 2008).

Progress continued to be made and by April 2008 these special measures were lifted when school inspectors claimed that that the school was continuing to improve. In spite of this, however, several teachers were given redundancy notices by Caerphilly local education authority. The pupils at the school objected strongly, arguing that their education would be disrupted and that their teachers deserved their support. Fifteen-year-old Cane Thomas, said 'There were banners and there were people with writing on their tops saying "Justice for the teachers" and some of the teachers' names. The teachers that have gone are really, really nice. I really am upset and my drama teacher has left – we need her for my GCSC. My course work is due in May and without the teachers there is no course work to be given in' (cited in BBC News Online, 2008).

Support for both pupils and teachers came from William Graham, Conservative AM for South Wales East. He said both teachers and pupils had worked 'tremendously hard over the past year to raise standards at Pontllanfraith Comprehensive. Together, they raised their school out of this situation, as acknowledged by Inspectors earlier this month. The bond of mutual support is demonstrated by today's protest.'

In the face of such united opposition, Caerphilly council backed down and put the cuts on hold, agreeing that 'appropriate consultation' was needed together with an 'ongoing positive dialogue with all parties'.

Note

[1] This section uses material from Chapter Five of my book *Children, Family and the State: Decision-Making and Child Participation* (Thomas, 2000, 2002).

References

Barton, C. and Douglas, G. (1995) *Law and Parenthood*, London: Butterworths.

BBC News Online (2008) 'Cuts "on hold" at protest school', 21 April, London: BBC, available online at http://news.bbc.co.uk/1/hi/wales/south_east/7358662.stm (accessed 3/08/08).

Bourdieu, P. (1992) *The Logic of Practice*, Cambridge: Polity Press.

Bradshaw, J. (2003) 'Poor children', *Children & Society*, vol 17, no 3, pp 162-72.

Bradshaw, J. and Bennett, F. (2007) *Tackling Child Poverty and Promoting the Social Inclusion of Children: A Study of National Policies (United Kingdom)*, Brussels: European Commission.

Cunningham, H. (2006) *The Invention of Childhood*, London: BBC Books.

Denzin, N. (1975) *Childhood Socialisation*, San Francisco, CA: Jossey Bass.

Dingwall, R. and Eekelaar, J. (1984) 'Rethinking child protection', in M. Freeman (ed) *The State, the Law and the Family: Critical Perspectives*, London: Tavistock.

Donzelot, J. (1980) *The Policing of Families: Welfare Versus the State*, London: Hutchinson.

Evans, M. and Scarborough, J. (2006) *Can Current Policy End Child Poverty in Britain by 2020?*, York: Joseph Rowntree Foundation.

Foucault, M. (2002) *The Archaeology of Knowledge*, London: Routledge.

Fox Harding, L. (1991) *Perspectives in Child Care Policy*, Harlow: Longman.

Frost, N. and Stein, M. (1989) *The Politics of Child Welfare*, Hemel Hempstead: Harvester Wheatsheaf.

Goldstein, J., Freud, A. and Solnit, A. (1973) *Beyond the Best Interests of the Child*, New York, NY: Macmillan.

Hart, J. (2009) 'Displaced children's participation in political violence: towards greater understanding of mobilisation', in N. Thomas (ed) *Children, Politics and Communication*, Bristol: The Policy Press.

Hendrick, H. (1994) *Child Welfare: England, 1872–1989*, London: Routledge.

Holman, B. (1988) *Putting Families First: Prevention and Child Care*, London: Macmillan.

Jordan, B. (1990) *Social Work in an Unjust Society*, London: Harvester Wheatsheaf.

Kamerman, S. and Kahn, A. (1978) *Family Policy: Government and Families in Fourteen Countries*, New York, NY: Columbia University Press.

Marson, D. (1973) 'Children's strikes in 1911', History Workshop Pamphlets, no 9, Oxford: Routledge and Kegan Paul..

Owen, M. (1992) *Social Justice and Children in Care*, Aldershot: Avebury.

Parton, N. (1991) *Governing the Family: Child Care, Child Protection and the State*, Basingstoke: Macmillan.

Pinchbeck, I. and Hewitt, M. (1969) *Children in English Society: Vol 1*, London: Routledge & Kegan Paul.

Richards, M. (1986) 'Behind the best interests of the child: an examination of the arguments of Goldstein, Freud and Solnit concerning custody and access at divorce', *Journal of Social Welfare Law* (March), pp 77-95.

Smith, A. (2007) 'The children of Loxicha, Mexico: exploring ideas of childhood and the rules of participation', *Children, Youth and Environments*, vol 17, no 2, pp 33-55.

Solomon, E. and Garside, R. (2008) *Ten Years of Labour's Youth Justice Reforms: An Independent Audit*, London: Centre for Crime and Justice Studies, King's College London.

Stedman Jones, G. (1971) *Outcast London: A Study in the Relationship between Classes in Victorian Society*, Oxford: Oxford University Press.

Steedman, C. (1986) *Landscape for a Good Woman*, London: Virago.

Stevens, O. (1982) *Children Talking Politics: Political Learning in Childhood*, Oxford: Martin Robertson.

Sutherland, H., Evans, M., Hancock, R., Hills, J. and Zantomio, F. (2008) *The Impact of Benefit and Tax Uprating on Incomes and Poverty*, York: Joseph Rowntree Foundation.

Thomas, N. (2000) *Children, Family and the State: Decision-Making and Child Participation*, London: Macmillan.

Thomas, N. (2002) *Children, Family and the State: Decision-Making and Child Participation*, Bristol: The Policy Press.

Tomlinson, S. (2003) 'New Labour and education', *Children & Society*, vol 17, no 3, pp 195-204.

UN (United Nations) (1989) 'Convention on the Rights of the Child', UN General Assembly, Document A/RES/44/25, available online at http://www.unhchr.ch/html/menu3/b/k2crc.htm (accessed 23/01/09).

Young, I.M. (2000) *Inclusion and Democracy*, New York, NY: Oxford University Press.

Two

Children and international politics

Karen Wells

Introduction

This chapter is about children's involvement in political movements that have had an international impact and that have been shaped by international structures and events. It is not about how international social policy frames childhood and nor is it an evaluation of the impact of international social policy and international law on children's lives. Although social policy and law are obviously key influences on children's lives, this chapter is concerned with how children act on international politics rather than how international policy acts on children. The distinction is an important one because, notwithstanding the attempts of child rights advocates to frame the UNCRC (UN, 1989) as an instrument that facilitates or even insists on children's right to participate in politics, the participation of children in political activism has not been a product of international policy and law but an effect of national political struggles.

Analysing children's involvement and impact on international politics is a very new endeavour for two reasons: first, the study of international relations has always privileged the study of relations between states and has not been concerned with what goes on within states; second, the presumption that children are incapable of participating meaningfully in political movements has obscured the role of children in politics, whether at an international or a national level. This view that children are incapable of meaningful political discourse and political activism persists despite a wealth of concrete evidence that shows that children do get involved in politics. Indeed, any significant conflict, whether intrastate or interstate, contemporary or historical, has involved children in political struggle. African American children and youth were involved in the civil rights movement, children were involved in the struggle for majority rule

in South Africa and they are actively involved in the Palestinian–
Israeli conflict. Nonetheless, the documented record of children's
engagement in political conflict has made very little impact on the
conceptualisation of childhood as a non-political space.

Children and politics

Political activism among children challenges some of the most dearly
held beliefs about childhood and children's capacities. The influence
of developmental psychology and pedagogy on our understanding
of contemporary childhood is critical for grasping why childhood
is viewed as a non-political space. The principles of orthodox
developmental psychology, which claim that children gradually
acquire intellectual and moral capacity throughout their childhood,
have become the common sense of our epoch. In particular, Piaget's
empirically derived claims that children cannot think logically before
the age of seven and are not capable of abstract reasoning before the
age of 12 has had an enormous influence on everyday understandings,
especially in the West, of children's intellectual and emotional
capacities. Similarly school-based pedagogies have been dominated
by a view that children have to understand and internalise a body
of knowledge before their beliefs can be given credibility. Piagetian
theory also claims that a child will move from one stage to another
in a total shift of perspective from concrete to abstract thinking. Since
many young children have a strong belief in magical thinking, it is
thought, from a Piagetian perspective, that they cannot hold this belief
alongside a meaningful understanding of politics.

This view of childhood as being an immanently non-political space
is reflected in the lack of research on children and politics. What
research there is tends to be concerned with how children learn about
political concepts and how they begin to form a political identity.
The most significant study of children's political understanding and
identities is probably still Coles' (1986) *The Political Life of Children*.
Coles' book is a study of national identity formation in children
written from a psychoanalytic perspective. Stephens (1995: 3), in
Children and the Politics of Culture, one of the few collections to
specifically address children's place in politics, glosses Coles' findings as
'a nation's politics becomes a child's everyday psychology'. His method
was to let children's narratives about politics and nationalism speak for
themselves and he offers little interpretative steer on their meanings.
In a sense, his work might be read as simply a general affirmation that
children's political and moral sensibilities are intuitive and complex.

Other studies of political socialisation have focused on the role of the family and the school in fostering political identity and attitudes, although there has been a recent interest in the role of the media – both news media and popular culture – in exposing children to political ideas (de Block and Buckingham, 2007).

A central concept in international relations and political science more generally is that war and politics are both strategies for resolving conflict between and within states. This is what is meant by Clausewitz's famous aphorism that war is the continuation of politics by other means (cited in Foucault, 2003:48). The study of conflict between states is the cornerstone of the major theoretical paradigms of international relations theory. This attention to conflict is very useful for understanding how and when children and young people come to be involved in politics; the character of state–society conflict, its longevity, its intensity and its intractability, is a determinant of the involvement of children and young people in politics. Another kind of conflict – intergenerational conflict – is also important in shaping the political interest and activism of children and young people. One of the questions we might ask about young political activism is: what difference does it make if political activists are children or adults? In other words, do children bring a different sensibility or different strategies and tactics to political life?

International relations theorists have recently entered the field of childhood studies and attempted to situate children in the field of international politics. Brocklehurst's (2006) *Who's Afraid of Children?* is a study of political conflict and international relations. As conflict is one of the central interests of international relations, it is hardly surprising that when international relations theorists start to think about how children might figure in its field of inquiry, they concentrate on conflict. The other main focus of international relations is in international law and this has also been an emergent area of inquiry in relation to children and the international system. The earliest endeavour in this field is probably Kent's (1995) *Children in the International Political Economy*, which is a plea for international actors to mobilise the UNCRC in support of children's welfare in developing countries. A more recent strand in theorising the impact of international child rights law critiques it as little more than an instrument of the foreign policy of hegemonic states in the international system. Pupavac (2001) has argued that international child rights law is being used to undermine the sovereignty of the state in the developing world.

This interest in political conflict links the emergent interest in childhood and the place of children in the international system with a more developed literature on the psychological impact of political conflict on children. Political conflict and violence has been one of the better-explored areas related to children and politics, although much of this literature is about war rather than politics. Cairns' (1996) review of the quantitative literature on the psychological impact of political violence on children is a valuable resource and synthesis of existing studies. His attention to children who initiate or contribute to political violence was an early sign of a turn away from children and youth as simply victims or suffering bystanders. Under the influence of the new social studies of childhood, and the evidence of children's participation in political violence in Northern Ireland, Palestine and, more recently, Afghanistan, there has been increasing recognition that children are active agents in political violence (Durham, 2000; Hart, 2000; Boyden and de Berry, 2004; de Boeck and Honwana, 2005).

The acknowledgement of children's political agency in conflict should perhaps be given a cautious welcome. On the one hand, it establishes that children and, especially, young people have been active participants – even initiators – of political conflict; indeed, the more recent literature on children and war shows that the participation of children and young people in war and political conflict is the norm (Marten, 2004; Rosen, 2005; Brocklehurst, 2006). On the other hand, this recognition has stripped children and young people of a degree of protection in contemporary conflicts. The Israeli government, for example, has justified its killing of young Palestinians by recourse to an argument that says they are active participants in the conflict and are therefore not entitled to the protection of international law, which is framed by the supposition that children are non-belligerents.

This chapter explores these questions about conflict and about strategies and tactics by focusing on:

■ the impact of state–society conflict on the political mobilisation of children and young people;

■ the role of intergenerational conflict in young political activism;

■ the role of school as a site for political mobilisation.

State–society conflict and interstate conflict

From this brief review of the literature on children and politics, it can be seen that there is a tendency to look at psychological development as the foundation of children's political engagement. The questions asked about children and politics tend to be questions about their intellectual competence and their emotional maturity; the degree to which they have the capacity for empathy or the ability to analyse complex situations. Often, children's political engagement is dismissed as merely 'parroting' the views of the adults around them. In contrast to this view of politics as internally or psychologically driven, I want to argue for the importance of the political and social contexts for understanding when, why and how children become politically active. In particular, I want to suggest that the degree of intranational and international conflict – that is, conflict within and between states – is critical to understanding the modalities of children's politics. In developing this argument, I discuss four sociopolitical contexts that have been particularly fertile ground for the political mobilisation of children and youth: revolutionary states in conflict with society; revolutionary societies in conflict with national state; interstate conflict; and war.

The widespread revolt of a society against the state is a relatively rare occurrence. When it does happen, young people are often perceived to be the most radical element in the struggle for a new society and the easiest for revolutionary parties to mobilise, if not always to organise. In the Iranian revolution of 1979, school and university students were important members of all the major political parties. In the struggle against Apartheid in South Africa, children and young people were members of political parties and participated in demonstrations and other anti-regime political actions. In entrenched political conflicts between state and society, as in Apartheid South Africa or the occupied territories in Palestine/Israel, the long-term assault on society by the state denudes political movements of experienced, adult activists who have been killed by the state, imprisoned or have fled into exile. In these extended political conflicts, over time the leadership of the movement is taken on by young activists.

Political movements may actively seek to involve children and young people in part because discourses of childhood innocence and children's right to protection from adult struggles can underscore the injustice of the situation that the movement is mobilised against. In her study of children in the US civil rights movement, de Schweinitz (2004) argues forcefully that the campaign for integrated education was chosen by the movement as a high-profile campaign because of the stark contrast between a widely legitimated discourse of childhood innocence protected by adults and the racist hatred directed by white adults against black school children as they attempted to integrate their local schools. Similarly, Singer (2006) claims that the involvement of children and young people in the *Intifada* was a political strategy intended to undermine the legitimacy of Israeli attacks against Palestinian insurgents by arguing that children's entitlement to protection and their innocence meant that they could not be treated as insurgents. One of the most iconic images of the struggle against Apartheid is of 12-year-old Hector Pieterson being carried through the streets of Soweto after he was killed by the police in a student demonstration. As of the images of African American children being threatened by white adults during the civil rights movement, this image owes its power to the terrible juxtaposition between the discourse of innocent and protected childhood and the reality of state violence perpetuated against children.

When revolutionary movements have gained control of the state, youth have played an important role in their strategies for consolidating power. Revolutionary regimes frequently perceive youth as both a threat to their secure control over government and a resource that can be deployed to entrench the revolution in the political hinterlands. Revolutionary regimes, including China after the Cultural Revolution (MacFarquhar and Schoenhals, 2006) or Cuba during the literacy campaign (Supko, 1998: 6), sent thousands of young people into the countryside to get support for the revolution and to make the governments' aims a reality, literally on the ground. In China, the 'send-down' campaign sent a generation of urban middle-class children to the countryside to learn 'revolutionary practice' from the peasantry.

As a generation, youth have responded ambivalently to these calls to propagate the revolution. Some have welcomed the opportunity to engage in what they think of as revolutionary action, extending the revolution to the rural 'masses'. In Ethiopia, the land and literacy campaign – the *Zemecha* – involved the entire body of secondary school and university students, some 50,000 young people. As Clapham (1988: 49) comments: 'Since it offered students the chance to participate in spreading the revolution to the countryside which they had demanded, they could scarcely refuse to take part, and many did so enthusiastically'. Others have gone reluctantly or have been coerced into going to the countryside. Whatever the reality of young people's propensity to radical political action, it is clear that regimes generally believe that young people are more radical, and therefore potentially more disruptive to post-revolutionary states, than adults. If the aim of sending young people to the countryside is to extend the revolutionary state's capacity outside of the urban centres, it also removes students from the cities, where they could threaten the regime (Clapham, 1988: 49).

Political conflict in states is often expressed sporadically and rarely intensifies into revolution or ongoing armed conflict; when it does, children and youth may be recruited into the armed forces on the rebel or government side. Arguably, many contemporary intrastate and regional conflicts in which children and young people are fighting are not political conflicts but struggles over the control of economic resources rather than over state power in itself (Berdal and Malone, 2000). This distinction between political or ideological and economic conflicts is important because the opposition forces in these conflicts have mostly been socialist and nationalist forces formally committed to gender equality. Revolutionary/rebel armies, including FRELIMO in Mozambique (West, 2000), FARC in Colombia (Cunningham, 2003; Gonzalez-Perez, 2006), the Tamil Tigers in Sri Lanka and Umkhonto-we-Sizwe in South Africa, have integrated women into the fighting forces; and girls and women have spoken of their hopes for a new role in the post-revolutionary society as motivating them to join the rebels (West, 2000; Cunningham, 2003).

Intergenerational conflict

The distribution of political power and control of economic resources along generational lines in Africa has led to an analysis of young people 'almost as a political class for themselves' (Shepler, 2005a: 125). Shepler (2005b), writing about the civil war in Sierra Leone, argues that young people in Africa think of themselves as a coherent class or group with shared experiences of exclusion and discrimination. In similar terms, Comaroff and Comaroff (2000: 291) have spoken of generational conflict as a 'fertile site into which class anxieties are displaced'. Many of these conflicts are expressed, these scholars are suggesting, in violent political confrontation and civil war. Hoffman (2003: 304), also writing about child soldiers in Africa, talks about how 'militarization increasingly presents itself to some as a way to opt out, to subvert the injustices of patronage by violently levelling the field'.

In an international context, these grievances against the older generation are not only seen by analysts as a consequence of the unequal distribution of land and power between a large population

of young people, in truth mostly young men, on the one side and
their fathers and grandfathers on the other. They are also seen as a
consequence of global political and economic flows in two respects:
the perception that globalisation has increased the scale of resources
available to Africans but these are not flowing to young Africans; and
the impact of international law on local conflicts over the relative
rights and duties of children and adults or juniors and seniors.

In this view, then, intergenerational political conflict is a
consequence of the unequal distribution of resources between the
young and the old and the growing perception of the young not only
that this is unfair but also that they have a right to protest against it.
The idea that young people have a generational identity that brings
them into conflict with older generations is hardly novel but it has
taken on a new significance in the contemporary global context.

An alternative view of the role of intergenerational conflict
in explaining how and why children and young people become
politically active is when young people perceive their elders to be
passive in the face of political injustice. Durham (2000: 113) claims
that 'youth enter political space as saboteurs; their potential for political
sabotage comes from their incomplete subjugation to contexts and co-
opters, and to their own power for action, response, and subversion in
contexts of political definition'. What she means by this is that young
people are not politically compromised because they are too young
or inexperienced to have been co-opted by hegemonic forces. Keddie
(2003: 218), writing about the Iranian revolution, makes a similar point
when she says that young activists were 'too young and idealistic to
have been co-opted by the regime'. Speaking specifically of the South
African struggle, Bundy (1987: 310) comments that:

> The youthful militants of the ICU [Industrial and
> Commercial Workers Union], the radicals who formed the
> Independent ANC [African National Congress], and the
> young intellectuals of the ANC Youth League all chafed
> against the restraint and moderation of their elders; they
> were the precursors of the Black Consciousness ideologues,
> the enrages of 1976, and the township comrades of the
> 1980s ... a self-aware age-group sought generational unity,
> [and] distanced themselves from their parents, and spoke for
> 'we, the youth of South Africa'.

However, it is equally clear that not all youth political activism
involves the severing of ties between parents and children. In the

cases of both South Africa and Iran there was, on the part of many activists, a frustration with the political tactics adopted by the older generation. However, this frustration did not always translate into a rejection of the older generation's rights over the younger generation or of the political or religious sensibilities of their parents' generation. Their disagreement was over tactics, not principles. In the context of Northern Ireland, Brocklehurst (2006) argues that conflicts between generations were less important than conflicts between Catholic and Protestant neighbourhoods and their political and military organisations. In Iran, the Mojahedin attracted young followers because of its adaptation of Shi'ism to a revolutionary programme. The young intelligentsia, many of whom were the children of the traditional middle class – tradespeople and shopkeepers, were deeply attached to Shi'ism but rejected its clerical interpretations. Joining the Mojahedin, unlike joining a secular Marxist party, 'did not necessitate severing ties to family values, household customs, or childhood beliefs' (Keddie, 2003: 230). In her study of youth identity in post-revolutionary Iran, Varzi (2006: 66) says that, during Friday prayers at the beginning of the Iran–Iraq war, 'teenagers were encouraged to ask their parents' permission to go to the front. Mothers were congratulated for giving up their sons'. In Nigeria, Nolte (2004) has shown that youth organisations are embedded in religious or ethno-nationalist movements and share a common agenda with older generations. Similarly, in Cape Town, children and young people who supported the ANC were reluctant to be seen to be critical of their elders, many of whom supported Inkatha (Dlamini, 2005). There is also substantial evidence that youth activists, particularly leaders, were politicised by their elders (Marks, 2001).

In this section I have discussed intergenerational conflicts where young people have confronted their elders or sought to be at the vanguard of a revolutionary movement. The third context in which intergenerational conflict is a significant dimension of young political activism is when revolutionary and radical states seek to mobilise support for their rule and overturn the old order by involving young people in smashing the symbols of that order. When children and young people have been offered the reins of power as new regimes seek to consolidate their rule, they have often taken up the offer with terrifying enthusiasm. The new regime seeks to mobilise young people in support of the new regime by breaking people's attachment to pre-revolutionary symbols and social relations. Central to this is breaking relations between children and their parents. Like other revolutionary states, before and since, the Chinese Communist Party sought to usurp 'the prerogatives of the family' (Gold, 1991: 597). In such moments, children and young people are encouraged to break their ties with their parents and other symbols of parental authority (teachers, for example) and to reorientate their sentimental or affective ties from their families to the symbols and actors of the new regime. Love, one might say, is transferred from the father/mother to the fatherland/motherland. This turning away from the mother/father to the *patrie* is often accompanied by extreme acts of violence and rage, many committed against precisely those persons, teachers and parents (perhaps especially fathers) who could have demanded respect from their young attackers before the revolution (see Brocklehurst, 2006, on the child–family relationship in Nazi Germany). One might say that at these points the state encourages the expression of generational resentment. In breaking their ties with their parents, they break with their parents' attitudes, with their parents' habituation with the old order and they refuse to countenance their parents' doubts about the morality of the new order.

The investment of a new regime in securing its rule through the inculcation in the ruled of a reinvented public morality is met by the investment of the young in asserting their 'will to power'; a will that is normally frustrated precisely by their youthful status. Young people should not be thought of as inevitably on the side of 'right'. Although they are often on the side of those whose claims to power are tenuous and fragile, a condition that echoes their own lives, and therefore more often on the side of the usurper or the contender than the incumbent or the established, it is as well to remember that the usurper is not always progressive.

School as a site of political mobilisation

The focus of this chapter so far has been on the social and political contexts that motivate children and young people to become politically involved. This is a perspective that is intended to take us away from the focus on internal or psychological development in explaining children's motivation and capacity for political organisation towards an external and indeed *political* explanation. It is also intended to shift us from understanding motivation and capacity as individual to understanding them as social. It is to the specific social context that I now turn to explain how children and young people might come to perceive themselves as a kind of class.

Political struggle is a collective endeavour. To understand how anyone, including young people, comes to be politically involved it is necessary to appreciate how they come to think of themselves as some kind of collectivity. Mannheim (1952 [1928]), whose theory of generation has been very important in explaining children's political activity, theorised the concept of a 'generational unit' as a group with a shared consciousness or understanding of society. School is one of the most important sites for this formation of a shared identity among a generation.

The role of the school as a site for the formation of political subjectivity is not limited to the forces of political opposition. Schools have always played an important role in the formation of the imagined community of the nation. Governments have self-consciously sought to organise the school in ways that would inculcate in children a sense of national belonging (Hobsbawm, 1975; Perko, 2003). Schools use an ensemble of technologies that produce a national sensibility in the school child. These technologies include:

- the use of the official language as the medium of instruction;

- the production and study of a national curriculum;

- the organisation of time and space within the school building in ways that are repeated across the territory of the nation;

- displays of nationalism in the extra-curricular activities of the school (such as saluting the flag, singing the national anthem or observing national holidays).

In the era of decolonisation, right across the postcolonial world, new meanings were mapped onto rituals, and new traditions were invented, with the intention of forming the national identity of the newly nationalised citizen. Schools were a favourite site for the practice of national rituals. Starrett (1998: 79) reminds us that in Egypt after independence:

> The conscious invention of public ceremonies became an important part of the state's mass mobilisation program, and schools began to capitalise on public events like the Prophet's birthday, Unity Day, and Mother's Day to clothe nationalist values like unity, cooperation and brotherhood with the appearance of important religious principles.

Nor are these practices now simply a matter of the historical record. Indeed, in many ways, ironically, the use of the school as a site for the production of a national sensibility has intensified in the contemporary period, despite regular proclamations of the death of the nation under the twin threats of globalisation and multiculturalism. In recent years, for example, the observance of St George's Day has become a regular fixture of the school calendar in many English schools, a national curriculum has been in place in England and Wales since 1988, and increases in school bureaucracy testify to attempts to homogenise across national space the organisation of schools. Debates about the role of religious schools in segregating communities and, conversely, the role of secular, government-funded (or community) schools in bringing communities together across religious, cultural and linguistic differences also testify to the importance of school as a site for the production of children's political subjectivities. Clearly, the work that has gone into imagining the nation continues to be necessary work, even in an era of globalisation, perhaps more so.

Once they are in school, children are not only children, they are also students with interests in common with other students and a shared experience of the world. This is not enough to turn children into political activists but if children do become politically conscious – often as a response to political conflict in the wider society – then schools are likely to be central sites for their mobilisation. In South Africa, for example, the history of youth activism is virtually inseparable from the history of education.

If students are more likely than other young people to be political activists, this is particularly true of university students. University students often take a leading role in politics and push emerging issues onto the top of the news agenda from where they may become mainstream political issues. This is what happened in the US during the civil rights and anti-Vietnam War movements (Kurlansky, 2005) and in Latin America in the 1930s through to the 1950s when student protests were 'the earliest and most significant bases of opposition to authoritarian governments' (Liebman et al, 1972: 25, cited in Bundy, 1987: 308). If youthful political activism takes this vanguard or leading role but then fails to engage the interest and involvement of a wider population, then it is likely to fizzle out.

In South Africa during the struggle against Apartheid, schools 'became an epicentre and vehicle of political mobilization' (Brocklehurst, 2006: 136); this was also what happened in pre-1979 Iran. The overt political interference in schools by government had the effect of politicising and mobilising students *against* the government.

The conflict between state and society was deep and sustained over many decades. This meant that many teachers, who had been involved in politics and who had experienced government oppression when young, felt that they had a duty to encourage and support students in taking a critical view of school life and of politics. Of course, not all teachers are potential revolutionaries! Nonetheless, when teachers are politically committed, school is more likely to become a site of political consciousness-raising and activity against the regime than a place for the smooth transmission of dominant ideologies to students.

Case study: young moral guardians

There is a substantial literature in developmental psychology that theorises the development of morality in children. Typically, these studies pose a causal and more or less linear relationship between increasing age and increasing moral understanding. Underlying these models is a supposition that children acquire moral understanding from adult members of society in socialising institutions, in particular the family and the school and, over time, internalise ethical codes into their own sense of self. In periods of intense political activism, particularly arising in the context of political conflict, especially war and revolution, the role of moral guardian is often taken up by children and young people.

Diamant (2000), in his study of politics, love and divorce in China from the revolution to 1968, proposes a thesis that sexuality – or more accurately sexual Puritanism – was an important element in explaining the role of young people in the Cultural Revolution. Furthermore, he suggests that the role of young people as moral guardians is a pervasive feature of strong religious or ultra-nationalistic political movements. Young people, Diamant (2000: 215) says, 'can easily cast themselves as "cleansers" of the national community largely because of their own naiveté, black-and-white worldview and innocence with respect to the complications of love and passion'. The Red Guards called for a ban on the under-24s smoking and drinking and denounced the vulgar language as 'intolerable to the ear and extremely shameless' (MacFarquhar and Schoenhals, 2006: 114). In China, it is evident that children and young people often perceived themselves as involved in a project of moral renewal. It is not that they rejected the normative values of their communities but that they felt that the older generation had forgotten or abandoned an ethical life – the ideals of communism in China. In this context, young people explicitly framed their role as that of moral guardians of the community, inverting the classic moral context governing parent–child or adult–young people interactions.

It is unsurprising that political movements that are legitimated by, and framed within, religious doctrine involve a moral discourse. In these revolutionary movements and their post-revolutionary regimes, the search for a transcendental ethics and the dualistic worldview of the young provide fertile soil for the formation of young people as the moral guardians of the revolution. In Iran, the Revolutionary Guard, the *Basij*, whose role is to protect the moral character of the revolution, is formed of young men who pursue their guardianship of the purity of the revolution with great fervour. The *Basij* are a very pertinent case study for the role of children and young people in international politics because political Islam is a significant force in shaping contemporary international politics.

The '*Basij*' (mobilisation) is the name of the militia of young men who were mobilised by the post-revolutionary regime to provide the 'human wave' in the 1980–88 war between Iran and Iraq (Varzi, 2006; Khosravi, 2008). The *Basij* continue to be a significant force in Iranian politics, especially in the cities where they have the role of policing moral conduct, especially of women and young people. They have access to work and education through a quota system that reserves 40% of university places to *Basijis*, their children and the families of martyrs (Khosravi, 2008: 39). In official speeches, *Basijis* are thanked on behalf of families whose 'immoral youth have been guided and corrected by them' (Khosravi, 2008: 29). They charge people with being 'vendors of western clothes', 'immodest veiling' and playing 'corrupt music and [having] unlawful relationships' (Khosravi, 2008: 30). There is an element of class resentment in their use of routine tactics of stopping rich young people and harassing them. It is not, of course, that all young people are policing the morality of public space. Indeed, it is women and other young people who are the targets of their moral surveillance (Amir-Ebrahimi, 2008).

Conclusion

Young protagonists engaged in political activity are more likely to be teenagers than children in early or middle childhood. While pre-teenage children have been involved in political activity, this generally only happens when there is a specific configuration of events. In particular, children are more likely to be mobilised for political activity by government interventions, as was the case with the young Red Guards in China, than they are to take up politics in opposition to the government. The exception to this – in a pattern that bears comparison with the mobilisation of children in war – is where the longevity of the conflict leads to the death or imprisonment of older generations, meaning that the leadership of the movement falls to young people and the mass mobilisation of the young brings with it children who would normally be considered too naïve and inexperienced to be directly involved in political activity. This was the case in the ANC's struggle against the Apartheid regime and is also evident in the changing age profile between the first and the second Intifadas in Palestine.

Young people are also more likely to be politically mobilised when they are in secondary school or university. This means that in most contexts politically active young people are likely to be better off than their generation as a whole. This also points to one of the clearest explanations for why young people are often more politically active than older generations: they have rising expectations that are frustrated by their material situation so that, for example, increased school enrolments (rising expectations) accompanied by diminishing opportunities or opportunities that do not keep pace with the increased numbers of high school and university graduates (frustration of expectations) provide fertile ground for young people to become politically active.

Generational conflict and resentment, which are widely regarded as a key reason for young people to become politically active, actually seem far from conclusive on the evidence offered here. While young people in many politically charged contexts accuse their parents' generation of quietism, this accusation only makes sense because of the presumption that their parents *should* be more politically involved with the (shared) cause. Young people and children were more likely to be politically active in the Red Guards if their parents were also politically involved or had been politically involved. When parents and children are on opposite sides of a political conflict it seems that they often (although by no means always) try to depoliticise or contain their relationship – as Dlamini (2005) found with young Zulu ANC members whose parents were affiliated to Inkatha, or the young Mojahedin in Iran who tried to integrate their politics with their parents' worldview (Keddie, 2003: 230).

The activism of young people in contrast to the quietism of their elders is often explained by the purity of young people in the political context – they have not been compromised or co-opted. However, before reproducing a well-trodden path of youthful political innocence and enthusiasm versus elders' political corruption and cynicism, it is as well to remind ourselves that in all the contexts discussed here, young people were, like their elders, a minority in political struggle and that not only were older generations also still involved in the struggle but that in many instances they provided the leadership for it. Indeed, when the leadership of political movements is only in the hands of young people – as with the Red Guards, the ANC during the notorious 'necklacing' period, the young *Basijis* policing Islamic morality in the Iranian revolution – it often displays a spectacular excess and a politics of terror that the protagonists may later look back on with incredulity and remorse. The innocence of young people does not mean that they are more politically engaged than their elders but it does often translate into a moral Manichaeism that allows them to take up the role of moral guardian with great enthusiasm.

The involvement of young people in spectacular acts of terror – often in the name of moral rectitude – should also alert us to the dangers of thinking of young people as the new political saviour. While there is, as this chapter has shown, ample evidence that young people are open to political mobilisation, there is nothing automatically progressive about their political engagements. They are as likely as adults are to be on the side of reactionary, conservative politics as they are to be on the side of progressive, radical politics.

References

Amir-Ebrahimi, M. (2008) 'Transgression in narration: the lives of Iranian women in cyberspace', *Journal of Middle East Women's Studies*, vol 4, no 3, pp 89-118.

Berdal, M. and Malone, D.M. (eds) (2000) *Greed and Grievance: Economic Agendas in Civil Wars*, Boulder, CO: Lynne Rienner.

Boyden, J. and de Berry, J. (2004) 'Introduction', in J. Boyden and J. de Berry (eds) *Children and Youth on the Front Line: Ethnography, Armed Conflict and Displacement*, Oxford: Berghahn.

Brocklehurst, H. (2006) *Who's Afraid of Children?: Children, Conflict and International Relations*, Aldershot: Ashgate.

Bundy, C. (1987) 'Street sociology and pavement politics: aspects of youth and student resistance in Cape Town', *Journal of Southern African Studies*, vol 13, no 3, pp 303-30.

Cairns, E. (1996) *Children and Political Violence*, Oxford: Blackwell.

Clapham, C. (1988) *Transformation and Continuity in Revolutionary Ethiopia*, Cambridge: Cambridge University Press.

Coles, R. (1986) *The Political Life of Children*, Boston, MA: Atlantic Monthly Press.

Comaroff, J. and Comaroff, J. L. (2000) 'Millennial capitalism: first thoughts on a second coming', *Public Culture*, vol 12, no 2, pp 291-343.

Cunningham, K. (2003) 'Cross-regional trends in female terrorism', *Studies in Conflict and Terrorism*, vol 26, no 3, pp 171-95.

de Block, E. and Buckingham, D. (2007) *Global Children, Global Media*, Basingstoke: Palgrave Macmillan.

de Boeck, F. and Honwana, A. (2005) 'Introduction: children and youth in Africa', in A. Honwana and F. de Boeck (eds) *Makers and Breakers: Children and Youth in Postcolonial Africa*, London: James Currey.

de Schweinitz, R. L. (2004) 'If they could change the world: children, childhood and African American civil rights politics', Unpublished PhD, University of Michigan.

Diamant, N.J. (2000) *Revolutionizing the Family: Politics, Love and Divorce in Urban and Rural China, 1949–1968*, Berkeley, CA: University of California Press.

Dlamini, S. N. (2005) *Youth and Identity Politics in South Africa, 1990–1994*, Toronto: University of Toronto Press.

Durham, D. (2000) 'Introduction: youth and the social imagination in Africa', *Anthropological Quarterly*, vol 73, no 3, pp 113-44.

Foucault, M. (2003) *Society Must be Defended: Lectures at the Collège de France, 1975–76*, ed by M. Foucault, M. Bertani, A. Fontana, F. Ewald and D. Macey, trans by D. Macey, London: Picador.

Gold, T.B. (1991) 'Youth and the state', *The China Quarterly*, no 127, pp 594-612.

Gonzalez-Perez, M. (2006) 'Guerrilleras in Latin America: domestic and international roles', *Journal of Peace Research*, vol 43, pp 313-29.

Hart, J. (2000) 'Contested belonging: children and childhood in a Palestinian refugee camp in Jordan', Unpublished PhD (Anthropology), Goldsmiths College, University of London.

Hobsbawm, E. (1975) *Age of Capital*, London: Weidenfeld and Nicolson.

Hoffman, D. (2003) 'Like beasts in the bush: synonyms of childhood and youth in Sierra Leone', *Postcolonial Studies*, vol 6, no 3, pp 295-308.

Keddie, N. (2003) *Modern Iran: Roots and Results of Revolution*, New Haven, CT, and London: Yale University Press.

Kent, G. (1995) *Children in the International Political Economy*, Basingstoke: Macmillan.

Khosravi, S. (2008) *Young and Defiant in Tehran*, Philadelphia, PA: University of Pennsylvania Press.

Kurlansky, M. (2005) *1968: The Year that Rocked the World*, London: Jonathon Cape.

Liebman, A., Walker, K. and Glazer, M. (1972) *Latin American University Students: A Six Nation Study*, Cambridge, MA: Harvard University Press.

MacFarquhar, R. and Schoenhals, M. (2006) *Mao's Last Revolution*, Cambridge, MA: Harvard University Press.

Mannheim, K. (1952 [1928]) 'The problem of generations', in K. Mannheim *Essays on the Sociology of Knowledge*, London: Routledge & Kegan Paul.

Marks, M. (2001) *Young Warriors: Youth Politics, Identity and Violence in South Africa*, Johannesburg: Witwatersrand University Press.

Marten, J. (2004) *Children of the Union: The War Spirit on the Northern Home Front*, Chicago, IL: Ivan R. Dee.

Nolte, I. (2004) 'Identity and violence: the politics of youth in Ijebu-Remo, Nigeria', *Journal of Modern African Studies*, vol 42, no 1, pp 61-89.

Perko, F. M. (2003) 'Education, socialization, and development of national identity: the American Common School and Israel defence forces in transnational perspective', *Shofar: An Interdisciplinary Journal of Jewish Studies*, vol 21, no 2, pp 101-20.

Pupavac, V. (2001) 'Misanthropy without borders: the international children's rights regime', *Disasters*, vol 25, no 2, pp 95-112.

Rosen, D. M. (2005) *Armies of the Young: Child Soldiers in War and Terrorism*, Piscataway, NJ: Rutgers University Press.

Shepler, S. (2005a) 'Globalizing child soldiers in Sierra Leone', in S. Maria and E. Soep (eds) *Youthscapes: The Popular, the National, the Global*, Philadelphia, PA: University of Pennsylvania Press.

Shepler, S. (2005b) 'The rites of the child: global discourses of youth and reintegrating child soldiers in Sierra Leone', *Journal of Human Rights*, vol 4, no 2, pp 197-211.

Singer, P. W. (2006) *Children at War*, Berkeley, CA: University of California Press.

Starrett, G. (1998) *Putting Islam to Work: Education, Politics and Religious Transformation in Egypt*, Berkeley, CA: University of California Press.

Stephens, S. (1995) 'Introduction', in S. Stephens (ed) *Children and the Politics of Culture*, Princeton, NJ: Princeton University Press.

Supko, R. A. (1998) 'Perspectives on the Cuban national literacy campaign', Paper presented at the LASA Conference, Chicago, IL, 24–26 September.

UN (United Nations) (1989) 'Convention on the Rights of the Child', UN General Assembly, Document A/RES/44/25, available online at www.hrweb.org/legal/child.html (accessed 18/02/05).

Varzi, R. (2006) *Warring Souls: Youth, Media, and Martyrdom in Post-Revolution Iran*, Durham and London: Duke University Press.

West, H. (2000) 'Girls with guns: narrating the experience of war of FRELIMO's "female detachment"', *Anthropological Quarterly*, vol 73, no 4, pp 180-94.

Three

Children and young people's participation

Mary Kellett

Introduction

The term 'participation', at its simplest, means to become actively involved in something. Davies et al (2006: 11) more specifically refer to it as 'involvement in a collective decision-making process with a recognisable social and/or educational outcome'. This definition implies agency and encapsulates its theoretical origins embodied in the UNCRC (UN, 1989). Historically, participation has been linked to active citizenship (Arnstein, 1969). Herein lie some of the tensions around the concept in relation to children because most adult constructions of child participation do not connect with child agency or active citizenship but are wedged in more passive agendas of listening and consulting. In this chapter I examine the multidimensional nature of children's participation from a UK perspective, exploring the myths, challenging the rhetoric and evaluating the impact on children's lived experiences. I conclude with a case study about a group of young people with learning difficulties who undertook their own research into barriers to their meaningful participation in youth decision-making forums. In this chapter the term 'children' is sometimes used for brevity but it also includes young people.

Theoretical frameworks

Participation has long been a contested concept in contemporary political and social dialogues. The reality of children's participation is neither singular nor simple and requires a process of continual adjustment to the changing needs of the societies that children inhabit. The shift towards increased involvement of children, in a variety of social and institutional contexts, not only in the making of decisions that affect them but also in research into their lives, has been driven by three main influences: the recognition of children as social actors, their concomitant recognition as consumers or 'users' of products and services and the increased attention paid to children's rights (Kirby et al, 2003; Coad and Lewis, 2004; Cairns and Brannen, 2005). To have an understanding of the complex and multifaceted nature of participation, it is necessary to examine how the theoretical frameworks have been constructed.

Historically, children have been denied the right to make decisions about matters that affect them, being viewed as morally incompetent, inexperienced and incapable of making rational decisions (Cunningham, 1996). This is epitomised in the paternalist stance of so-called 'child savers' (Archard, 2004) who took decisions on children's behalf as a protection against them making potentially harmful mistakes (Mayall, 2002; Cockburn, 2005). This perspective has been robustly challenged by liberationists who argue that even young children can make rational decisions (Hyder, 2002; Lansdown, 2004). Wyness (2001) takes a broader view, arguing that children's right to involvement in decision making threatens to destabilise the adult paternalist stance since it requires a shift of power and may openly conflict with adults' claims that they have the child's 'best interests' at heart. Franklin (2002: 24) further weakens the paternalist argument by claiming that children need to be given opportunities to gain experience and points out that adults, who are deemed to have the necessary experience, often make the wrong choices but are not excluded from doing so on the same grounds. In response to some of these theories, it is worth noting that the age of participation has been lowered from 12 to 7 in Norway. It is a legal requirement that at 7 years of age, children must be given the opportunity to express themselves and at 15 years of age they can make decisions about their own education, religion and membership of organisations in addition to being recognised in their own right in legal cases (Skivenes and Strandbu, 2006).

The rise of liberationist, and wane of paternalist, theories set participation on a rights course, which culminated in the UNCRC. In the years since this edict, the concern has been on how to translate its articles into meaningful practice. Hart's (1992) 'Ladder of children's participation' was the first real attempt to do this and his work is cited and criticised in equal measure. He refers to the first three rungs on his ladder – *manipulation*, *decoration* and *tokenism* – as non-participation and describes four further rungs – *assigned but informed*, *consulted and informed*, *adult-initiated shared decisions with children* and *child initiated and directed* – before the eighth and top rung of the ladder – *child-initiated shared decisions with adults.* Some (for example, Pridmore, 1998) have found it to be a powerful evaluation tool. Others (for example, Reddy and Ratna, 2002) criticise the implicitly sequential nature of the model. John (1996) asserts that Hart's ladder is a bestowing of rights to the powerless and passive child by the powerful adult, an outdated model of rights. A further criticism of Hart's ladder is that its structure implies a 'hierarchy of values' (Hart et al, 2004: 48), which is likely to lead to participatory activities being unfairly and misleadingly judged against particular levels. Treseder (1997) critiques the failure to acknowledge cultural contexts. His own model of participation takes the top five levels from Hart's ladder but arranges them in a circle, demonstrating that they are different, but equal, forms of good participation.

Shier is the other seminal author of participation frames of reference. Shier's model (2001) focuses more on the adult roles than the status of children within projects. From the lowest level – children are listened to – to the highest – children share power and responsibility for decision making – Shier frames questions for adults to consider when planning or evaluating participatory projects around 'openings', 'opportunities' and 'obligations'.

Level 1: children are listened to:

■   Are you ready to listen to children?

■   Do you work in a way that enables you to listen to children?

■   Is it a policy requirement that children must be listened to?

Level 2: children are supported in expressing their views:

■   Are you ready to support children expressing their views?

■   Do you have a range of ideas and activities to help children express their views?

■   Is it a policy requirement that children must be supported in expressing their views?

Level 3: children's views are taken into account:

■   Are you ready to take children's views into account?

■   Does your decision-making process enable you to take children's views into account?

■   Is it a policy requirement that children's views must be given due weight in decision making?

Level 4: children are involved in decision-making processes:

■   Are you ready to let children join in your decision-making processes?

■   Is there a procedure that enables children to join in your decision-making processes?

■   Is it a policy requirement that children must be involved in your decision-making processes?

Level 5: children share power and responsibility for decision making:

■   Are you ready to share some of your adult power with children?

■   Is there a procedure that enables children and adults to share power and responsibility for decisions?

■   Is it a policy requirement that children and adults must share power and responsibility for decisions?

Shier places a lot of emphasis on the collaborative activity of adults and children to bring about the most effective participation, reflecting a Vygotskian approach to scaffolded outcomes. Participation in joint activity with more knowledgeable adults or peers can support children in developing particular areas of competence through a bridging of that gap. This was what Vygotsky (1962) referred to as the *zone of proximal development*, or ZPD, the gap between a child's existing and potential levels of performance. It is the experiences that children encounter that determine their personal trajectories of development and the acquisition of particular competencies.

Kirby and Gibbs (2006) criticise both Hart and Shier's models on the basis that each participation initiative or task cannot be assigned a single level of participation when, in reality, levels of decision-making power constantly shift within projects and within tasks. Other criticisms of the models centre around the absence of any guidance on how adults can support children in participation work to make decisions and take action, or any problematising of different levels of empowerment that children might experience. In stark contrast, the stance adopted by the National Youth Agency (NYA, 2005) focuses on advocacy and outcome by adopting two core principles of participation: first, children have the right to have their views heard *and taken seriously* through a process of *dialogue*; and second, this dialogue should lead to *tangible* change (my emphases).

Political frameworks in the UK

The UNCRC was a catalyst for change, charging its membership with ensuring that children were listened to and consulted on matters affecting their lives. However, the UNCRC was not an initiator of participation, as some myths appear to perpetuate – participation existed as a human right long before this – but the UNCRC did throw a spotlight onto the concept and bring it into the political arena. Despite ratifying the Convention, the UK government entered a number of reservations and no new legislation was initially drawn up to support its undertaking. Instead, the government retreated behind the 1989 Children Act, claiming that this was sufficient to address the issues. Rights activists were unhappy with this stance (Freeman, 2002) and Mayall (2002) pointed out that the Act only required local authorities to take account of the views of children in their care – a small minority. The UNCRC recommended increased attention to Articles 3 and 13 about listening and consulting and charged governments to establish further participation mechanisms in state, family and community (UN, 1995), but it was not until 2002 that the UK government finally adopted a new approach and a commitment to listen to children. This was the start of the *Every Child Matters* agenda (DfES and the Chief Secretary to the Treasury, 2003; Children Act, 2004; DfES, 2004). Five outcomes were identified as being important to children leading happy lives ('being healthy', 'staying safe', 'enjoying and achieving', 'making a positive contribution' and 'achieving economic well-being').

The participation agenda in the UK evolved in three phases:
listening, consulting and ultimately involving children in decision-
making processes. With the roll-out of *Every Child Matters*, several
initiatives mushroomed, such as the Children's Fund, targeting children
aged 5 to 13 years at risk of social exclusion (Coad and Lewis, 2004);
Participation Works (2006), an online facility to help adults and
children access and share information about children's involvement in
decision making; and *Hear by Right* (Badham and Wade, 2005), which
provided standards for both statutory and voluntary organisations to
help improve the ways in which they involve children in decision
making.

Article 42 of the UNCRC required state parties to make public the
principles and provisions of the Convention. The UK government
complied with this in the creation of an *Every Child Matters* website
(www.everychildmatters.gov.uk) but fell short of the 'fundamental
rights and freedoms' expressed in the Article, drawing attention only
to 'the need for children to have special assistance and protection due
to their vulnerability' (DfES, 2006). The right of children to express
those views freely in all matters affecting them was not made explicit.
By taking this entrenched protectionist stance, the government set
itself on a collision course for conflict between adults' and children's
priorities where the needs felt by children were at risk of being
supplanted by the needs attributed to them by adults – a reflection
once again of children's perceived incompetence and inability to make
rational decisions. However, the Department for Education and Skills
(DfES, 2005) did acknowledge the difficulties in transforming this
rhetoric into long-term 'meaningful' participation for children, which
could bring about institutional change. If the outcomes identified
in *Every Child Matters* were to be effective, organisations had to be
clear what this meant in practice and how progress towards this could
be measured. Middleton (2006), drawing on her own experiences
of Youth Councils, confirms that while targets can instigate the
setting up of projects, they alone cannot guarantee good practice.
This situation is compounded by confusion about what the aims of
children's participation are and by the fact that any expectations about
these are likely to vary according to the roles of those involved in
participatory initiatives (Murray and Hallett, 2000).

Impact and meaningful outcomes

Listening to children's views is not the same as sharing decision-making processes. The rhetoric belies the reality that children's participation, as yet, is having little or no impact on policy making (Alderson and Morrow, 2004). Skivenes and Strandbu (2006: 16) have outlined four procedures they consider essential to facilitating effective child participation, and which ensure that children participate in the same decision-making process as the adults involved:

- Children have the opportunity to form their opinions in the first place – this requires adequate, age-appropriate prior information, including details of the consequences of any decisions they take for themselves and for others.

- Children have the opportunity to express their viewpoints in a decision-making situation – being invited to voice their opinions, and having the choice to express these for themselves or through a trusted adult.

- Children's arguments must be taken seriously – with equal opportunities to voice their views and sound reasons given if those views are not to be acted on.

- Children are informed after a decision has been taken – what result has been reached, how it has been reached and what the result actually means, including opportunities for questions and appeals.

This ideal is rarely implemented in practice, however, and while it is possible to find some pocketed evidence of improvements in services attributable to children's participation (Sinclair, 2004), there is much less evidence of substantial impact and long-term benefit for children's lives. Indeed, there is a danger that the current wave of 'participation activity' may lead to a bigger wave of disillusionment among children. For participation to be meaningful, it has to be accessible and there are instances where adult language and behaviour can exclude children from participating at the outset, as can lack of sensitivity to culturally appropriate contexts. The case study at the end of this chapter addresses some of these issues. The point is also usefully illustrated in an example from South Africa cited by Moses (2008). In 2002, Save the Children Sweden commissioned the *Children's Poll: A South African*

Child Rights Survey (Save the Children Sweden, 2002) to investigate
South African children's views and experiences of their rights and
violations of those rights. The South African constitution is among the
highest advocates of children's rights (Moses, 2006) yet participation
was ranked by the children as the third highest rights violation.
The reality, rather than political rhetoric, is that cultural norms, not
political edicts, are dictating actualities. Here, power relationships
between adults and children undermine any decision-making activity,
as expressed in simple terms by one boy who said: 'adults make the
decisions because they have the power' (Save the Children Sweden,
2002: 10). Children also reported being unable to make informed
decisions because adults deny them access to relevant information for
cultural or religious reasons. This is particularly common in relation to
information about safe sex.

There are differences between outcomes for organisations and/or
adults and outcomes for children. Moreover, there are differences
between outcomes for children as individuals and children as a social
group and these differ further according to the social and cultural
compositions of those groups. Children are not a homogenous group.
Like adults, they differ from one another in terms of their physical,
emotional and cognitive make-up. They have different histories and
different lived experiences. Varying degrees of self-development are
often cited in the literature as important outcomes of participation for
children (Roche, 1999; Shier, 2001; Kellett, 2005a). However, unless
activities are truly participatory, involvement might just as likely lead
to disempowerment and disillusionment as self-development. A note
of caution needs to be heralded because, despite all this debate, a
substantial body of evaluation literature on participation impacts and
outcomes is as yet only embryonic (Percy-Smith, 2006; Skelton, 2007).

Deconstructing children's participation

What is participation? Can we 'do' participation? Is children's
participation different from adults' participation? How do we measure
their participation? Confusion still abounds as to what children's
participation really means. It is interpreted both passively and actively.
The former suggests taking part in the sense of 'being present at' and
the latter suggests taking part as knowing one's participation may
be acted on (Morrow, 1999), exposing a wide gap between rhetoric
and reality. As Cairns (2001: 357) argues, 'young people's experience
has been of consultation as an event, in which the powerful (adults)
consult and the powerless (children) are consulted'. Children have

grown tired of endless tokenistic consultations that lead to no measurable change for them (Stafford et al, 2003). Power held by adults seeking children's views is evident in their control over topic, the methods used to ascertain their views, the timeframe in which consultation takes place and the impact of the consultation (Miller, 1997). Thus, children are still, to a large extent, dependent on adults to interpret and represent their perspectives. Processes of consultation, involvement and participation become blurred. It is possible, for example, to *participate* in consultation or to be *involved* in participatory activities. Some methods used to elicit children's views may be participatory or not since it is entirely dependent on the context and way in which the views are used. Lansdown (2001) groups approaches to participatory work with children into three broad categories: consultative processes, participative initiatives and the promotion of self-advocacy.

The semantic debate about what we mean by participation is fuelled by words like 'empowerment', 'agency', 'negotiation' and 'partnership', which are often used interchangeably. Clark and Percy-Smith (2006) consider that there are two important areas for debate: (1) critiques of the impact and efficacy of participation activities and processes and (2) a wider questioning of participation discourses. The first addresses how children's participation is impacting on services, structures and organisations. This embraces diverse economic, cultural and political issues. Differences within multicultural contexts raise some challenging dilemmas. For example, cultural, gendered and/or religious expectations in the family may be at odds with some state service providers' approaches to participation, engendering conflict between different values and agendas. The second requires a widening of discourses to include more critical reflections on participation. Criticism is levelled at the rhetoric of agency and the danger of exaggeration where too much responsibility is placed on those who may not have the power to implement change. Other critical reflection claims that children's involvement merely provides a vehicle for 'tick box' managerial approaches.

Putting the child at the centre of the participation debate

Amid all the rhetoric and debate, we are in danger of forgetting the child. What do children think about participation? Graham and Fitzgerald's (2008) study in Australia sheds some light on this. The children in their study (aged 13-18) view participation as a status issue. To them, participation is about being recognised, for who they are in the here and now, for their place in social and cultural life. Such recognition is accompanied by increased levels of self-confidence, self-respect and self-esteem. Graham and Fitzgerald maintain that due recognition of children should not be a 'bolt on', it is a vital human need and core to any rights agenda.

A coda to the recognition assertion is aspiration to citizenship. This is another hotly contested concept in the UK. Can children with their minority legal status genuinely enjoy citizenship status? Is citizenship the ultimate embodiment of participation? Does the current practice of positioning children mainly in the private arenas of family and school rather than the public arenas of policy and decision making render such questions redundant? Increased citizenship is frequently cited as a beneficial outcome of children's participation – but is the reality yet another semantic fudge? While the present English Children's Commissioner, Al Aynsley-Green, might insist that children are citizens, the UNCRC briefing document interprets the status of 'child' as having no political rights (John, 1996). The concept of citizenship in the UK seems closer to notions of responsibility and control than participation. Setting the age of criminal responsibility in the UK at age 10 is a prime example of this (for further details, see Chapter Eight). Children are among the highest users of state services in minority world societies, yet one of the most governed groups (Hill et al, 2004) and participation sits uncomfortably within such a paradox.

Participation facilitated by children as researchers

A recent initiative from within participation activists is the empowerment of children as researchers in their own right (Sinclair, 2004; Kellett, 2005b). The UNCRC is commonly cited in relation to listening and consulting children about matters affecting their lives; much less common is reference to the clauses in Article 3, which uphold the right of children to high standards of research about their lives. Outlawed is research where adults misinterpret data collected from children. Equally rejected are studies that claim generalisations about children's lives with supposed authentic children's voices when close scrutiny reveals population samples that are tokenistic and dangerously unrepresentative (Ennew, 2008). One way to privilege children's voice, minimise adult filters and ensure meaningful participation is to empower them as researchers in their own right (see Chapter Fourteen). Much participatory research is still adult-led, adult-designed and conceived from an adult perspective. It is not uncommon for children to be involved in data collection but play no part in design, analysis or dissemination. Children are party to the subculture of childhood, which gives them a unique 'insider' perspective critical to the design of methods that will generate appropriate data. Insight into their peer culture is just as valuable in the analysis of these data.

In a similar way to children's meaningful participation in South Africa being curtailed by parents restricting their access to information, access to quality research training is an example of another such participation gatekeeping. A genuine barrier to children engaging in, and leading their own, research is their lack of research knowledge and skills. Reflecting on the skills needed to undertake research, it is apparent that these attributes are not necessarily synonymous with being an adult; they are synonymous with being a researcher, and most researchers have undergone some form of training. Many, perhaps most, adults would not be able to undertake research without training. The task of distilling the complexities of the research process for children without compromising its core principles is extremely challenging but has been shown to be possible (see Kellett, 2003, 2005a; Kellett et al, 2004). The Children's Research Centre (http://childrens-research-centre.open.ac.uk) at The Open University is a centre dedicated to supporting and promoting research *by* children. There is a similarly empowering school-based initiative in Hungary (Jaeger and Zsolnai, 2004; Zsolnai, 2004) where 51 schools in Hungary have research methods as a taught part of their national curriculum for 10- to 14-year-olds and students are given dedicated curriculum time to undertake their own research. Six countries in Europe and one in the Middle East are currently piloting children-as-researcher projects.

Power dynamics are at work at a number of levels. Adults still control which children access research training and there is a danger of articulate, middle-class children getting a disproportionate slice of the cake. Marginalised groups and the less cognitively able are at risk of being excluded. Concerns about inclusion extend to children choosing to opt out as well as in. If we accept participation as an integral part of a rights agenda, we also have to respect the right of children to opt out. Not all children want to engage in participatory activity, not all children want to engage in political decision making and not all children want to engage in their own research. However, what all children would appear to want is a level of self-determination and control over the immediacy of their environment.

On a positive note, there have been some very successful outcomes where young people have undertaken their own research and effected political or institutional change across the globe and these instances are growing in number and global scale. Ghanaian child researchers investigating transport and accessibility problems were invited to share their findings with the Ghanaian Cabinet Minister for Transport (Lolichen, 2006) in the same year that a group of 11-year-old researchers in the UK were presenting their findings about mobility issues for young people to the Department of Transport (Patil, 2006). This chapter is not the place to discuss such projects in depth but it would be remiss not to refer readers to an initiative that is taking participation into pioneering territory (see http://childrens-research-centre.open.ac.uk).

Case study: WeCan2

Taking due note of earlier allusions to marginalised groups of children, this case study will focus on participation by young people with learning disabilities. Between 2005 and 2008, young people in Blackpool and Devon, assisted and funded by Mencap, researched some of the difficulties they faced when seeking meaningful participation – difficulties in translating theory into practice and rhetoric into reality. For this project, called WeCan2, Allan Aoslin, Ross Baines, Alice Clancy, Lizzie Jewiss-Hayden, Ryan Singh and Josh Strudgwick looked at some of the barriers and problems faced by themselves and other young people when trying to participate, wrote a report on what they had found and suggested solutions to some of the difficulties they encountered. For an account of the project in their own words, and to see video clips of the children speaking, go to the Children's Research Centre web page.

Before they started their research, these young people undertook training in research methods, shaping their proposal and deciding on the best methods to carry out this research. They then went on to examine the barriers they faced when trying to participate. Although they, and other young people like them, were very keen to participate, they found that it was not always easy. Based on 70 hours of attendance at youth meetings (young people's councils, anti-bullying meetings and Youth Opportunity Fund panels) and interviews with young people, Youth Parliament Members and youth participation workers, they found that difficulties occurred when:

- people spoke too fast;

- minutes of meetings were not sent out in advance and had to be read during the meeting;

- minutes and agenda papers were produced with small print and no pictures and were hard to read;

- people used too many 'big words': for example, in one youth council meeting one of the researchers drew attention to the example of the phrase 'ethnically diverse';

- meetings were often scheduled straight after school and the young people were hungry and tired, which affected how well they could participate;

- meeting places frequently did not have good disabled access.

Having carried out this research the young people then designed a toolkit giving the adult organisers of youth group meetings simple practical solutions to some of these problems, such as big writing and pictures on the papers, breaks for food and drinks and a set of traffic-light cards for young people with a disability to use in meetings to let people know when there was a problem. If people spoke too fast or if a young person did not understand something, they could hold up a red card. If a young person needed to ask a question, they could hold up a card with a question mark on it. The red, green and yellow cards could also be used as voting cards for no, yes and unsure.

The WeCan2 group then went on to evaluate these measures and found increased levels of understanding, participation and a sense of being listened to. They found that, in general, people were taking the time to explain things more clearly, were giving out simplified information and were taking their views on board. Young people were sometimes asked to co-chair meetings, were consulted about the recruitment of adult workers and when they suggested changes to leaflets or web pages, they were made (Aoslin et al, 2008).

Conclusion

It is only relatively recently that the concept of children's participation is being comprehensively addressed. Article 12 of the UNCRC introduced a radical and profound challenge to traditional attitudes

(Lansdown, 2001), which many governments have struggled to accommodate. Much has been at a tokenistic level, since there is no onus on those who organise initiatives to produce evidence that children's participation has led to successful outcomes, only that participation 'has occurred' – at least at the minimum level of children being listened to. Children are under no obligation to participate, indeed some children do not want to participate. Stafford et al's (2003) research showed that children are often reluctant to spend time taking part in consultation exercises or in decision making that they regard as either futile or an adult responsibility. The extent to which this is due to disillusionment is still unclear. What is abundantly clear, however, is that participation is a multifaceted and complex process predicated on a human right, integral to which is children's right to informed choice about participating in participation activity. The crucial factor is that when children do make that informed choice, power dynamics, gatekeeping and mediated interpretations are not mobilised to undermine them. The new sociology of childhood celebrates children as social actors and agents in their own lives. Facilitating meaningful participation is a further endorsement of this position, finally laying to rest sepulchral perspectives of children as 'adults in waiting' or 'human becomings'.

References

Alderson, P. and Morrow, V. (2004) *Ethics and Social Research with Children and Young People*, Ilford: Barnardo's.

Aoslin, A., Baines, R., Clancy, A., Jewiss-Hayden, L., Singh, R. and Strudgwick, J. (2008) 'WeCan2 Research', available online at http://childrens-research-centre.open.ac.uk (accessed 11/11/08).

Archard, D. (2004) *Children: Rights and Childhood*, London and New York, NY: Routledge.

Arnstein, S. (1969) 'Eight rungs on the ladder of citizen participation', *Journal of the American Institute of Planners*, vol 35, no 4, pp 216-24.

Badham, B. and Wade, H. (2005) *Hear by Right: Standards for the Active Involvement of Children and Young People*, Leicester: National Youth Agency/LGA.

Cairns, L. (2001) 'Investing in children: learning how to promote the rights of all children', *Children & Society*, vol 15, no 5, pp 347-60.

Cairns, L. and Brannen, M. (2005) 'Promoting the human rights of children and young people', *Adoption and Fostering*, vol 29, no 1, pp 78-87.

Children Act (1989) London: HMSO.

Children Act (2004) London: HMSO.

Clark, A. and Percy-Smith, B. (2006) 'Beyond consultation: participatory practices in everyday spaces', *Children, Youth and Environments*, vol 16, no 2, pp 1-9.

Coad, J. and Lewis, A. (2004) 'Engaging children and young people in research: literature review for the national evaluation of the Children's Fund (NECF)', available online at www.necf.org/core_files/Elicitingchdrnsviewsjanecoadannlewisoct2004.doc (accessed 24/11/06).

Cockburn, T. (2005) 'Children's participation in social policy: inclusion, chimera or authenticity?', *Social Policy and Society*, vol 4, no 2, pp 109-19.

Cunningham, H. (1996) 'The history of childhood', in C.P. Hwang, M.E. Lamb and I.E. Sigel (eds) *Images of Childhood*, New Jersey, NJ: Lawrence Erlbaum Associates.

Davies, L., Williams, C., Yamashita, H. and Ko Man-Hing, A. (2006) *Inspiring Schools: Impact and Outcomes*, London: Carnegie Young People's Initiative and the Esmée Fairbairn Foundation.

DfES (Department for Education and Skills) (2004) *Every Child Matters: Change for Children in Schools*, London: DfES, available online at www.teachernet.gov.uk/publications (accessed 16/01/09).

DfES (2005) *Every Child Matters: Change for Children: Participation of Children and Young People*, London: DfES, available online at www.everychildmatters.gov.uk/participation (accessed 16/01/09).

DfES (2006) *Every Child Matters: Change for Children: UN Convention on the Rights of the Child: Background*, London: DfES, available online at www.everychildmatters.gov.uk/strategy/uncrc/background/ (accessed 16/01/09).

DfES and the Chief Secretary to the Treasury (2003) *Every Child Matters*, Norwich: HMSO.

Ennew, J. (2008) 'Children's rights in the driving seat? Muddles in the interface between policy, programme and information about children since 1989', Paper presented at the conference 'Child and Youth Research in the 21st Century: A Critical Appraisal', European University, Nicosia, Cyprus, 28–30 May.

Franklin, B. (2002) 'Children's rights and media wrongs: changing representations of children and the developing rights agenda', in B. Franklin (ed) *The New Handbook of Children's Rights: Comparative Policy and Practice*, London and New York, NY: Routledge.

Freeman, M. (2002) 'Children's rights ten years after ratification', in B. Franklin (ed) *The New Handbook of Children's Rights: Comparative Policy and Practice*, London and New York, NY: Routledge.

Graham, A. and Fitzgerald, R. (2008) 'Conversations with children: theoretical possibilities for progressing participation', Paper presented at the conference 'Child and Youth Research in the 21st Century: A Critical Appraisal', European University, Nicosia, Cyprus, 28–30 May.

Hart, J., Newman, J., Ackerman, L. and Feeney, T. (2004) *Children Changing their World: Understanding and Evaluating Children's Participation in Development*, Woking: Plan International.

Hart, R. (1992) *Children's Participation: From Tokenism to Citizenship*, Florence: UNICEF.

Hill, M., Davis, J., Prout, A. and Tisdall, K. (2004) 'Moving the participation agenda forward', *Children & Society*, vol 18, no 2, pp 77-96.

Hyder, T. (2002) 'Making it happen: young children's rights in action', in B. Franklin (ed) *The New Handbook of Children's Rights: Comparative Policy and Practice*, London and New York, NY: Routledge.

Jaeger, P. and Zsolnai, J. (2004) 'Research training program in primary schools of Hungary', Paper presented at Research in Schools Conference, University of Vesprem, Hungary, 20 July.

John, M. (1996) 'Voicing: research and practice with the silenced', in M. John (ed) *Children in Charge: The Child's Right to a Fair Hearing*, London: Jessica Kingsley Publishers.

Kellett, M. (2003) 'Empowering ten-year-olds as active researchers', Paper presented at the British Educational Research Association Annual Conference, Herriot-Watt University, Edinburgh, 6 September.

Kellett, M. (2005a) *How to Develop Children as Researchers: Step-by-Step Guidance to Teaching the Research Process*, London: Paul Chapman Publishers.

Kellett, M. (2005b) *Children as Active Researchers: A New Research Paradigm for the 21st Century?*, NCRM/003, Southampton: ESRC National Centre for Research Methods, available online at www.ncrm.ac.uk/publications (accessed 8/01/07).

Kellett, M., Forrest, R., Dent, N. and Ward, S. (2004) 'Just teach us the skills please, we'll do the rest: empowering ten-year-olds as active researchers', *Children & Society*, vol 18, no 5, pp 327-43.

Kirby, P. and Gibbs, S. (2006) 'Facilitating participation: adults' caring support roles within child-to-child projects in schools and after-school settings', *Children & Society*, vol 20, no 3, pp 209-22.

Kirby, P., Lanyon, C., Cronin, K. and Sinclair, R. (2003) *Building a Culture of Participation: Involving Children and Young People in Policy, Service Planning, Delivery and Evaluation*, London: DfES.

Lansdown, G. (2001) *Promoting Children's Participation in Democratic Decision-Making*, Florence: UNICEF.

Lansdown, G. (2004) *Evolving Capacities and Participation*, Victoria, BC: International Institute for Child Rights and Development, available online at www.iicrd.org/cap/files/CAPevolvingcapacities_0.pdf (accessed 2/05/06).

Lolichen, P. J. (2006) 'Children as informed partners in governance', *International NGO Journal*, vol 1, no 1, pp 3-13.

Mayall, B. (2002) *Towards a Sociology for Childhood: Thinking from Children's Lives*, Maidenhead: Open University Press.

Middleton, E. (2006) 'Youth participation in the UK: bureaucratic disaster or triumph of child rights?', *Children, Youth and Environments*, vol 16, no 2, pp 180-90.

Miller, J. (1997) *Never Too Young: How Young Children Can Take Responsibility and Make Decisions*, London: Early Years Network in Association with Save the Children.

Morrow, V. (1999) '"We are people too": children's and young people's perspectives on children's rights and decision-making in England', *International Journal of Children's Rights*, vol 7, no 2, pp 149-70.

Moses, S. (2006) 'An overview of children's participation in South Africa', Paper presented at the conference 'Theorising Children's Participation', University of Edinburgh, 4-6 September.

Moses, S. (2008) 'Children's public participation in the South African context', Paper presented at the conference 'Child and Youth Research in the 21st Century: A Critical Appraisal', European University, Nicosia, Cyprus, 28–30 May.

Murray, C. and Hallett, C. (2000) 'Young people's participation in decisions affecting their welfare', *Childhood*, vol 7, no 1, pp 11-25.

NYA (National Youth Agency) (2005) *The NYA Active Involvement Team*, Leicester: National Youth Agency, available online at www.nya.org.uk/Templates/internal.asp?NodeID=89411&ParentNodeID=89141 (accessed 18/06/07).

Participation Works (2006), www.participationworks.org.uk (accessed 16/01/09).

Patil, M. (2006) *Getting Around as the Child of a Wheelchair User*, Milton Keynes: The Open University, available online at http://childrens-research-centre.open.ac.uk (accessed 16/01/09).

Percy-Smith, B. (2006) 'From consultation to social learning in community participation with young people', *Children, Youth and Environments*, vol 16, no 2, pp 153-79.

Pridmore, P. (1998) 'Ladders of participation', in V. Johnson, E. Ivan-Smith, G. Gordon, P. Pridmore and P. Scott (eds) *Stepping Forwards: Children and Young People's Participation in the Development Process*, London: Intermediate Technology Publications.

Reddy, N. and Ratna, R. (2002) *A Journey in Children's Participation*, Bangalore: The Concerned for Working Children.

Roche, J. (1999) 'Children: rights, participation and citizenship', *Childhood*, vol 6, no 4, pp 475-93.

Save the Children Sweden (2002) *Children's Poll: A South African Child Rights Survey*, Stockholm: Save the Children Sweden (Radda Barnen).

Shier, H. (2001) 'Pathways to participation: openings, opportunities and obligations', *Children & Society*, vol 15, no 2, pp 107-17.

Sinclair, R. (2004) 'Participation in practice: making it meaningful, effective and sustainable', *Children & Society*, vol 18, no 2, pp 106-18.

Skelton, T. (2007) 'Children, young people, UNICEF and participation', *Children's Geographies*, vol 5, no 1-2, pp 165-81.

Skivenes, M. and Strandbu, A. (2006) 'A child's perspective and children's participation', *Children, Youth and Environments*, vol 16, no 2, pp 10-27.

Stafford, A., Laybourn, A., Hill, M. and Walker, M. (2003) '"Having a say": children and young people talk about consultation', *Children & Society*, vol 17, no 5, pp 361-73.

Treseder, P. (1997) *Empowering Children and Young People*, London: Save the Children.

UN (United Nations) (1989) 'Convention on the Rights of the Child', UN General Assembly, Document A/RES/44/25, available online at www.hrweb.org/legal/child.html (accessed 18/02/05).

UN (1995) 'Concluding observations of the Committee on the Rights of the Child: United Kingdom of Great Britain and Northern Ireland', 15/02/95, Geneva: Office of the High Commissioner for Human Rights, available online at www.everychildmatters.gov.uk/_files/C1924FB899147873CC82E9B309CB507B.doc (accessed 16/01/09).

Vygotsky, L. S. (1962) *Thought and Language*, Cambridge, MA: MIT Press.

Wyness, M. (2001) 'Children, childhood and political participation: case studies of young people's councils', *International Journal of Children's Rights*, vol 9, no 3, pp 193-212.

Zsolnai, J. (2004) 'Kutatóvá nevelés már tízéves kortól', *Magyar Tudomány*, vol 49, pp 147-62.

Four

Children, young people and their families in the UK

Virginia Morrow

Introduction

Children in the UK grow up in a diverse range of families, but up until the mid-1990s, very little research had been carried out directly with children themselves about their views of family life and close relationships. This chapter introduces recent trends within the sociology of childhood that have attempted to incorporate children's accounts of family life into childhood and family sociology, by drawing on two empirical studies conducted by the author (one in 1990, the other in the mid-1990s), and updated with references to more recent studies by other researchers.

This chapter makes two claims. First, it suggests that children's views about what is important in family life may differ from those of adults (whether parents, policy makers or researchers). Second, it suggests that the tendency within sociology to construct children as 'burdens' on adults, and particularly women's, time, has meant that the contributions (whether practical or emotional) that older children may be making to the 'work' of family life have been overlooked.

Sociology is the study of social change and social divisions and patterns of difference between social groups. Sociologists analyse the consequences of divisions such as social class, gender, ethnicity and, more recently, childhood and old age. Mainstream, or classical, sociology, for a long time constructed 'the family' as nuclear, that is, two parents and their children, and characterised the role of 'nuclear family members' in the family division of labour as divided along the lines of gender and age, with (adult) women mainly caring for (immature) children. However, as Douglas (2004: 2) points out, family may be understood from a range of perspectives:

including the genetic, focusing on the blood-tie; social, emphasising the functions carried out by those standing in a family relationship to each other; psychological, exploring the ties of affect and emotion between individuals; legal, defining the family for the purposes of legally binding decisions and rules; and ideological, promoting a particular form of family structure and behaviour as the desirable norms.

Family sociology arguably had very little to do with children, therefore, but focused rather on parenthood, marriage and divorce, with the consequence that 'so-called family theories might be more accurately called partnership or parent theories' (Hill and Tisdall, 1997: 71). Milkie et al (1997: 220), US researchers, point to the irony in this:

> One might argue that children are simultaneously at the centre and the periphery of social scientific scholarship on the family. Although a great deal of work focuses on the family's effect on children (e.g. the consequences of parents' divorce), most sociological scholarship ignores children's understandings, portrayals, and evaluations of families.

Thus, within family sociology, children tended to be excluded, and where they were included, they were peripheral to marital relationships or construed as passive or as burdens. Children were interesting in so far as they became adults, not for what they were. This had two consequences for the way sociology conceptualised children in families: first, it meant that the importance of a range of significant others in children's lives (such as siblings, wider kin, friends, even pets) had been overlooked, as 'the family' (often merely defined as 'family structure' and the presence of parents) became reified as the most important source of influence on children. Where children's relationships with others, such as friends, were considered, such relationships were almost invariably seen as negative. Research tended to look at children in families predominantly from a perspective that placed children in a particular family setting and extrapolated from there. In other words, there was a tendency to describe and define children as being in particular family forms: children in 'single-parent' families, lone-mother families, stepfamilies and so on (of course, from a child's point of view, there is no such thing as a 'single parent').

These ideas were challenged by the 'new' social studies of childhood, which grew out of a dissatisfaction with the general neglect of children within sociology. The Danish sociologist Qvortrup (1987: 3) was the first to break with the sociology of the family in the mid-1980s, arguing that there were plenty of 'sociologically *relevant* discussions of children's problems and problem children' (emphasis in original) but few studies that were grounded in children's experiences of their daily lives. Following on from this, during the late 1980s and early 1990s, sociologists and anthropologists increasingly acknowledged that *sociological* research (as opposed to psychological/behavioural/medical research) with children was underdeveloped and needed rethinking (Qvortrup, 1987; Mayall, 2002). Social anthropologists Alan Prout and Allison James (1997) proposed a framework that moved beyond psychologically based models of childhood as a period of socialisation. They claimed that childhood (like the concept of family) is socially constructed, and that children's roles and activities are differentiated according to historical period and cultural context. They argued that children should be seen as active social agents, who shape the structures and processes around them, at least at the micro level. Furthermore, their 'social relationships and cultures are worthy of study in their own right, independent of the perspectives and concerns of adults' (Prout and James, 1997: 8). This paradigm involved moving on from the narrow focus of socialisation and child development (the study of what children will *become*) to a sociology that attempted to take children seriously as they experience their lives *in the here and now*. This presents a challenge not only to mainstream sociology, but also to developmental psychology, which is the discipline that still tends to dominate the training of professionals who work with children, whether in social work, education, or healthcare work.

Until the late 1990s, there was remarkably little research into how children make sense of contemporary patterns of family life. For a long time, most knowledge of children's experiences of their families came from adults, from parents, from professionals such as social workers, lawyers or psychologists, or from adults' recollections of their own difficult childhood experiences (for example, Walczak and Burns, 1984; Mitchell, 1985). Much quantitative research focused on 'family structure effects' (such as the effects of parental separation on children; for example, Dunn and Deater-Deckard, 2001; Smart et al, 2001), which fed powerful popular debates about the harmful effects of family breakdown on children, generating a discourse that portrayed children in the 'wrong' kinds of family as being damaged, and leading to political rhetoric about the 'parenting deficit' (Etzioni, 1993). While parental conflict undoubtedly has a deleterious effect on children, the possibility that there may be benefits from living in complex family forms, or that non-nuclear family structures may expand the potential for sources of social support, was rarely explored.

By the new millennium, researchers had begun to raise questions about how far it is appropriate to try to analyse data from, or about, children according to their family structure when talking about their experiences of family life. Rather, they argued, researchers need to focus on what families mean to children, and what family members do for each other (see Morrow, 1998a; Mayall, 2002). Other research began to focus on children's own accounts of family life, including their views on parental separation and stepfamily life (Moore et al, 1996; O'Brien et al, 1996; Brannen et al, 2000; Dunn and Deater-Deckard, 2001; Smart et al, 2001; Mayall, 2002). There have also been important moves within sociology towards acknowledging a diversity of family forms, including 'non-traditional' family forms (see, for example, Gabb, 2005, in relation to lesbian parenting).

Case study 1: children's notions of family

This section of the chapter draws on data collected for a research project that explored children's conceptualisations of family. The research was set in the context of two recent social phenomena. The first is that contemporary children are likely to experience a variety of family settings as they pass through childhood; the second relates to changes in social policy that have prioritised the need to 'listen to children' and elicit their views when matters about their futures are being decided.

Sample and setting

The research was based on data gathered in schools in the mid-1990s from 183 children aged between 8 and 14 in two areas of East Anglia. The first area was largely rural with a predominantly white population and the second was a large town with a large population of British Muslims originating from Pakistan (referred to here as children of Pakistani origin). The research explored how children's notions of family differed according to family background and compared children from the majority cultures with those from a minority ethnic group, thus exploring the 'diversity of childhoods' arguments coming from the sociology of childhood. Data were gathered through drawings, written accounts, sentence completion and group discussions; see Morrow, 1998b, for a description of the methods and ethics of the research. For the purposes of this chapter, children have been divided into 'younger' (aged 8-11) and 'older' (aged 12-14) groups. All names have been changed to protect anonymity. Children chose their own pseudonyms. Place names have also been changed.

Children's definitions of family

Children's beliefs about what counts as family appeared to vary according to age and ethnic background. Marriage, the presence of children, or geographical proximity, were the key components of a family for younger children, while in general, older children seemed more likely to generalise beyond their own experiences, without referring to concrete examples. They were more likely to see the quality of relationships between family members as being the defining feature rather than formal contractual relations. The themes that emerged from the children's definitions of family were broken down into the following three categories: roles (what family members do for each other); the quality of relationships (love and affection); and structure (the people involved, for example 'a group of people who live together'). It was in their descriptions of roles that their active contributions emerged, particularly from the older children's definitions. The italicised emphases in the following extracts highlight this.

Nisa, aged 13, defined family as 'a group of people who are related who respect, love and value one another. Families are for helping you through bad times, cheering you up when you feel down, *caring for one another.*' Bob, aged 14, wrote: 'A family is related to me in some way. Mum, dad, grandparents, brothers, sisters, aunts, uncles, cousins, half-brothers/sisters, stepsisters/brothers are all family. Families are for giving me stuff; food, clothes, presents. Loving, caring for me and *for giving things back to.* And for people to talk to.' Some older children used the terms 'related' and 'relations' in their definitions of family, but they were not necessarily taking 'related' to mean genetic links, and some were clear that people are connected to each other in different ways, through marriage as well as blood ties. Rather, caring and love, the quality of the relationships involved, and fulfilling expected roles, defined family and this was the case regardless of age, gender and ethnicity. Older children's definitions emphasised abstract notions such as the quality of the relationships and reciprocity more than those of the younger children: nearly half of the older children included elements of mutual support in their definitions of what families are for, using words like '*caring for each other*', '*sharing*' and '*looking after each other'*. Several mentioned how they undertake tasks such as looking after siblings or nieces and nephews, and two 14-year-olds, one girl and one boy, described how they were helping their mothers who both had physical health problems. Another boy, Jack, aged 14, mentioned how the most important person to him is his father: 'because he is the only parent I have got left and he struggles to look after me *so I help* as well'.

These comments also reveal how much family members do for children, as well as how much children might think they do things for their families. It would be misleading to suggest that children are independent social actors, when they are clearly the recipients of more care than the givers of it, especially when they are very young, but what these data show is that family relationships are more than a one-way process of parents giving to and caring for children (as they have tended to be conceptualised in family sociology).

Who is important to children?

Parents, especially mothers, provide physical and emotional care and this was explicitly acknowledged by children. However, any discussion of the centrality of parents to children's lives probably needs to be balanced, because a range of 'significant others' were also described, such as siblings and pets.

Recent sociological research has begun to explore children's sibling relationships in their everyday lives (Edwards et al, 2005; Mason and Tipper, 2008; McIntosh and Punch, 2009). In my research the presence of one or more children was an important element in children's definition of what a family is, particularly for the younger children. Many children drew their brothers and/or sisters in their pictures and mentioned them in descriptions of 'who is important'. The comments by children of Pakistani origin about their siblings were positive, and included many examples of what brothers and sisters *do for* each other: Wassim, aged 10, described how 'My big sister is important to me because she *helps me* on my homework and sometimes on my reading books'; Wyed, aged 10, wrote: 'I love my sisters because *they care* for me. I love my brothers because *they care* for me.' Two differences emerge between the accounts of children of Pakistani origin and other children's accounts. First, some of the children of Pakistani origin described large families, almost hierarchically arranged in age order, for example:

> My [big] brother is important to me *because without him I*
> *would not be able to do my work.* My [big] sister is important
> to *me because without her I could not do the housework.*... My
> little sister is important to me because without her I would
> have nothing to do. My little brother is important to me
> because without him I would have no one *to play with.* My
> littlest sister is important to me because she always makes
> something for me to do. (Shazia, aged 10)

Second, Shazia's description may also illustrate a preference for
playing with siblings among families of Pakistani origin. It is also
possible that there may not be the same expectation of going round
to friends' houses as there is among white families. This is reflected
in other accounts, for example Nakila, aged 11, described how 'My
baby sister is important to me because she is smaller than me and I
got every right to look after her.... My brothers are important to me
because [without them] I will not have anyone to play with.' Saifullah
Khan (1979: 44) comments that (for adults of Pakistani origin) 'the
closest bonds of friendship and emotional attachment are within
the family and close kin'. It is also important to note that Pakistani
kinship patterns are based on extended family groups and wider 'clan'
networks and children's ideas about family need to be seen in this
context. According to Hylton (1995: 15), 'group cohesion and links
with family networks are very strong, resulting in a strong aversion and
stigma to divorce, and restrictions on remarriage'. Issues of family and
kinship are further complicated by strong Islamic principles contained
in the Qur'an, 'which emphasise the importance of family obligations
and interdependence' (Hylton, 1995: 15). There may also be more
control over Pakistani origin children's (especially girls') freedom of
movement, in that they may not be allowed to play outside (see also
Shaw, 1988); further, a fear of racial harassment may inhibit some
children from using public spaces in the same way as white children
so they may be more 'home-centred' in their leisure pursuits (Morrow,
2000).

Older (white) children wrote mostly positively about their siblings,
and some described how they provide support to each other. Tara,
aged 13, described how 'My sister *helps me* with what I look like when
I go to parties. She's pregnant at the moment so her baby is very
important to me. If my sister goes through any distress *I cheer her up.*'
Fred, aged 14, described how 'My brother and sister [are important]
as we *do things for each other* and do things together' and Tiffany,
aged 12, wrote: 'My older brother is important ... I can talk to him about

most things and I care about him'. Stepsiblings were included here by some children. Danielle, aged 13, described how 'My stepbrother is very important to me as when I have problems *he really does care and stick up for me*. When we were younger we used to fight but now we're more grown-up we can be really close.' There were some examples of more conflict-ridden relationships with siblings, but these were usually qualified by an indication that the children 'love them really'. Charlotte, aged 13, described how 'My brother is [important] too, although I don't say it because we're always fighting, but I don't think I could live without him'. Callum, aged 12, wrote: 'My little sister is important to me because I can sometimes trust her. She does get very annoying, though.' It is important to acknowledge that sibling relationships can be sources of stress, as well as support (see McIntosh and Punch, 2009; Punch, 2008).

Pets were frequently drawn in pictures or mentioned by the rural children, markedly less so by the urban children, and it seems likely that pet ownership is more common in rural areas. When asked to draw or write about who is important, the children in the rural location all asked 'can we include our pets?' to which I responded 'yes'. This may have skewed subsequent responses as children widened the range of 'who' they described. However, from children's point of view, their pets are part of their families, and for some children pets remain very important into mid-teens. Many children described how pets are 'always your friends, they can't say anything back'; 'you trust them and they trust you'; 'in a way they're sort of part of your family, so you like respect 'em, love them'. One boy said, 'well, when they die, it's kind of like a family member dying, so you get all sad'. Pets represent a source of emotional comfort for some children, and this is frequently overlooked in accounts of British children's social lives. Pets were not mentioned at all by the children of Pakistani origin (dogs in particular are seen as polluting and not kept within houses) – again this alerts us to the diversity of childhood experiences.

In summary, this study revealed not only the centrality of parents from children's point of view, but also the importance of various relationships beyond parents. It also highlighted children's active contributions to these relationships, and a diversity of children's experiences of family life.

Case study 2: children's contributions to family labour

The second case study explored children's involvement in work, broadly defined, and highlighted children's contributions to family businesses and domestic labour. The research was based on an analysis of 730 children's written accounts (essays) describing their everyday life outside school (children aged between 11 and 16, in Birmingham and West Cambridgeshire); interviews with a small number of children (n=5); and school-based discussions on the meaning of 'work' with two small class groups of children in inner-city Birmingham (see Morrow, 1994 for more detail). In general sociology, children tend to appear as burdens on women's time, and while there has been some acknowledgement of girls' contributions to family labour, this is usually seen as a kind of apprenticeship for future adulthood, part of their socialisation (for example, Oakley, 1974) rather than as intrinsically useful. Seeing this kind of work as a direct rehearsal of an adult role leaves us unable to explain why boys ever do anything at all to help around the house. There has also been increasing acknowledgement that large numbers of children and young people act as carers who look after ill or disabled parents and siblings (see Aldridge and Becker, 2003). However, even here there has been an emphasis on seeing child carers as 'children in need' or 'victims', rather than acknowledging and respecting their contributions as intrinsically useful (Olsen, 2000; Warren, 2007).

What reciprocal support do children give to families?

In terms of family labour, the research found that children whose families run small businesses are likely to help in those businesses, regardless of ethnic background. There were examples of children working in a range of businesses belonging to parents or other relatives, such as shops, repairing goods, building and construction, restaurants, outwork (specifically, making jewellery, framing prints). To give two examples: one 15-year-old Birmingham girl, of African Caribbean origin, described how she worked at her aunt's bakery in Leeds in the school holidays:

> Sometimes I help in the restaurant, or sometimes I work in the takeaway. My aunt owns the bakery, her husband owns the restaurant, and he's a part manager in the takeaway. They are all Caribbean shops on *** Road. I help out

voluntarily, but surprisingly I had £100 this six weeks holiday.

The following example is by a 15-year-old Cambridgeshire boy, who described working in his family butchers business:

> After school, I go straight home on the bus. When I get home I watch television for about an hour before having my dinner. After my dinner I go out with my dad to where I work at my brother's butchers shop. I usually help my brother and my dad for about two hours most evenings.... In the mornings before school I usually get up quite early and bike to a nearby village to a field, which my dad owns. I have to go there to check that the sheep which are there are ok.... At the weekends, I work for my brother at his butchers shop.... On a Sunday I work in the morning and I go out with my friends in the afternoon. My work involves cutting up joints of meat and boning out meat. Also clearing up.

Domestic labour

Thirty-one per cent of the boys (n=106) and 53% of the girls (n=153) mentioned some form of domestic labour. (Their precise contributions in terms of time cannot be 'measured', and it is important to remember that these were children's accounts, not their parents'.) Children mentioned a range of chores, which were categorised under the following topics:

- general domestic chores, such as washing up, ironing, tidying, dusting and hoovering;

- care of or babysitting siblings;

- care of/helping other relatives such as grandparents or babysitting younger cousins;

- shopping for the household;

- outdoor tasks such as gardening, lawn-mowing, washing the car.

Self-maintenance (for example 'I get my own breakfast', 'I tidy my room') was excluded from the analysis, but is an example of children's agency. Not surprisingly, there were clear gender differences, in that girls described doing more housework than boys and boys tended to describe outdoor tasks, such as shopping, washing cars and cutting the grass. Children tended to describe 'helping mum', like this 13-year-old girl: 'I help my mum with the cooking and changing my baby brother and giving him baths.... I have to go up the shop for my mum as she and my dad has very bad arthritis.' There were instances where they described helping their fathers, where there was apparently no adult female at home, for example a 15-year-old boy described how:

> Before I can go out I must do all my work.... I put
> shopping away with the help of my brother. That is on
> Monday and Friday that is the days when my dad does the
> shopping. The rest of the days I do the washing up and the
> hoovering and I do my bedroom with my brother's help,
> when we have done our work we can go out, but we have
> our dinner, then wash up ... our dad sometimes does dinner,
> but we would do it normally.

Other children mentioned helping their grandparents, for example a 12-year-old girl wrote: 'My nan isn't well so I have to help look after her and keep a check on her in case anything happens'. A 15-year-old boy described how:

> Then if no one has been to see my gran, I call in to see
> her for a couple of minutes. I also keep her garden tidy, cut
> her grass, plant her vegetables. My other gran and grandad
> live out in a small village so I only see them at weekends.
> Grandad has an old car, so when that needs some work
> doing to it, I help my dad to repair it.

One 14-year-old girl mentioned in discussion that 'I started doing babysitting but I don't do any more work like that now, because I *look after* my nan'.

   Birth order, age, family composition, parental employment patterns, parents' health status, ethnic background and religious beliefs are all likely to interact with gender to influence whether or not children contribute to domestic labour or to family businesses. In other words, the context in which these processes are negotiated is of central importance. There may be a continuum, from children who make no contribution whatsoever to the domestic economy, to children whose contribution is crucial to the functioning of the household, with many children making contributions that fall somewhere in between the two extremes. The social construction of children as 'dependants' requiring socialisation (which has tended to dominate family sociology) has arguably prevented us from acknowledging the extent to which children have agency and responsibility in the here and now. This dependency assumption leads us to see them as merely consumers (of goods and services) rather than as possible contributors. It seems likely that sociology and practice could well move forward, away from dualistic conceptualisations of childhood as the polar opposite of adult independence, towards a model that sees family members as interdependent at different stages of the lifecourse (see Jones, 1992; Morrow, 1996).

The second case study deliberately highlighted the *practical* contributions that older children make to their families. More recently, research has shed some light on the *emotional* contribution that children may be making in the running of households. Smart et al (2001: 72), in their study with children about their everyday lives after their parents divorced or separated, suggest that children's positions 'as "dependants" can mask their contribution to the work of sustaining relationships with other family members after divorce'. They found:

> What was interesting about the accounts of the children and young people we spoke to was how many of them voiced a belief that divorce had intensified their appreciation of their parents, and their desire actively to help them. They suggested that, as a result of the divorce or separation, they no longer took their parents for granted or saw them simply as an accustomed backdrop to more immediate concerns of their daily lives. Instead, they had become more consciously aware of their attachment to their parents, perceiving the intimacy that they shared with them as potentially vulnerable, and therefore as something to which they wanted to give time and commitment.
> (Smart et al, 2001: 73)

Children's contributions to family life, whether in working in family businesses, in household chores and the day-to-day running of homes, or in the emotional contributions they may make to family life, all remain somewhat under-researched.

Conclusions and implications

In conclusion, adult-dominated accounts of family life (based on traditional sociology of the family) have tended to conceal, rather than illuminate, children's active roles within families. An approach from the 'new' social studies of childhood presents a contrasting picture. When asked about the important defining features of family, children emphasised the quality of the relationships within the family, rather than family structure. When asked about activities they undertake, it is apparent that many children contribute to the day-to-day practices of family life. Thus, a sociological analysis of families from children's views finds an account that is not defined by structure, but which is pivoted around the quality of relationships, and one in which the division of labour is not solely based on gender and age, but is flexible and dynamic, in other words, changes according to family members' needs and capabilities.

There are a number of implications for policy and practice from the two case studies. First, in relation to the first case study, as noted, social policy conceptualisations of childhood tend to depict children as a unitary, homogenous category. In practice, the study suggested that children have a wide range of experiences and backgrounds. Children of different ages described 'family' in differing ways, and younger children tended to use concrete examples and their own experiences in discussions, while older children were more abstract. However, there was wide variation between children, and some young children showed a clear capacity to step outside their own circumstances to generalise, and to see things from others' points of views.

Second, children's emphasis on wider social relationships, including those with their extended family members, friends and even pets, needs to be taken into account when decisions are being made about their care. The fact that pets are important to children is often noted, but rarely explored in depth, possibly because it is seen as trivial and essentially childish. This in turn may enable adults to trivialise other expressed wishes or views from children.

Third, debates about the effects on children of family breakdown and reconstitution have generated an image of children as passive and vulnerable, which exemplifies an inherent tension between protecting children from the harmful effects of family conflict, and enabling children to be active participants in decisions about their welfare.

In the second case study, it was argued that children actively contribute to family life in many ways, but that their agency and responsibilities within families are not widely recognised or valued.

This denial of children's agency in a positive sense in turn fails to acknowledge interconnections between family members, generations and others in their communities (see Morrow, 1998b). Social policy rhetoric emphasises responsibility in relation to good citizenship, but misses the point that many children already actively contribute in various ways. Neoliberalising tendencies to withdraw the welfare state intentionally overemphasise the importance of parents in children's lives, with enormous emphasis being placed on parents to socialise their children 'responsibly'. This is in contrast to a weaker shift towards recognising children as people with rights in line with the UNCRC (UN, 1989). This links to ideas about rights and responsibilities in relation to children in English social policy (see also Chapter One). The more that parents' responsibilities are emphasised, and the more the importance of parents in children's lives is reified, then the more the contributions that children already make may be rendered invisible or slip from view.

References

Aldridge, J. and Becker, S. (2003) *Children Caring for Parents with Mental Illness: Perspectives of Young Carers, Parents and Professionals*, Bristol: The Policy Press.

Brannen, J., Heptinstall, E. and Bhopal, K. (2000) *Connecting Children: Care and Family Life in Later Childhood*, London: Routledge Falmer.

Douglas, G. (2004) *An Introduction to Family Law*, Oxford: Oxford University Press.

Dunn, J. and Deater-Deckard, K. (2001) *Children's Views of their Changing Families*, York: Joseph Rowntree Foundation/YPS.

Edwards, R., Mauthner, M. and Hadfield, L. (2005) 'Children's sibling relationships and gendered practices: talk, activity and dealing with change', *Gender and Education*, vol 17, no 5, pp 499-513.

Etzioni, A. (1993) *The Spirit of Community: Rights, Responsibilities and the Communitarian Agenda*, London: Fontana Press.

Gabb, J. (2005) 'Lesbian motherhood: strategies of familial-linguistic management in lesbian parent families', *Sociology*, vol 39, no 4, pp 585-603.

Hill, M. and Tisdall, K. (1997) *Children and Society*, London: Longman.

Hylton, C. (1995) *Coping with Change: Family Transitions in Multi-Cultural Communities*, London: National Stepfamily Association.

Jones, G. (1992) 'Short-term reciprocity in parent–child economic exchanges', in C. Marsh and S. Arbour (eds) *Families and Households: Division and Change*, Basingstoke: Macmillan.

McIntosh, I. and Punch, S. (2009) '"Barter", "deals", "bribes" and "threats": exploring sibling interactions', *Childhood*, vol 16, no 1, pp 49-65.

Mason, J. and Tipper, B. (2008) 'Being related: how children define and create kinship', *Childhood*, vol 15, no 4, pp 441-60.

Mayall, B. (2002) *Towards a Sociology for Childhood: Thinking from Children's Lives*, London: Open University Press.

Milkie, M., Simon, R. and Powell, B. (1997) 'Through the eyes of children: youths' perceptions and evaluations of maternal and paternal roles', *Social Psychology Quarterly*, vol 60, no 3, pp 218-37.

Mitchell, A. (1985) *Children in the Middle: Living through Divorce*, London: Tavistock.

Moore, M., Sixsmith, J. and Knowles, K. (1996) *Children's Reflections on Family Life*, London: Falmer Press.

Morrow, V. (1994) 'Responsible children? Aspects of children's work and employment outside school in contemporary UK', in B. Mayall (ed) *Children's Childhoods: Observed and Experienced*, London: Falmer Press.

Morrow, V. (1996) 'Rethinking childhood dependency: children's contribution to the domestic economy', *Sociological Review*, vol 44, no 1, pp 58-77.

Morrow, V. (1998a) *Understanding Families: Children's Perspectives*, London: National Children's Bureau/Joseph Rowntree Foundation.

Morrow, V. (1998b) '"If you were a teacher, it would be harder to talk to you": reflections on qualitative research with children in school', *International Journal of Social Research Methodology: Theory and Practice*, vol 1, no 4, pp 297-313.

Morrow, V. (2000) '"Dirty looks" and "trampy places" in young people's accounts of community and neighbourhood: implications for health inequalities', *Critical Public Health*, special issue on health inequalities, vol 10, no 2, pp 141-52.

Oakley, A. (1974) *The Sociology of Housework*, London: Martin Robertson.

O'Brien, M., Alldred, P. and Jones, D. (1996) 'Children's constructions of family and kinship', in J. Brannen and M. O'Brien (eds) *Children in Families: Research and Policy*, London: Falmer Press.

Olsen, R. (2000) 'Families under the microscope: parallels between the young carers debate of the 1990s and the transformation of childhood in the late nineteenth century', *Children & Society*, vol 14, no 5, pp 384-94.

Prout, A. and James, A. (1997) 'A new paradigm for the sociology of childhood', in A. James and A. Prout (eds) *Constructing and Reconstructing Childhood: Contemporary Issues in the Sociological Study of Childhood* (2nd edition), London: Falmer Press.

Punch, S. (2008) '"You can do nasty things to your brothers and sisters without a reason": siblings' backstage behaviour', *Children & Society*, vol 22, no 5, pp 333-44.

Qvortrup, J. (1987) Introduction, Special Issue 'The sociology of childhood', *International Journal of Sociology*, vol 17, no 3, pp 3-37.

Saifullah Khan, V. (1979) *Minority Families in Britain: Support and Stress*, London: Macmillan.

Shaw, A. (1988) *A Pakistani Community in Britain*, Oxford: Blackwell.

Smart, C., Neale, B. and Wade, A. (2001) *The Changing Experience of Childhood: Families and Divorce*, Cambridge: Polity Press.

UN (United Nations) (1989) 'Convention on the Rights of the Child', UN General Assembly, Document A/RES/44/25, available online at www.hrweb.org/legal/child.html (accessed 18/02/05).

Walczak, Y. and Burns, S. (1984) *Divorce: The Child's Point of View*, London: Harper and Row.

Warren, J. (2007) 'Young carers: conventional or exaggerated levels of involvement in domestic and caring tasks?', *Children & Society*, vol 21, no 2, pp 136-46.

Five

Children and families in an international context

Heather Montgomery

Introduction

The family is one of the most studied, debated and analysed concepts in the social sciences. How the word is defined, what constitutes a family and what roles and responsibilities families should take are all issues that have concerned educationalists, anthropologists, sociologists and historians as well as economists and politicians. Discussing the family is also highly emotive. Everyone has some experience of families and usually has strong views on what is an ideal family, even if their own experiences are negative or unhappy. Analysing the family therefore involves discussing the ideal and the reality, the personal as well as the cultural, the theory and the practice. Families are also inherently contradictory; they are a private space away from public life and the outside world yet they are also profoundly concerned with, and affected by, events outside themselves. While sometimes sentimentalised as a haven in a heartless world, the family is also the site of conflict and ideological strife between individual members and between itself and the state. Issues such as how to balance the rights and interests of children with those of adults, how to deal with certain freedoms and choices, such as divorce, and the place of cultural diversity within this struggle are all played out in debates over the family.

Analyses of children's roles within families have changed dramatically over the last 30 years and the rise of the new sociology of childhood, which has foregrounded children's experiences of families, was discussed in more detail in the previous chapter. Before this shift in emphasis, however, children's role was assumed to be a transformative one with research focusing on the ways in which the birth of a child altered the social status of their parents, for example, or changed a married couple into a family. These studies were also based on an underlying assumption that biological ties between parent and child brought with them caring responsibilities and duties.

Looking cross-culturally, however, it is clear that many of these 'natural' ideas are not universal and that families in other parts of the world are formed very differently and care for their children in different ways. Social scientists have described enormous variations in family types, the ways in which they are established, the relationships between the people in them and, perhaps most importantly, how conceptualisations of family ties affect the ways in which adults act towards children. They have found that while 'the family' may be a universal institution in that all societies recognise family relationships, there is no universal family form. Families may be nuclear, extended, polygamous and even in very rare cases polyandrous (when a woman lives with several husbands). Husbands and wives may live separately and children may trace their descent from either their mother or their father or from both. Families may be recognised as such because there are blood or biological ties between their members or because there are social ties.

It would be possible to write a whole chapter on different family structures cross-culturally and the basis on which these are made but this chapter seeks to do something different and will examine, using one particular example, how different ideas about the family clash in a transnational context and in the globalised societies that make up the contemporary world.

Relatedness

For many years, theories about kinship lay at the heart of anthropological theory but had limited impact outside academia. In general, ideas about the family are so ingrained, involve so much 'common sense' and are often so emotive that they are rarely deconstructed. Children are seen as being related to their parents by biology (thought of as 'blood ties' in the early part of the 20th century but now more likely to be seen in terms of genetics). As Schneider (1980: 23) argues about the US (but also applicable to the UK):

> [K]inship is defined as biogenetic. This definition says that kinship is whatever the biogenetic relationship is. If science discovered new facts about biogenetic relationship, then that is what kinship is and was all along, although it may not have been known about.

Following on from this, not only does biology define kinship but it is also fundamental to Western notions of identity and affiliation. As Strathern (1999: 68) puts it, 'Parentage implies relatedness; facts about birth imply parentage. Euro-Americans cannot ignore these connections. The information forms ("constitutes") what they know about themselves.'

Studies from other societies, however, have shown that this insistence on blood, genetics or other biological linkages between parents and children is not universal. Ideas about shared substances do not form the basis of the relationship between parents and children and there is no belief that those who give birth are necessarily the ones who should raise the child. Anthropologists have long pointed to examples of cultures where biological paternity is downplayed and even denied. They have drawn a distinction between the social mother or father, that is, the mother or father who raises the child (referred to as *mater* and *pater*) and the biological/genetic mother or father (*genetrix* or *genitor*).

Whatever the basis of family ties, however, the care and socialisation of children continues to be one of the central roles of families and families remain at the heart of children's experiences of growing up. Anthropologists have started to look, therefore, not only at the structures of family life, but also at the individuals who make up families and the difficult and messy emotions that being in a family inevitably entails. Carsten (2004: 9) has argued that, despite their emphasis on kinship, anthropologists have ignored the 'close-up, intimate and experiential dimension of kinship', preferring to examine interactions between groups instead of the nurturing that goes on between individuals in the domestic sphere (see Chapter Four for a fuller account of children's own views of their emotional attachments within the family).

Alongside this new interest in the daily, domestic sphere and the affective side of relationships is the acceptance that while there can be no universal definition of what a family *is*, it is possible to draw broad generalisations of what families *do*. Goody (1982: 7–8), for instance, has argued that there are five aspects of parenthood that 'appear to receive social recognition, as well as a patterned, institutionalised response, in all societies … i. bearing and begetting, ii. endowment with civil and kinship status, iii. nurturance, iv. training and v. sponsorship into adulthood'. Using this model, it is clear that parenthood is not simply about giving birth to a genetically related child, it is also about fulfilling the roles required to reproduce the next generation by raising useful and productive children, giving them a name and status within their society, and training and socialising them to the point when they are socially recognised as adults. Furthermore, Goody points out that the exact personnel who perform these roles differ across cultures and that in many instances the tasks of parenthood are assigned to people other than the biological parents. Relatedness, therefore, is not only about how people are connected but is also about generating kinship through care, nurturance and emotional ties. Kinship is not only something a child is born with, it is also something that can be created.

The 'problem' of African families

These differences between families exist not solely in the pages of obscure anthropological journals but are also relevant to problems in contemporary multicultural societies. Using the example of fosterage in West Africa, this chapter will now analyse one non-Western childrearing practice, describing both its historical forms and its present incarnations. By comparing these it is possible to see not only the potential for clashes and misunderstandings, but also the impact that globalisation and migration have had on complicating understandings of 'traditional' practices.

In May 2005, *The Guardian* ran a story with the headline 'Hundreds of African boys go missing in London' (Left, 2005). It was followed by a flurry of reports in other newspapers and on the BBC. The story went on to examine the case of 'Adam', the young West African boy whose torso was found in the Thames and who is believed to have been ritually murdered. The police have been unable to solve the crime, or even identify the child, and there were concerns that 'Adam' may not be the only child who was killed in this way. Against this backdrop, the police began to look at the apparent numbers of 'missing' African boys in London; those who had gone to school for a short while but had then unaccountably vanished. Scotland Yard asked all London education authorities how many black boys between the ages of four and seven had disappeared from school registers and could not be traced and found that 300 boys, 299 from Africa and one from the Caribbean, had vanished from official records between July and September 2001. The police were eventually only able to find two of these boys while the rest were said to have returned to Africa (BBC News Online, 2005).

The BBC, on its website, claimed that these missing children may be indicative of a serious social problem. It suggested that these boys were victims of 'child trafficking, sometimes for labour or benefit fraud' and quoted journalist Yinka Sunmonu who claimed 'They are being trafficked, they are being emotionally abused, there are incidences of domestic slavery, there is physical abuse, sexual abuse'. Another journalist alleged that 'part of the problem lies with the custom in many African communities of placing children with distant relatives' and there were calls to end the practice of private fostering in which relatives took in a child, often from overseas (BBC News Online, 2005).

The report left no room for doubt as to the seriousness of the situation. These young African boys, sent thousands of miles away to live with near strangers, with no safeguards and unknown to the authorities, were obviously vulnerable and it seems inexplicable that parents would expose their children to such risks. However, on looking at the problem in its wider cultural context, the situation becomes more complex. It is necessary to examine whether this concern is partly a consequence of ethnocentric thinking, which sees certain aspects of non-Western childcare as inherently pathological.

Systems of fosterage in West Africa

In general, keeping biological families together is seen as the best way of caring for children and the British state attempts to support and help parents (and mothers in particular) keep and care for their own children (Modell, 2002). As suggested earlier, there is a deep-seated belief that biology and identity are closely intertwined and that carers should ideally share biological or genetic relatedness to the children they care for. There are, however, cases where children cannot live with their natural parents, either temporarily or permanently. In the latter cases, they are usually put up for adoption and their new parents are treated in law as if they are the child's natural parents. Adoption thus involves 'the transfer of an individual from one filial relationship to another, from a "natural" relationship to a "fictional" one, but one which is in most respects legally equivalent' (Goody, 1969: 58). Social scientists draw a conceptual distinction therefore between adoption and fostering, arguing that adoption involves a change of identity and a move from one family to another, giving up rights of inheritance and support from the former while gaining new ones in another family. In Western societies it usually occurs when someone is a legal minor and involves a full legal recognition of the change in identity (Modell, 2002). Fostering, on the other hand, involves no such change of identity. Even in cases where children live away from their natural parents for long periods, their social and legal status is unaffected.

Systems of fosterage are found in many places but some of the best studied have been among West African cultures such as the Gonja, the Yoruba or the Mende. These studies have shown a great variety of fostering relationships, ranging from children being sent away at a young age and not seeing their parents again for years, to those where a family sends a child away for only a week or two. In many instances there are ongoing relationships between the biological and foster parents (Goody and Goody, 1967). Parents give many different reasons for these practices, citing cases where marriages have broken down and children cannot, or do not want to, remain with stepparents. They also talk about children being needed in other households as domestic labour or being fostered by couples who are childless. Fostering can also offset the cost of raising children during periods of economic hardship while the households into which they are fostered gain practical help, particularly if girls are fostered as they can then look after smaller children or perform household chores.

Fostering is part of wider cultural beliefs about the relative roles and responsibilities of parents and children and ideas about who are the best people to raise children. Sometimes it is taken as a matter of course that parents are not the right people to raise their own children, and indeed parents go to great lengths to downplay any sense that they do, in fact, 'own' their children. Some communities believe that parents are too sentimental to discipline their own children and lack the hardness that is necessary to train and socialise them (Goody, 1982). Verhoef (2005: 370), in a more recent study of fostering in Cameroon, sums up the very different understandings of family ties and parental responsibilities:

> As children belong not only to birth parents but to this kin group as well … it follows that conceptions of 'parenthood' are relatively more inclusive than those of nuclear families…. 'Motherhood' might be central to the female identity throughout sub Saharan Africa, but rarely is it assumed that the birth mother alone can raise competent children…. Instead, the 'motherhood' concept allows for various 'relatives' to participate in different aspects of nurturing, socializing and educating children…. Grandmothers may be involved in feeding children, older 'brothers' and 'sisters' in instilling cultural values, aunts in introducing them to marketing skills, and wealthier relatives in contributing to their school fees. In this context, it is understandable why the practice of fostering children is

> rarely questioned ... : other 'mothers' are merely 'holding',
> 'minding', or 'taking care of' the family's collective children.

Bledsoe (1990a, 1990b) has looked at the reality behind culturally stated ideals of fosterage. Based on fieldwork conducted among the Mende of Sierra Leone, she describes how fostering arrangements are explained as a way of promoting social mobility so that children are sent to more powerful or prestigious family members as a political act. Mende society has an elaborate system of patronage and parents see sending their children off to be servants to their patrons as a way of appealing to an influential supporter who may later be in a position to help them. This traffic is not one-way and parents may pay for other children's schooling as well as their own or send their own children out to others to foster, while taking in other children themselves, thereby building up many layers of indebtedness and influence over time (Bledsoe, 1990b).

In much of the literature, the long-term outcomes of these placements are presented positively and claimed as successful. Children appear to feel no long-term negative consequences from having been fostered and show no apparent difficulties in forming long-term relationships when they grow up (Goody, 1982). Indeed, contemporary studies from Sierra Leone have shown that many adults believe that 'the truly unfortunate children are those who have not been sent away from home to advance' (Bledsoe, 1990a: 85). Children's own views of the situation may be less positive, however, and some children describe being fostered as a miserable experience that brings them into conflict with both their birth parents and their foster parents (Bledsoe, 1990a, 1990b; see also Notermans, 2008). Bledsoe cites examples of children being treated harshly and worked hard by their foster parents and of parents being generally unsympathetic to their complaints. There may be a clash, therefore, between children's and parents' views on fostering: it is seen by parents as a way of training children for the future, teaching them that life is a struggle that they must work hard to overcome, but by some children it is regarded as a form of parental neglect (see Notermans, 2008).

Much of the literature on fostering looks at it from an adult perspective, asking what the benefits are for adults and for society in general. Yet, often there are benefits for the child in many of the above scenarios and fosterage is not entirely about adult needs or adults being cavalier with their children's futures. There are instances where children may actually choose to be fostered against their mothers' wishes, they may gain social advancement, a better education or greater opportunities, or even a family with siblings near their own age (Verhoef, 2005). Children can, and do, make decisions about with whom they wish to live and the opportunities available to them. Few studies, however, have analysed children's own views of the situation. Those that have, found that children, when asked, often express negative opinions about fostering. Notermans (2008), for example, showed that Cameroonian children were highly ambivalent about being fostered and claimed that they experienced being fostered as a time of conflict and tension.

Ideas about the correct care of children, and the best people to provide it, are subject to change and cultures are not static entities impervious to influences from the outside world. Globalisation and the impact of television and international agencies have had profound effects on every aspect of life in West Africa and there is evidence that this is affecting how children are raised. Among the Yoruba in Nigeria, for instance, both parents and children are reconsidering ideas about fostering. Here parents speak of their concerns about sending their children away or taking in others, despite the long traditions of child fosterage in the area, while children are running away from what they perceive as abusive foster carers (Renne, 2005). The younger generation of parents feel that they are the best people to raise children and are limiting their family sizes so that they have only those children they can care for themselves. Verhoef (2005) makes similar points in her study of 20 families in Cameroon who fostered their children out to others. She describes families who, while valuing the cultural norm of having 'many mothers' in theory, were much more ambivalent in practice and expressed doubts about letting others raise their children, resenting their children's foster mothers and believing that they could raise their own children better.

Case study: Victoria Climbié and transnational fosterage

The case of Victoria Climbié is extremely well known and there is no need to go into much detail here of either her murder or the subsequent inquiry by Lord Laming (2003), which pointed out endemic shortcomings in the social and medical services that contributed to her death. However, there is another aspect of the case that is less often addressed and that is the question of what Victoria was doing in the UK. Lord Laming (2003: 1) said little about this in his report, other than Victoria had come to the UK for a 'better life'.

Others, however, were considerably more vocal on the subject and her parents were severely criticised by some commentators in the media, and by social workers involved in the case, for allowing eight-year-old Victoria to leave the Ivory Coast and come to the UK with a woman she barely knew. Lisa Arthurworrey, one of the junior social workers at Haringey council, said in a newspaper interview: 'I can't stand Mrs Climbié. At the end of the day, parental responsibility begins and ends with her. She gave her daughter away' (Fairweather, 2008). A columnist in *The Sunday Times* wrote even more truculently:

> When you [Berthe Climbié] cheerfully handed over your own daughter for keeps to an almost complete stranger, a convicted fraudster who, with your blessing, intended to take her out of the country – did any money change hands, Berthe? If so, do you have a receipt? Is giving away your child to a fraudster recommended in the Ivory Coast Good Parenting Guide? … According to you, there is a 'tradition' among West African parents of sending children to Britain to 'better themselves'. Isn't it more the case that these children are shipped in as a lucrative investment, enabling their guardians to mop up all available child welfare benefits? (Liddle, 2008)

For a Westerner, with Western understandings of family duties and responsibilities, these are reasonable (if emotively expressed) questions. However, from a West African perspective, they become more problematic. The studies discussed above show that fostering there is seen very differently and far from being a betrayal of family relationships is a way of strengthening and supporting them. This appears to be the position of Victoria's parents. When asked whether he felt any responsibility for her death because he had entrusted her to her great aunt, Marie Therese Kouao, Victoria's father Francis replied:

> I have said again and again that that was not so. She [Kouao] is a member of our family and her role is to give assistance when she can and she gave us assistance in times of difficulty.…This is not uncommon at all. Everyone was excited about Victoria going because there was a possibility that other family members could follow. (Philpot, 2002)

Fostering for Victoria Climbié was supposed to be a step out of poverty for herself and her family. By sending her to Europe her parents believed that they were giving her opportunities for advancement, with the possibility that once she was successfully established, she could facilitate her siblings' entrance into the UK, where they too could get an education. They believed that they were doing their best for all their children and using the traditionally, culturally sanctioned means of fostering in order to do so. As her mother said in response to criticism that she gave her child away, 'We don't have a benefits system, [in Africa] we have extended family' (Harding, 2008).

Both commentators and Victoria's parents are arguing from positions based on their own understandings of family roles and responsibilities. Highlighting this aspect of the case is not intended as a defence of childrearing practices that pose risks to children. Clearly in this case the result was horribly tragic. Berthe Climbié has said that Kouao 'broke a tradition that went back for generations. She broke promises. She broke our culture' (Harding, 2008). This case does show, however, the difficulties involved in balancing the rights of children from different cultural traditions while also ensuring the highest possible standards of child protection. Cultural difference should never be used as a justification for harming children nor as a 'trump card' over human rights but neither should it be assumed that anything that does not fit with Western ideas of 'normal' families is necessarily wrong.

This case also shows the importance of properly understanding the cultural context and not assuming that 'African', 'African Caribbean' or 'black' are meaningful adjectives. Lord Laming (2003: 345–6), in his discussion of cultural relativity and social context, explicitly criticised the assumption that there is any one 'African Caribbean' or 'black' culture against which to make legal or any other judgements. He concluded:

> Cultural norms and models of behaviour can vary considerably between communities and even families. The concept of Afro–Caribbean behaviour referred to in Victoria's case illustrates the problem. The range of cultures and behavioural patterns it includes is so wide that it would be meaningless to make generalisations, and potentially damaging to an effective assessment of the needs of the child. The wisest course is to be humble when considering the extent of one's own knowledge about different 'cultures' and to take advice whenever it is available. (Laming, 2003: 345–6)

Conclusion

With a better understanding of the cultural background, both the news story about the vanishing African boys and the case of Victoria Climbié take on different meanings. That abuses can occur among children who are fostered by relatives is not in doubt, but it is not a problem unique to West African families, and the cultural practice of fostering by supposedly distant family members does not necessarily lie at the heart of the problem. What in Western terms are 'distant' relatives are understood very differently in other cultures and may well be seen as part of close kin networks with recognised and acknowledged responsibilities towards children.

It may be that the 'problem' of hundreds of disappearing African boys is not as it seems and the most likely explanation is that they have indeed returned to their home countries after periods of being fostered in the UK. It would be helpful to have a register of these children so that this could be checked and it would be even better to know their cultural and ethnic background in order to ascertain whether they were being fostered in line with identifiable traditions of their home communities. Doing this would make it easier to identify children from communities with no history of fostering who may well be more vulnerable.

This is speculative, however, and it is as important not to romanticise non-Western childcare practices as it is to avoid pathologising them. It is evident from many of the ethnographic accounts given in this chapter that there is ambivalence about fostering among both parents and children and that the actual realities of an individual child's placement do not always match up with the cultural ideals. Families under pressure in the UK may well see their African relatives as an unwelcome burden on overstretched households, who they feel compelled to take in, but do so unwillingly. In such instances, abuses are more likely to occur. Children too may resent or fear being sent overseas to be fostered by people they barely know and may run away. The harshness of childrearing, so prized by the Mende of Sierra Leone, may also be incompatible with a Western society that is struggling to support and implement children's rights and which promotes very different conceptualisations of the relationship between carer and child. Questions of cultural relativity and state interference in family and cultural life lie at the heart of such dilemmas and there are no easy answers. In a multicultural society like Britain, the family life of 'others' is not simply some anthropological curiosity to be read about at a distance but has an impact on policy choices and social interventions. Transnational fostering carries risks but it can also bring rewards and benefits. Weighing up the possible benefits with the potential risks is never easy. It is important to take account of wide variations in childrearing practices across the globe, different understandings of family relationships and acknowledge that what is 'natural' and 'normal' in Western terms may not be elsewhere. This enables discussion of the 'best interests of the child' to be undertaken with greater cultural sensitivity and a fuller understanding of the risks that children might face.

References

BBC News Online (2005) 'Hundreds of children "vanishing"', 13 May, London: BBC 13/05/2005, available online at http://news.bbc.co.uk/1/hi/uk/4541603.stm (accessed 26/01/09).

Bledsoe, C. (1990a) 'The politics of children: fosterage and the social management of fertility among the Mende of Sierra Leone', in W. P. Handwerker (ed) *Births and Power: Social Change and the Politics of Reproduction*, Boulder, CO: Westview Press.

Bledsoe, C. (1990b) 'No success without struggle: social mobility and hardship for foster children in Sierra Leone', *Man (N.S.)*, vol 25, no1, pp 70-88.

Carsten, J. (2004) *After Kinship*, Cambridge: Cambridge University Press.

Fairweather, E. (2008) 'I don't dream about murdered Victoria Climbié', *The Daily Mail*, 14 June, available online at www.dailymail.co.uk/femail/article-1026441/I-dont-dream-murdered-Victoria---I-live-day-says-social-worker-scapegoat.html (accessed 26/01/09).

Goody, E. (1982) *Parenthood and Social Reproduction: Fostering and Occupational Roles in West Africa*, Cambridge: Cambridge University Press.

Goody, J. (1969) 'Adoption in cross-cultural perspective', *Comparative Studies in Society and History*, vol 11, no 1, pp 55-78.

Goody, J. and Goody, E. (1967) 'The circulation of women and children in northern Ghana', *Man (N.S.)*, vol 2, no 2, pp 226-48.

Harding, L. (2008) 'Victoria Climbié's mother speaks out', *The Mail on Sunday*, 17 July, available online at www.mailonsunday.co.uk/you/article-1034908/Victoria-Climbi--8217-s-mother-speaks--8216-I-shocked-I-attacked-I-did-8217.html (accessed 26/01/09).

Laming, W. H. (2003) *The Victoria Climbié Inquiry*, London: HMSO.

Left, S. (2005) 'Hundreds of African boys go missing in London', *The Guardian*, 13 May, available online at www.guardian.co.uk/society/2005/may/13/children (accessed 26/01/09).

Liddle, R. (2008) 'Before you damn us all, Mrs Climbié, I've a few questions too', *The Sunday Times*, 1 June, available online at http://www.timesonline.co.uk/tol/comment/columnists/rod_liddle/article4039884.ece (accessed 26/01/09).

Modell, J. (2002) *A Sealed and Secret Kinship: The Culture of Policies and Practices in American Adoption*, Oxford: Berghahn.

Notermans, C. (2008) 'The emotional world of kinship: children's experiences of fosterage in East Cameroon', *Childhood*, vol 15, no 3, pp 355-77.

Philpot, T. (2002) 'Interview with Victoria Climbié's parents', www.communitycare.co.uk, available online at www.communitycare.co.uk/Articles/2002/02/07/35285/interview-with-victoria-climbies-parents.html (accessed 26/01/09).

Renne, E. (2005) 'Childhood memories and contemporary parenting in Ekiti, Nigeria', *Africa*, vol 75, no 1, pp 63-82.

Schneider, D. (1980) *American Kinship: A Cultural Account*, Chicago, IL: University of Chicago Press.

Strathern, M. (1999) *Property, Substance and Effect: Anthropological Essays on Persons and Things*, London: Athlone Press.

Verhoef, H. (2005) '"A child has many mothers": views of child fostering in northwestern Cameroon', *Childhood*, vol 12, no 3, pp 369-90.

Six

Race, ethnicity and young people

Anoop Nayak

Introduction

It is perhaps not an overstatement to declare that the burning question of the 21st century is how to live with difference. This chapter considers this challenge through an analysis of race and ethnicity in young lives. The chapter begins by outlining why race must be thought of as an 'empty sign', rather than meaningful category. It then considers what is meant by ethnicity and why the concept should be opened out beyond a fixation with minority ethnic communities. The remainder of the chapter focuses on children and young people's relationships to race and racism, beginning with an exploration of racism in children's lives, where the focus is on the contradictory nature of racist expression and complex attitudes to blackness, whiteness and 'mixedness'. The chapter then turns to consider how young people are forging new ethnicities through creative local–global dialogues with music, language, sport and fashion. This is seen to offer the potential for them to move beyond at least some of the strictures of racial 'absolutes'. Finally, the chapter concludes with a case study of Chinese youth and the impact that disco culture is having on their ethnicities as it gives rise to a new flexible, cosmopolitan sense of being and becoming in global times.

Race – the empty sign...

Race is one of the most controversial concepts in the English language. Broadly speaking, it is premised on a belief in innate human difference. This derives from a profound misconception that fixed biological distinctions exist between, say, 'Arabs', 'Africans' or 'Europeans'. Scientists suggest that even in those circumstances where a minor genetic difference can be traced within parts of a national population, this is a consequence of environment, regional diet, health and close intermarriage over time. This means that the genetic differences between, for example, a Nigerian and an English child, melt into insignificance when compared to the differences within each of these respective national populations. There is, then, little evidence to support the idea of any essential 'racial' characteristics let alone anything approaching the existence of definitive or unique species within humankind. For this reason, race can be seen as a fallacy – a human invention used to make sense of a complicated social world.

Although race may be an empty category, it has achieved an almost cinematic quality in popular culture. We can easily feel drawn to participate in this luminescent fiction with the power to put into motion strangely elusive yet at once familiar racialised images. As Back (2007: 119) intimates, 'race and racism operate within ocular grammars of difference'. One of the common ways in which young people 'see' race – and render it as-if-real – is through skin colour, 'the most visible of fetishes' (Bhabha, 1983: 30). Differences in pigmentation have led young people to think of race as natural, yet the application of race signs through colour is both an arbitrary act and a modern phenomenon. As C.L.R. James (1994) explains in his majestic book *Beyond a Boundary*, exploring class, colour and cricket in the West Indies, 'historically it is pretty well proved now that the ancient Greeks and Romans knew nothing about race. They had another standard – civilized and barbarian – and you could have white skin and be a barbarian and you could be black and civilized' (cited in Alexander, 1987: 5).

But if race is no more than a modern myth, why is it such a compelling fiction for successive generations? Part of the explanation rests with the divisive way in which race has been used in the past. The invasion of distant lands, the acquisition of local resources and the butchery of native peoples have all taken place in the name of race. This has entailed the elucidation of an imaginary hierarchy of human 'types' on which ideas of civilised/primitive, superior/inferior, developed/undeveloped, clean/dirty and so on were rapidly ascribed. The use of race categories operates to justify oppression and exploitation. It concerns the way somatic or phenotype markers reflect *perceived* differences between people; for example, how they might look or sound, comes to stand in for who they 'really are'. Race can then be seen as an *organising principle* in modern society; it is the grammar through which nations are constructed, territories are designated and claims to human rights, citizenship and belonging are iterated.

While the concept of race may be theoretically bankrupt, it retains a high material currency in young people's everyday world. The idea of race has come to shape educational opportunities, labour market structures, neighbourhood choices and attitudes to such wide-ranging topics as sport, crime and mental health. The idea that some people are biologically superior to others as a consequence of 'racial' difference is largely redundant. However, if biological forms of racism are in decline, recent years have witnessed a proliferation of new race signs expressed through *cultural* forms of racism. Youth culture has been a primary site for the discursive explosion of race signifiers in which language, image, text, music and other symbols perform the work of race. Discourses communicate meaning and, in producing the objects of knowledge, may in time come to form common-sense beliefs. For example, on MTV, hip-hop music is often deeply enwrapped in signifiers of race spoken through the encoded tropes of sex, violence, drugs, urban culture and excessive forms of black masculinity. Here, race can appear an inescapable truth – a 'sticky' sign that attaches itself to particular bodies, spaces and practices. This bringing-into-being of race in cultural or popular racism is one of the most pernicious ways in which race thinking is sustained, kept alive and made new again.

Seen in this light, the seemingly permanent signs of racial authenticity, inscribed most potently by way of skin colour – black, yellow, red or brown – need to be understood as socially constituted and relationally connected categories. We might consider how marketing advertisements, films and scenes in video games work with a palette of race signs in which ideas about blackness and whiteness are produced through and against one another. Furthermore, race signs may change over time and place, taking on different meanings and new significations as seen in the recent demonisation of South Asian Muslim youth as new 'folk devils' (Alexander, 2000; see also Chapter Twelve). As such, there is no 'inner truth' to the values accorded to skin pigmentation, only a set of socially ascribed attributes or deficiencies. In this respect, we might consider race to be an empty sign; what Barthes (1973) would term a 'myth'. This presents something of a tautology – race may not be real but its effects within youth culture certainly are. Ultimately, race is a modern invention, an arbitrary sign that has become imbued with particular meaning in late modernity. When it comes to the reality of race, it appears that all that is solid melts into air…

... Opening out ethnicity

Anthropological studies have often focused on ethnicity as a marker of difference between human societies. In its broadest sense, the term 'ethnicity' refers to the cultural practices of a community such as its diet, dress, religious beliefs, traditions, rituals and ceremonies. Many early anthropologists were frequently compelled to produce 'spectacular' ethnographies featuring tales of tribal cannibalism, headhunting, voodoo rituals and taboo sexual practices. A problem of this approach is the tendency to abstract culture out from social relations by focusing on difference. The act of reifying culture – or at least selecting out those aspects designated as 'cultural' – became a means of rendering these ethnicities as 'Other'. This enabled comparisons to be made between native cultures in colonised lands and an unquestioned and (presumably superior) white Western norm.

While these early ethnographic testimonies may tell us little about the communities under study, they often have a great deal more to impart about whiteness and the construction of 'the West'. These dark, colonial fantasies inform us of the repressed fears and desires of Western subjects. Archetypal examples of this can be seen in popular media representations of South Asian people in Britain throughout the 1970s and 1980s. In television comedies such as *It Ain't Half Hot Mum*, *Mind your Language* or *Carry On Up the Khyber*, South Asians come to be represented through a repertoire of well-worn cultural stereotypes that appear to crystallise their 'ethnicity'. They have funny accents, play bizarre music, eat 'foreign muck', dress peculiarly, hold curious superstitions, abide by antiquated religious beliefs and indulge in excessive sexual practices, such as having harems or multiple wives. For Said (1995 [1978]), these are vivid examples of what he classically terms 'Orientalism'. In Said's (1995 [1978]: 73) critical readings, Orientalism is the product of a deep and enduring set of Western power relations elicited through a 'collection of dreams, images, and vocabularies available to anyone who has tried to talk about what lies east of the dividing line'. In such colourful accounts, ethnicity appears a timeless, unchanging essence when in actuality it is frequently adapted and reinvented.

If we were to consider Englishness as an ethnicity – and there is no reason why we shouldn't – we might be inclined to remark how a quintessential aspect of English identity is the ritual of tea drinking. Yet, tea is hardly an English commodity. It was first grown in China and later exported to India as the British East India Company wished to harvest yields that could be sold throughout the Empire. The British were actually slower than many other European nations in taking up tea and even when they did, for some time it remained the sole preserve of wealthy English aristocrats. Only by around 1750 can tea be seen to be becoming the popular national drink. More recently, the rise in multinational American-style coffee houses has seen coffee overtake tea in terms of sales, suggesting that this seemingly stalwart 'English' tradition is once again being reinvented, displaced and transformed. We can conclude from this that ethnicity is not a fixed or static marker but a flexible, open-ended practice that is made meaningful through collective repetition. The ritual of tea drinking reveals that ethnicities can be invented and often carry with them the traces of other cultures. For Hall (1995), ethnicity is then a contested term, forever in the making, being subject to the play of history, language and culture. This suggests a need to uncouple ethnicity from dominant notions of nationhood and any lingering idea of race. It also entails the recognition that ethnicity is a promiscuous category so is neither homogenous nor 'bounded', as we shall go on to discover in our discussion of children and young people.

Racism in children's lives

Childhood is frequently imagined as a wide-eyed state of innocence, favourably contrasted with the turbulence of 'troublesome' teenage years and adolescence (Kehily and Montgomery, 2003). If 'childhood' is constructed as innocent, vulnerable and in need of protection then 'youth' is its dangerous 'Other' – unruly, threatening and a potential source of moral panic, as recent media debates on 'binge drinking', 'happy slapping', 'hoodies' and 'knife gangs' testify. However, we would be mistaken in assuming that while racism might feature in contemporary urban youth culture it is entirely absent from the safe, pastel-coloured world of small children. Instead, a closer examination of children's cultural worlds reveals a more complex picture in which childhood friendships, fall-outs, name-calling and abuse are formative practices in the overarching landscape of childhood. For example, in a study of racism in an inner-city, multi-ethnic, English primary school, Connolly (1998: 192) reveals how, 'at the ages of 5 and 6 children appear to be already actively involved in appropriating, reworking and reproducing racialised discourses'.

But racism is not only an issue within the energetic urban areas in which young people rub up against one another on a daily basis. In a meticulous account of children's racism within mainly white English primary schools, Troyna and Hatcher (1992a) investigate the role that racist ideas perform. Their study dispels common myths about childhood innocence by demonstrating the contingent and multiple functions racism serves in the playground cultures of white children; for example 'hot' name-calling, where insults are hurled in heated exchanges, often between friends, which may later lead to regret, guilt and apologies. They also encountered more calculated 'cold' name-calling where racism is clinically deployed as a vehicle of harassment. Another common reason children gave for engaging in racist insults was to 'act tough' and assert dominance, suggesting a link between racism and particular displays of masculinity. Sometimes racism travelled beyond individual encounters and was 'taken up, animated and amplified by peer group social processes' (1992a: 129). The complex manner in which racism operates also meant that some white children participated in cultural acts of 'refencing' in which particular black friends could be 'bracketed out' from the general racist abuse going on: 'You're alright, you're not like the others – you're one of us'.

So what are we to make of such unpredictable racist encounters? Are they just 'child's play' or something more pernicious? A familiar adult response to children who are rude, use bad language or deploy racist words might be the refrain, 'I blame the parents', thus exonerating children of agency. However, Troyna and Hatcher (1992a) disclose the short-sightedness of this approach. They divulge how children are active and discerning subjects: some are capable of dismissing the racist views of their parents, others readily engage in racist acts that parents would strenuously disapprove of.

While Troyna and Hatcher's study expertly points to the *ambiguity* of racist practice, this does not appear to extend to the subjectivities of children themselves. In an accompanying paper (Troyna and Hatcher, 1992b) they make a distinction between 'racist' name-calling (committed by white children against black peers) and 'racial' insults (committed by children from minority ethnic backgrounds against white peers or one another). Their definition foregrounds the 'asymmetrical power relations' (1992b: 495) between black and white people and appears a welcome improvement on liberal, power-evasive models of racism that imply everyone has equal potential to deploy racism. Yet in this reading there is an immediate reification of race as a 'proper object' (Butler, 1994), an insurmountable point of difference that too readily equates whiteness with oppression and blackness with victimhood. Here, white people are endowed with being the central architects of history, and the key agents of social change. The multiple positions that white and black people may come to occupy, and how these subjective locations are nuanced by ethnicity, class, gender, sexuality and generation, are subsequently condensed into a dichotomy of powerful/powerless.

This rationalist, anti-racist account of the effects of power and how it is lived out has been thoroughly critiqued by Foucault (1980, 1988). For Foucault, power is not uniformly experienced, nor is it a wholly negating activity. Instead, power is conceptualised as *productive* since it 'doesn't only weigh on us as a force that says no … it induces pleasure, forms of knowledge, produces discourses' (1980: 119). Here, power relations are continually produced and reproduced in often unpredictable ways, as the contours of oppression and resistance shift and intertwine. Rather than seeing power as a simple matter of closed binaries – white/black, men/women, straight/gay, middle class/working class – where the former categories come to dominate and subsume the latter elements of the dichotomy, post-structuralist analyses of race investigate the multiple interconnections between gender, ethnicity, sexuality and social class, to ask how these processes can be seen to interact, and so inflect one another (see Chapter Thirteen).

These analytic tools are likely to be especially productive in the light of the new racisms and contemporary global migrations influencing young people's social worlds. Where concerns surrounding early post-war migration to Britain had largely centred on immigrants from former Commonwealth countries (parts of Africa, the Caribbean, India, Bangladesh) as well as Pakistan, these dynamics are further diversifying beyond once familiar postcolonial routes. World disasters, conflict and genocide in Iraq, Afghanistan, Bosnia, Rwanda, Montenegro and so on have seen numbers of displaced people seeking refuge and asylum across the globe, usually in neighbouring countries. The accession of new nation states into the European Union (EU) from 2004, granting freedom of movement to citizens throughout the EU, has resulted in further population flows from Central and Eastern Europe. In Britain and other parts of Europe, recent arrivals, refugees and children from asylum-seeking families may face new forms of state and popular discrimination. This means that having white skin is no guarantee against racist hostility where being of a particular religious faith, wearing a headscarf or lacking appropriate English language skills can emerge as new markers of race difference. Children from socially excluded and asylum-seeking families, Gypsy, Romany and Traveller communities may similarly be cast as 'not quite white' as their claims to whiteness and its unspoken privileges diminish. These new racisms can be felt in some multi-ethnic working-class neighbourhoods in Britain where the arrival of newcomers has led to hostility and resentment from more established minority ethnic communities who perceive a further struggle for resources.

It is evident that in the light of new migrations and contemporary racisms it is now necessary to move beyond the black/white binary of race utilised in Troyna and Hatcher's memorable account of children's lives. A thought-provoking illustration of this can be seen in a study of 'mixed-race' identities conducted in three schools in the South of England by Ali (2003), with children aged 8-11. Ali noticed how many children could hold claims to 'mixedness', based on colour, culture, stepparents or a whole host of other shifting configurations and alliances, which go beyond genetic inscription. In conversations with children, Ali found that popular 'mixed-race' characters such as the Hollywood actor Will Smith or the singer Mel B, otherwise known as 'Scary Spice', could momentarily transcend the negative ascription of race signifiers through appearing sexually attractive. We might also consider how 'mixed-race' sporting celebrities such as the racing driver Lewis Hamilton or the golfer Tiger Woods can similarly appear to surpass the limited rubric of race and present as individual neoliberal subjects.

It is tempting to suggest that nothing whitens more than money: fame, talent, beauty, high status and being relatively fair skinned further enable cosmopolitan, 'post-race' subjectivities to perform. While it may appear that certain 'mixed-race' celebrities can traverse the limits of race, in interviews with teachers, parents and children Ali discovered that her participants were forced to position themselves through 'racial' absolutes. Although these categories often involve a partial denial of their mixed heritage, many children utilise these categories for their unambiguous simplicity, or a palpable desire to 'belong'. In this way Ali (2003: 2) recounts that 'though we live in the increasingly post-race world – a world concerned with struggles for ethnic, national, religious and cultural meaning – the irrational and corporeal ground of "race" can still be a powerful force in social relations'. Indeed, in popular press and media terminology, 'ethnicity', 'culture' and 'nationality' are often synonyms for avoiding the inconvenient 'truth' that race purports.

Abolishing race as an idea, and even as a point of political mobilisation, remains deeply controversial. Nevertheless, Gilroy (2001: 14) has argued for abandoning 'the rational absurdity of race' in favour of what he describes as a 'planetary humanism' (2001: 2). But can we really forget race, leave behind its tortured history and start out afresh on a post-race journey to a global future? (See Nayak, 2006, for a discussion.) Perhaps race is a more resilient concept in late modernity than we may have thought? And if so, are there any advantages in speaking in the name of race – for example when it comes to monitoring youth employment, encouraging diversity and representation, or dismantling inequality, prejudice and racism? There are probably no easy answers to these questions, but both Troyna and Hatcher's (1992a, 1992b) sobering account of racism in primary schools and Ali's (2003) post-race study of 'mixedness' illuminate the value of empirical research and the role of power in social relations. For most children the term 'mixed-race' merely elides the reality that many are treated as 'black' in contemporary British society, and will be unable to escape what Frantz Fanon (1967 [1952]) ironically termed 'the fact of blackness', especially as they grow older. Ali (2003: 180) concludes: 'The challenge for the ['mixed-race'] children is whether they can use post-race thinking to provide new spaces for identity within societies for which the idea of "race" still has real and profound effects'. If recent political events are anything to go by, we are still some distance from going 'beyond race', but this does not make the goal any less desirable or achievable.

New ethnicities: young people, race and cultural hybridity

The term 'new ethnicities' was first used by Hall (1995: 224-5) to mark what he calls 'the end of the innocent notion of the essential black subject'. The challenge stemmed from postmodernist theories of identity and new forms of representation in the arts and popular culture. The postmodern challenge asserts that there is no coherent 'self' from which meaning can be derived since 'the question of the black subject cannot be represented without reference to the dimensions of class, gender, sexuality and ethnicity' (Hall, 1995: 226). Instead, we might consider what subject positions matter at what moments and why, in order to appreciate the constant interplay between ethnicity and other social relations of power. The postmodern idea that identities are multiple and fragmented suggests that there is no authentic essential 'black experience' to fall back on. For Hall (1995: 225), what once appeared a necessary fiction – the myth 'that all black people are good or indeed that all black people are *the same*' – has imploded as diverse representations, politics and practices have come to the fore.

Hybridity has a dubious place within race and ethnic studies as Young (1995) has carefully exposed. The term suggests a mixing of

two distinct 'species' to form a third, new genetic type, known as a
'hybrid'. Debates about hybridity are premised on the myth of racial
'purity' and pseudo-biological explanations of race difference. In
colonial times, many white masters had forced as well as consensual
sexual relations with slaves and the colonised subjects of the Empire.
The relations were always marked by differences in power such as
men/women, coloniser/colonised, white/black, plantation owner/
domestic worker and so on. Unsurprisingly, as a consequence of
sexual union a number of native women gave birth to illegitimate
offspring, who were deemed as the products of 'miscegenation' and
the inheritors of 'mixed blood'. There remained an abiding fear within
colonial authority that this new 'breed' of children, as they were seen
to be, could 'pass' as white and gain legitimacy within colonial circles,
which would eventually lead to the degeneration of the supposed
'white race'. Underlying this fear of 'passing' is a sense that 'race'
may not be an immutable category. If it can so readily be altered and
made degenerate, whiteness may be more precarious, and at least for
some a more precious emblem, than may have been imagined. And if
racial difference is not real then a major justification for the exertion
of colonial superiority, conquest and subjugation dissipates as it is
revealed for the brutal act of barbarism it really is.

More recently, postcolonial writers have attempted to displace these
biological theories by considering the uses of hybridity as a cultural
term. For example, Bhabha (1990: 211) views cultural hybridity as a
new terrain of resistance and negotiation, a 'third space which enables
other positions to emerge'. In these more recent debates on hybridity,
a starting point is the belief that all cultures are impure, that there is
no a priori, 'authentic' culture there to be salvaged. Youth cultures can
also be seen as sites of cultural production where new hybrid styles
and ethnicities are brought into being. These vibrant new ethnicities
are illuminated in Back's (1996) fascinating youth ethnography of
racism and multicultural living in South London. In the multi-ethnic
neighbourhood district he calls 'Southgate', he identifies a strong and
racially inclusive localism. This has resulted in emergent languages
and ethnicities where a number of teenage white youth combine
American slang with Caribbean Creole and local patois to form
a distinct black South London vernacular. These new cultures are
forming at the nexus of what Gilroy (1993) has termed 'the Black
Atlantic', where the polyglot influences of Africa, Europe, America and
the Caribbean float and intermingle. Within these spaces, certain white
youth can be found 'nicing up' their language as Standard English is
transformed into a new culturally syncretic working-class style. For

these white youth, their speech is peppered with the rich inflections of black linguistic codes as they come to embody a new ethnicity, which marks the becoming of a negotiated and culturally hybrid way of being. For example, 19-year-old Debbie (quoted in Back, 1996: 136) reflected on her immersion into black friendship circles and how from the ages of 12-15 years she adopted the full blazonry of black style:

> I used to cane-row [parallel plaiting] my hair, always
> plaiting my hair, my black friends would do it for me. I
> made sure that the beads were always red, gold and green.
> Also I used to have my little, what was it, I had a cap and it
> had Africa on it and all the colours and I used to wear all
> African, all Rastafarian badges. I had Gucci shirts and you
> had suede collars, that's what black people wore.

What is apparent in Debbie's account is that in parts of South London 'black' and 'white' culture can no longer be set apart, but are inscribed within one another and are formative of new ethnicities. At these points the potential of cultural hybridity is to 'turn the gaze from the discriminated back upon the eye of power' (Bhabha, 1984: 97). In this way, attempts to fix ethnicity to racially marked bodies are rendered obsolete.

Much of the new ethnicities research has focused almost exclusively on the cosmopolitan urban metropolis. As a global city, London in particular has spawned various youth ethnographies of 'thick' multicultural interaction (Hewitt, 1986; Wulff, 1995; Back, 1996; Cohen, 1997). This has enforced what Watt (1998: 688) depicts as a 'hegemonic discourse in relation to race and space'. Here, multiculturalism and the 'problem' of race relations somehow become confined to those spaces inhabited by minority ethnic people (Gilroy, 1987). There is now a greater need to engage with the particularity of place and the way it can come to shape race encounters. The 'global sense of place' (Massey, 1996 [1991]) that is celebrated in London accounts may have little meaning, or at least be differently constituted, in other spaces beyond the metropolis.

This is certainly the case in ethnographic research undertaken in the mainly white, postindustrial region of North East England. In the absence of a significant black population, a minority of white youth adopted signifiers of blackness outside of the day-to-day multicultural intimacies of the neighbourhood present in other cities to proclaim themselves 'B-Boyz' (Nayak, 2003). This identity was achieved through the 'flows' of global culture, including music, sport, media and filmic representations of urban black street-style. A few local sites, including independent record stores, sports arenas, dancehalls and clubs, became the social hubs around which these new ethnicities could materialise. However, many white youth who experimented with black culture in this way claimed to have experienced 'prejudice' and 'discrimination', pointing out that they could rapidly be deemed 'wiggers' ('white niggers') and argued that the label B-Boyz could be used disparagingly to impart that they were 'wanna-Bes' or, even more emphatically, 'Black Boyz'. The contradiction of this identity was further illuminated when it appeared that some B-Boyz could continue to espouse racially charged opinions concerning black people's hyper-masculine athleticism or 'natural' musical prowess – characteristics they believed were missing in whiteness. At the same time, few had made any meaningful connections with the city's largest minority ethnic population – South Asians.

This raises questions concerning the limits of cultural hybridity where white youth have the ability to embody socially desirable aspects of black 'cool', while avoiding or denigrating other elements. This postmodern 'pick-n-mix' attitude enables white youth to act as mobile citizens in the supermarket of style, cosmopolitan consumers who have the freedom to move through black culture to claim or disown it as they see fit. As Pieterse (1995: 54) states, 'what is not clarified are the terms under which cultural interplay and crossover take place ... what is missing is acknowledgement of the actual unevenness, asymmetry and inequality in global relations'. In such encounters it is seldom recognised that these new subject positions have come about through the historical struggles of black youth within the British nation state, whose once disparaged status as outsiders and rebels is now deemed a desirable subject position to inhabit (CCCS, 1982).

A further illustration of the way in which new ethnicities emerge can be seen in the performance of British South Asian *bhangra* music. British *bhangra* has developed from Punjabi folk music and dances, which were especially popular among rural farming communities in Northern India and Pakistan. These place-specific rituals have been transformed through South Asian diasporas to multicultural urban spaces such as Southall in London or Handsworth in Birmingham where a number of Punjabi Sikh families have settled. British *bhangra* combines Punjabi lyrics with music from popular Hindi and Bollywood film as well as black urban sounds including reggae, hip-hop and house. Modern *bhangra* has numerous subgenres such as '*bhangra*-muffin', in which ragga beats are combined with the heavy, lyrical 'toasting' of MCs and layered across the bass and the *dhol*, the latter being a Punjabi percussion instrument similar to a drum. This hybrid and eclectic sound has enabled diverse British South Asian young people to use *bhangra* as a new site of community and diasporic identification, forming what Sharma (1996: 39, emphasis in original) describes as 'an *affirmative moment* in the formation of Asian identity'. As a site of collective identification, *bhangra* is in part a bridge between generations, connecting a migratory past with the immediate present. In the body of the nation state, British *bhangra* music forms a pulse emanating from the beating heart of multicultural Britain whose veins and arteries connect to cultural flows to and from the Indian subcontinent. It is a product, then, of new local–global relations, as Dudrah (2002: 370) explains:

> Inner city areas with black social groups are comprised of layers of multitexual sounds, images and feelings. These layers jostle and blend with each other to produce a unique postcolonial experience of the city which is both indicative of the residents that dwell in the urban metropolis as multiple citizens and of how they make sense of each other.

The idea of 'community' is, then, a contested and imaginary construct situated in time and place. As with other large musical events such as the Notting Hill Carnival or the English nightclub scene, *bhangra* events have occasionally been the scene for violence between local youth 'gangs', religious groups and young people from different areas (Bennett, 2000). As Dudrah (2002) reveals, further divisions can be signalled in the lyrics to certain *bhangra* tracks, which may privilege caste, patriarchy and heterosexuality. However, when it comes to 'decoding' these messages, Dudrah reflects on the importance of placing lyrics within the context in which they are heard – the dancehall. At *bhangra* events, these faultlines tend to be negotiated and traversed through dance, where feeling, rhythm and movement give way to overriding pleasure. At these moments the practice of new ethnicities offers a productive means from which to unhinge the deadlock of British identities as constituted through race, nationhood and whiteness. As Gilroy (1987) poignantly asserts, this popular multiculturalism means that blackness and Britishness can no longer be seen as mutually exclusive.

Case study: globalisation, ethnicity and culture – Chinese *di-si-ke*

Globalisation has drawn attention to the interconnected world in which we live. The intensified global flow of music, image, finance, style and media signs beyond the borders of the nation state is thought to have a 'disembedding' effect on youth cultures in late modernity. They offer possibilities for more cosmopolitan forms of belonging and postmodern styles of consumption that transgress the boundaries of the local (Featherstone, 1998 [1991]). Through detailed observations of *di-si-ke* (that is, Chinese disco) in Shanghai and beyond, Farrer (1999) provides a fascinating insight into the global spectacle of club culture among young people in China. According to Farrer, *di-si-ke* is a fantasy space that allows young people to travel beyond the mundane world of neighbourhoods, work or family life. It enables young women to participate in what he depicts as a 'glamorous modernity', where 'one does not distinguish oneself by class or locality' (1999: 149), but instead can lose oneself in the immediate and intense spectacle of dance. The cosmopolitan spaces of *di-si-ke* become sites for new sexualised imaginaries in which the global is not so much resisted but appropriated, localised and transfigured into new modes of being.

Chinese disco culture operates here as a porous sexual arena in which Western migrants, global videos, urban music and other commodities leak and pass through. Rather than being the passive conduits of Westernisation, Chinese youth decipher, pilfer and make anew these mediated signs of global culture. By drawing on the sexualised imagery of dance, dress and musical lyrics, Farrer suggests that Chinese girls may perform as sexual cosmopolitans. Here, scantily dressed 'young women – whose modesty had been encouraged in Chinese society – simulate sexual excitement with lithe pelvic motions' (1999: 159). This simulation of image and sound occurs by mimicking the media signs of Western video and the cacophony of musical and cultural forms that interplay and overlap across one another. This heady, sexual 'inter-textuality' between throbbing music, video pop stars, dancers and youthful bodies reveals Shanghai *di-si-ke* to be a multisensory arena in which Chinese young women are adept 'textual poachers' of Western images using these resources to reflexively enhance their own projects of self. This is not simply a taking on of global mass media images. Instead, as Farrer (1999: 157) reflects, 'Foreigners became the objects of sexual fantasy and occasional sexual adventures, but even more so were the mirrors for the construction of a cosmopolitan sexual self-image'. Evidently,

Westerners and Western sexual imagery can each be transformed into mutable props through which a new cosmopolitanism can transpire. It would appear that in a world of signs, image is everything. Here, 'The disco is a place for the visual consumption of others but even more for offering oneself up for visual consumption' (1999: 162), a willing transformation of subjects into objects, selfhood into signs.

As China engages in a post–Socialist transition – poignantly marked by the 2008 Olympics – new youth cultures can be seen emerging. Where homosexuality had, until 1997, been classed under 'hooligan acts', Beijing now has a thriving number of gay bars. One travel writer reporting in *The Guardian* (28 June 2008) comments on how, up until 2001, homosexuality had been classified as a mental disorder, but now one can enter into spaces where 'several dozen young men, mostly Chinese with a sprinkling of foreigners, sit on red and grey sofas sipping cocktails and eating water melon slices', freely hugging and kissing.

This brief case study of Chinese *di-si-ke* illustrates how young ethnicities are changing under the impulse of globalisation and the cosmopolitan flows within and between nation states. This is seen in the new sexual practices of Chinese young women and young gay men. Furthermore, it appears that global processes can connect with local cultures in the formation of new ethnicities beyond Western frames. What is evident is that Chinese young people are not seeking to replicate the West but are negotiating a cosmopolitan ethnicity that heralds a new moment of being in the lives of future generations.

Conclusion

This chapter has shown that while race is a social construct it continues to be deployed as a deeply dividing practice in human society. Children and young people are not immune to the power of these ideas but invoke racism in a highly ambiguous fashion that is subject to situation and context. The idea of race operates to bestow privilege or disadvantage to us on the basis of skin colour, language, nationality, dress, faith and so on. Whiteness remains a contingent but central locus of power in youth cultures. It is a dominant, unspoken norm: the blank canvas of experience across which 'Other' ethnicities and cultures are so vividly painted. If we peer more closely, whiteness remains the formative category that designates 'Other' practices as different or 'exotic'.

Ethnicity should not, then, be seen as a fixed category tied to a 'bounded' notion of culture but as an open construct forever in the making. The new global practices of many young people suggest that their ethnicities are constantly refigured beyond the boundaries of race, colour and nationality. It is evident that young people are 'doing' ethnicity in many different ways and are producing new forms of being and attachment befitting of global times. Several studies document the emergence of new ethnicities that may be expressed through dance, dress, changing musical expressions, hairstyles and new sporting cultures. It is increasingly apparent that these new markers of identification are both the product of multicultural living and also stem from the cultural flows of globalisation 'made sense of' in local spaces. As the case account of Chinese *di-si-ke* reveals, debates on youth, ethnicity, culture and globalisation should not be restricted to the West. New youth identities are being formed in the 'third space' of local–global relations and these cultures will have a bearing in the postcolonial world.

References

Alexander, C. (2000) *The Asian Gang: Ethnicity, Identity, Masculinity*, Oxford: Berg.

Alexander, P. (1987) *Racism, Resistance and Revolution*, London: Bookmarks.

Ali, S. (2003) *Mixed-Race, Post-Race: Gender, New Ethnicities and Cultural Practices*, Oxford: Berg.

Back, L. (1996) *New Ethnicities and Urban Culture: Racisms and Multiculture in Young Lives*, London: University College London Press.

Back, L. (2007) *The Art of Listening*, Oxford: Berg.

Barthes, R. (1973) *Mythologies*, London: Jonathan Cape.

Bennett, A. (2000) *Popular Music and Youth Culture: Music, Identity, Place*, Basingstoke: Macmillan.

Bhabha, H.K. (1983) 'The other question: the stereotype and colonial discourse', *Screen*, vol 24, no 4, pp 18–36.

Bhabha, H.K. (1984) 'Signs taken as wonders: questions of ambivalence and authority under a tree outside Delhi, May 1817', in F. Baker, P. Hulme, M. Iversen and D. Loxley (eds) *Europe and Its Others*, vol 1, Essex: Essex Sociology of Literature.

Bhabha, H. K. (1990) 'The third space – interview with Homi Bhabha', in J. Rutherford (ed) *Identity: Community, Culture, Difference*, London: Lawrence and Wishart.

Butler, J. (1994) 'Against proper objects', *Differences: A Journal of Feminist Cultural Studies*, vol 6, no 2-3, pp 1-26.

CCCS (Centre for Contemporary Cultural Studies) (1982) *The Empire Strikes Back: Race and Racism in 70s Britain*, London: Hutchinson.

Cohen, P. (1997) *Rethinking the Youth Question: Education, Labour and Cultural Studies*, Basingstoke: Macmillan.

Connolly, P. (1998) *Racism, Gender Identities and Young Children: Social Relations in a Multi-Ethnic Inner-City Primary School*, London: Routledge.

Dudrah, R. (2002) 'Drum "n" dhol: British bhangra music and diasporic South Asian identity formation', *European Journal of Cultural Studies*, vol 5, no 3, pp 363-83.

Fanon, F. (1967 [1952]) *Black Skin, White Masks*, New York, NY: Grove.

Farrer, J. (1999) 'Disco super-culture: consuming foreign sex in the Chinese disco', *Sexualities*, vol 2, no 2, pp 147-66.

Featherstone, M. (1998 [1991]) *Consumer Culture and Postmodernism*, London: Sage Publications.

Foucault, M. (1980) 'Truth and power', in C. Gordon (ed) *Power/Knowledge: Selected Interviews and Other Writings 1972–77*, Brighton: Harvester Press.

Foucault, M. (1988) 'Technologies of the self', in L. Martin, H. Gutman and P.H. Hutton (eds) *Technologies of the Self, a Seminar with Michel Foucault*, London: Tavistock.

Gilroy, P. (1987) *There Ain't No Black in the Union Jack*, London: Hutchinson.

Gilroy, P. (1993) *The Black Atlantic: Modernity and Double Consciousness*, London: Verso.

Gilroy, P. (2001) *Against Race: Imagining Political Culture Beyond the Colour Line*, Cambridge, MA: The Beknap Press of Harvard University Press.

Hall, S. (1995) 'New ethnicities', in B. Ashcroft, G. Griffiths and H. Tiffin (eds) *The Post-Colonial Studies Reader*, London: Routledge.

Hewitt, R. (1986) *White Talk Black Talk*, Cambridge: Cambridge University Press.

James, C.L.R. (1994) *Beyond a Boundary*, London: Serpentine Press.

Kehily, M. J. and Montgomery, H. (2003) 'Innocence and experience', in M. Woodhead and H. Montgomery (eds) *Understanding Childhood: An Interdisciplinary Approach*, Chichester: John Wiley/Open University Press.

Massey, D. (1996 [1991]) 'A global sense of place', in D. Massey (ed) *Space, Place and Gender*, Cambridge: Polity Press.

Nayak, A. (2003) *Race, Place and Globalization: Youth Cultures in a Changing World*, Oxford: Berg.

Nayak, A. (2006) 'After race: ethnography, race and post-race theory', *Ethnic and Racial Studies*, vol 29, no 3, pp 411-30.

Pieterse, J.N. (1995) 'Globalization and hybridization', in M. Featherstone, S. Lash and R. Robertson (eds) *Global Modernities*, London: Sage Publications.

Said, E.W. (1995 [1978]) *Orientalism: Western Conceptions of the Orient*, Harmondsworth: Penguin.

Sharma, S. (1996) 'Noisy Asians or Asian noise?', in S. Sharma, J. Hutnyk and A. Sharma (eds) *Dis-Orientating Rhythms: The Politics of the New Asian Dance Music*, London: Zed Books.

Troyna, B. and Hatcher, R. (1992a) *Racism in Children's Lives: A Study of Mainly White Primary Schools*, London: Routledge.

Troyna, B. and Hatcher, R. (1992b) 'It's only words: understanding "racial" and "racist" incidents', *New Community*, vol 18, no 3, pp 493-6.

Watt, P. (1998) 'Going out of town: youth, race and place in the South East of England', *Environment and Planning D: Society and Space*, vol 16, no 16, pp 687-703.

Wulff, H. (1995) 'Inter-racial friendship: community and youth styles, ethnicity and teenage femininity in South London', in V. Amit-Talai and H. Wulff (eds) *Youth Cultures: A Cross-Cultural Perspective*, London: Routledge.

Young, R. (1995) *Colonial Desire: Hybridity in Theory, Culture and Race*, London: Routledge.

Seven

International children's rights

Afua Twum-Danso

Introduction

The UNCRC (UN, 1989), adopted by the United Nations General
Assembly in 1989, provides the 'fullest legal statement of children's
rights to be found anywhere' (Freeman, 2000: 277). While there had
been previous Declarations on children's rights such as those adopted
in 1924 and 1959, these were non-binding, aspirational and very
paternalistic. Their focus was on the welfare and protection of the
child, who was still simply as an object within international law. For
example, the 1924 Declaration placed duties directly on men and
women instead of making children the holders of rights that they
can claim against adults. Although the 1959 Declaration went further,
its emphasis was still firmly on protection and welfare. There was
no recognition of children's autonomy and no understanding of the
importance of children's wishes and feelings (Freeman, 1996, 2000).

Therefore, the UNCRC was different from its predecessors in a
number of ways. Not only was it the first binding treaty on children's
rights, it also focused on 'children's welfare as an issue of justice rather
than one of charity' (Veerman, 1992: 184). Hence, for the first time,
there was recognition of children as autonomous individuals and
holders of rights, as subjects rather than objects of international law.
As a result of this focus, for many, the Convention led to the first
faltering steps towards recognising children as 'human beings' and it
was supposed to mark the beginning of a new way of dealing with
children (Verhellen, 1996). This new focus in international law was,
in part, influenced by the children's rights movement, which emerged
in the 1960s (see Archard, 2004). The philosophy underpinning the
arguments of the key thinkers within the movement was that children
are full-fledged citizens. John Holt and Richard Farson (whose work
is discussed in Freeman, 1996), for example, argued that children
should be regarded as individuals with their own human rights who
are competent to exercise them independently. Farson, in particular,

claimed that self-determination was at the root of all other rights to which children were entitled. He argued that whether such a right was good for children was beside the point and that children should be granted rights for exactly the same reason as adults (see also Archard, 2004).

However, it is important to take note that while the Convention is greatly influenced by the children's rights movement, it also takes into consideration the arguments of critics who claimed that children are not sufficiently mature physically, intellectually or emotionally and lack the necessary experience to make rational judgements (Freeman, 1996). Thus, at the same time as granting children equal value to adults, it also provides them with the protection they require because of the vulnerability and special support that the modern Western conception of childhood believes they require. Thus, in order to be able to enjoy the rights to which they are entitled as human beings equal to adults, they also require rights that protect and make provisions for their welfare. It is for this reason that the rights articulated in the Convention can be grouped under four general principles:

- the participation of children in decisions that affect them;

- the protection of children against discrimination and all forms of neglect and exploitation;

- the prevention of harm to children;

- the provision of assistance for their basic needs.

These four principles guide the interpretation and implementation of the Convention and are reflected throughout the treaty in the articulation of specific rights, which include the right:

- to life;

- to a name and identity;

- to be raised by their own parents within a family or cultural grouping and to have a relationship with both parents even if they are separated;

- to express their opinions and to have those opinions heard and acted on when appropriate;

- to be protected from abuse or exploitation;

- to have their privacy protected.

Thus, the Convention marked a turning point in dealing with children – at least conceptually. It provided a vision and, as Freeman (2000: 278) states, it 'excited the world'. However, turning this landmark treaty in international law into reality has been a journey full of pitfalls. Therefore, this chapter seeks to assess the progress of the Convention and explore the extent to which its implementation fulfils the vision behind the drafting. Specifically, I will examine both the achievements and the challenges that the Convention has faced, with a particular focus on Ghana, which is offered as a case study to highlight the practical realities of implementing the Convention's standards in a developing country context. As a result of the limitations that have dogged the implementation phase of this treaty, I will explore key criticisms that have emerged in the years since the Convention was adopted in 1989.

Assessing the progress of the Convention 20 years after its adoption

Recognising achievements

The Convention does, indeed, represent an achievement in a number of respects and has now been ratified by all countries in the world except the US and Somalia. As a result, it is the most widely ratified, and indeed the most rapidly ratified, convention in the history of the United Nations. These achievements have led Muscroft (1999: 21) to conclude that 'compared with other human rights treaties, this is a remarkable feat and reflects a profound common desire to achieve a better world for children'.

Furthermore, the Convention is a key step forward as it creates a real opportunity for public scrutiny of government performance in regards to the fulfilment of children's rights (Muscroft, 1999: 22). As a binding treaty, the Convention places a legal obligation on state parties to fulfil requirements laid down in its contents. In ratifying the treaty, governments voluntarily accept the obligations it sets out and hold themselves accountable for their success or failure in executing its provisions. This has led Temba and de Waal (2002: 207) to claim that 'states' obligations to children have never been so clearly defined in international law'. As a result of ratifying the Convention, numerous governments have initiated the process of law reform. In at least 50 countries, the Convention has been incorporated into the national legal framework by legislative reform, including constitutional amendments (Santos Pais and Bissell, 2006: 689). In the years following the adoption of the Convention, Children's Acts or Codes were introduced into the legislative framework in a number of countries such as Bangladesh, Brazil, Ghana, Mauritius, Nepal and Uganda.

Independent children's rights watchdogs have been set up in 38 countries worldwide (Santos Pais and Bissell, 2006), acting as catalysts for the realisation of children's rights as they monitor legislative proposals, review the impact of government initiatives, increase public and official awareness of children's rights and provide a means for children's voices to be heard on issues affecting them (Muscroft, 1999: 23-4). An example is the children's rights watchdog in Uganda, which also comprises subnational institutions that monitor children's rights within provincial or municipal bodies. The Convention has thus been used by governments and non-governmental organisations as an additional tool to push for advances for children in their specific contexts. According to Woll (2000: 26), the ratification of the Convention emphasises the concept of children as people with rights, beginning a transformation of public policy from one based on needs to one based on rights. As a result, children's rights and human rights more generally are more visible in society today than they were 20 years ago.

Despite these achievements to date, no country has fully realised the Convention's provisions. According to Freeman (1992: 40-1), 'much of the world has as much chance of implementing the Convention as sending its citizens to the moon…. Unfortunately most countries would also rather do the latter.' Elsewhere, Freeman (2000: 278) refers to Sgritta's (1997) claim that despite the Convention, the plight of children worldwide has not got better, but worse. Several reasons are behind this limited implementation of the Convention in countries around the world, some of which are related to its inherent limitations while others are related to external factors.

Underlying challenges

First, with regards to limitations inherent in the Convention, there is a general consensus that its chief weakness lies in the mechanisms for its implementation, which are governed by the principle of the best interests of the child (Article 3). The constraints on implementation are not helped by the fact that the Committee on the Rights of the Child, the main body monitoring implementation, has found it increasingly difficult to manage its workload. As Muscroft (1999: 189) argues, 'Even with the assistance of civil society organisations, it [the Committee] faces a major challenge in effectively scrutinizing and challenging the actions and behaviour of all the world's governments.'

Moreover, the five-year gaps (which, in reality, are often longer) between the progress reports submitted by governments to the Committee on the Rights of the Child mean that the state of children's rights is seen only in snapshot, rather than in the ongoing flux of progress and setbacks. Thus, the Committee is not provided with a holistic picture of the lives of children in a particular country. Hence, as delays build up in the examination of the reports submitted by governments, the credibility of the monitoring process may begin to be challenged by civil society groups.

Even after submitting reports to the Committee, governments tend to pay little attention to the Committee's concluding observations and in many instances it is unclear which government department is responsible for follow-up (see Woll, 2000: 35). This situation is worsened by the fact that implementing agencies often have little knowledge of the Convention and do not feel that it is their responsibility to implement its provisions. Furthermore, they have very limited budgets and a high turnover of staff, which limits their capacity to deliver services and tackle pressing policy-related issues. They also lack basic data on children, which prevents effective monitoring (Woll, 2000: 38). In addition, local governments, in light of the decentralisation policies of many countries, have increasingly become responsible for the implementation of children's rights. However, generally they have low levels of awareness about the Convention and do not make much effort to implement it, particularly in rural or marginal areas.

Second, external factors have undoubtedly been significant in limiting the effectiveness of the Convention. Even in cases where governments were committed to its vision, they were charged with implementing its provisions at precisely the time when their ability to do so was being most rapidly eroded. The 1990s were a period in which the capacity of governments to bring about change was increasingly constrained by cutbacks in resources and social welfare expenditure due to Structural Adjustment Programmes (SAPs), the competitive pressures of globalisation and the growing power of giant corporations whose wealth far exceeded that of many developing countries. Writing of Africa in particular, Temba and de Waal (2002: 215) argue that declining aid levels, unsustainable levels of debt, obstacles to access to world markets for African products, and the requirement of African governments to meet stringent austerity conditions in order to qualify for debt relief have made it impossible for governments in the region to fulfil important provision rights to which children are entitled. Related to this is the poor governance and economic mismanagement that have slowed the progress of development and thereby adversely impacted the life chances of children around the world.

Widespread and systemic poverty, not least as a result of the implementation of economic reform programmes such as SAPs, proved a significant barrier to the realisation of rights such as access to health, education and social services. Also, poverty forced many children to engage in hazardous labour in order to ensure their survival and also that of their families (see Mulinge, 2002). The ability of governments at the national level to manage their own affairs continues to be increasingly challenged, while the mechanisms of global governance are as yet too weak to control market forces. This has led Freeman (2000) to state that it is doubtful whether poorer countries can, by themselves, afford to implement the UNCRC as they have large populations, smaller incomes and a higher percentage of their populations tend to be children. Therefore, there is a need for policy makers (both national and international) to explore flexibilities within the Convention and devise practical and realistic strategies to enable countries in the majority South to realise children's rights, taking into consideration the socioeconomic realities of their countries.

In addition, the Convention has operated in a hostile sociopolitical environment since its adoption. Polarised political conditions or instability have impeded the progress of implementation. The end of the Cold War unleashed a series of brutal, prolonged intrastate conflicts, which killed and displaced millions of people. Not only have children borne the brunt of these conflicts as the victims of violence, but they have also been the perpetrators of the violence that is part and parcel of such conflicts (see Twum-Danso, 2003; see also Chapter Two). Furthermore, the HIV/AIDS pandemic continues to wreak havoc on populations across the world, but especially in sub-Saharan Africa, where it claims thousands of lives every year, including many children.

Case study: implementing the UNCRC in Ghana

Ghana became the first country to ratify the UNCRC on 5 February 1990, only three months after its adoption by the United Nations General Assembly. As ratification of the Convention requires governments to take steps to ensure that all children within their national boundaries are able to enjoy their rights as stipulated, governments are expected to harmonise their national laws with the standards articulated in the treaty. Hence, the government of Ghana began to review its policies and legislation after 1990. In 1995, the government initiated a comprehensive law reform process in order to ensure full compatibility between national laws and the Convention. The result of this process was the passage of the 1998 Children's Act, which brought together all laws relating to children into a single piece of child-focused legislation that at the same time domesticated the Convention into the national laws of the country. The provisions of the Act, which are largely all in accordance with the Convention's principles, include the following: the right to education and well-being; the right to express an opinion on decisions affecting their welfare; the right to protection from torture, exploitative labour and forced betrothal; and prohibitions on hazardous employment by children under the age of 18.

Although it was envisaged that the Children's Act would represent a change in the lives of children in the country, the reality of children's experiences remains in stark contrast to the picture the legislation sought to draw. The reality on the ground points to a hostile environment for child protection and the implementation of children's rights. Children are subjected to various forms of physical, mental and sexual abuse. While it is difficult to assess the exact nature and scope of this phenomenon due to lack of official data, information from the media, courts and the Ghana Police Service point to a number of violations of children's rights, including defilement or statutory rape (very often by people closest to children such as uncles, teachers or neighbours), incest and harassment, harmful corporal punishment, abandonment, child abduction or stealing, trafficking, intentional neglect and commercial exploitation for domestic servitude or sexual purposes and the engagement of children in hazardous labour. With regards to the last of these, information collected for the 2003 Ghana Child Labour Survey indicates that children under the age of 18 remain very visible as labourers, including in work that has now been defined by the Children's Act as exploitative and hazardous, namely mining, quarrying, fishing, agriculture and the hotel industry, which altogether employ an estimated 242,074 children (Ghana Statistical Service, 2003).

It is worth exploring Ghana's experience of implementing one particular right in order to highlight the challenges that the Act has faced. Education has long been considered a birthright in Ghana. Basic education, which was defined as the first nine years of school (that is, from age 6 to 15) by the 1987 Education Reform Programme, was made compulsory and free for all in the 1961 Education Act. Thus, many believed that with regards to this provision, Ghana had had 'a head start in appreciating the value of the Convention' (see Tengey, 1998). The Children's Act itself makes clear provisions with regard to education, which are further reinforced by the Free and Compulsory Universal Basic Education (FCUBE) policy, a provision of the 1992 constitution. The policy, which was launched in 1996, stipulated that the government should progressively work towards making public basic education free within 10 years of implementation. In order to achieve this, in 2005, the government introduced a school-feeding programme and a small grant for every child (up to the age of 15) in government basic schools. The aim was to reduce the burden on parents in catering for their students. The abolition of school fees did see a sharp rise in the number of children in basic schools. Enrolment of 6- to 11-year-olds in primary schools jumped by 400,000 in 2005/06, which was an increase of 14% on the previous year (Atafori, 2006). However, the FCUBE policy has also faced a number of challenges since the first week of its implementation. Public basic education in Ghana is still not free since there are hidden charges and levies such as school uniforms, exercise books and food. The last of these is particularly important in parts of the country such as the north where food security is not guaranteed. Despite this, the school-feeding programme is still at the pilot stage and only covers two public basic schools in each of the 138 districts in the country's 10 regions. Many parents complain that the government's allocation for each child is not sufficient and that they still bear the financial burden of educating their child. As a result, large numbers of children remain out of school – and very visibly so. This is further compounded by challenges pertaining to gender and geographical considerations, particularly in the north of the country where families may prefer to send a boy child to school and where children who do attend schools have to walk miles before reaching their destination.

Central to understanding the limited implementation of the Children's Act, and as a result, the Convention, is the lack of resources – both human and financial – which has severely impeded the ability of key institutions charged with enforcing the Act to fulfil their mandates. For example, although district assemblies, the basic unit of government administration, are charged with ensuring that the relevant sectors liaise with each other on matters concerning children, many have yet to be sensitised or educated on the UNCRC or the Children's Act. As a result of this widespread lack of knowledge at local authority level, it is difficult for the district assemblies to appreciate the importance of children's rights and this limits their ability to incorporate these principles into their medium-term plans. In addition, those members of the district assemblies who have been sensitised often have difficulty in understanding and comprehending the law. Even when aware and willing, most district assemblies lack the capacity to implement the law effectively due to the sheer magnitude of local government responsibilities that have been placed on them at a time when they are facing severe staff shortages and high personnel turnover. Therefore, they have difficulty apportioning their time and resources adequately and are unwilling to take on new assignments (see Tengey, 1998; Woll, 2000).

Studies have shown that, as a result of these challenges, an extremely limited proportion of the District Assemblies Common Fund, which is allocated by the central government for the development of districts, is used for the protection of vulnerable groups such as children while the bulk goes to capital projects such as building roads (UN and Government of Ghana, 2004: 42). The Department of Social Welfare, which is part of the Ministry of Manpower, Development and Employment, is particularly responsible for children in need of care and protection, who are defined in the Act as those who are neglected, ill-treated, abandoned, orphaned and begging on the streets. However, the capacity of the department to fulfil its mandate is severely restricted. Like the district assemblies, conditions of service are poor and this, in turn, further demoralises the already disillusioned staff and results in a high turnover. Hence, there is a severe shortage of personnel to handle the workload of the Department, which has increased tremendously since the passage of the Children's Act in 1998. As a result, instead of being able to investigate or follow up cases and monitor violations of children's rights, district social workers are reduced to sitting at their desks and being forced to wait for cases to be brought to them. This is problematic in a context where state intervention in family affairs is not welcomed and families rarely take the initiative in reporting cases of abuse to social workers (Gagnon, 2005). The restrictions the Department faces in its work are further compounded by the fact that district social welfare offices do not have vehicles at their disposal, restricting their mobility and making it difficult for them to reach families in more remote places.

In addition, the establishment of the Ministry of Women and Children's Affairs has had an impact on the work of the Department. There has been lack of clarity in oversight responsibilities, particularly between the Ministry of Manpower, Development and Employment, the sector ministry in which the Department of Social Welfare is based, and the Ministry of Women and Children's Affairs. The mandates of the two agencies regarding the protection of children overlap in several areas, leading to duplication of efforts and gaps in services (UN and Government of Ghana, 2004).

Lack of awareness among the general public is also an impediment to the implementation of the Children's Act and the Convention, as most members of the public have no knowledge of these laws. Even in cases where the public are aware of the Act or the Convention, they do not recognise their importance or relevance and many reject the concept of children's rights as it attacks and threatens the very premise on which Ghanaian cultural values, such as reciprocity, are based. Such values are antithetical to the idea of inalienable rights for anyone, let alone children. The idea of children having rights a priori was often met with rejection by many adults I interviewed during the data collection process for my PhD fieldwork in Ghana (between May 2005 and March 2006). According to several participants in different focus group discussions and interviews that I organised, 'we do not want Western children here in Ghana'. The implication behind this statement is that they believe that in Western countries children expect their entitlements, but do not give anything in return – an attitude that they strive hard to ensure that their children do not adopt. What is evident here is the belief that rights, or better still entitlements, come along with duties.

Critiquing the Convention

The limitations that have faced the implementation of the Convention in Ghana and elsewhere require further examination. A number of critiques have been put forward since the Convention was adopted, many of which focus on its Western bias.

Cultural critiques of the Convention

First, as a treaty that is very much rooted in Western conceptions of childhood, the Western bias of the Convention has dominated the debate on implementation from its earliest days. Relativists who believe that childhood is a concept that changes according to historical time, geographical environment, local culture and socioeconomic condition (Dasberg, 1989) argue that the definition of childhood outlined in the Convention is culturally and historically bound to the social preoccupations and priorities of the capitalist countries of Europe and the US (Boyden, 1997). Thus, they attack international children's rights lawyers who crystallised in international law a universal system of rights for the child based on notions of childhood that emerged and were consolidated in the West in the 19th century (Boyden, 1997). According to de Waal (2002: 14): 'The idea of a single (gender neutral) age of legal maturity [evident in the Convention] reflects the western juridical tradition and concepts of citizenship built around the universal franchise and eligibility for conscription into the army'.

Indeed, when we explore different societies we do find evidence to support the claim that childhood is a relative concept. According to Twum-Danso (2008), in numerous African societies, as in other non-Western cultures, chronological age as an indicator for the termination of childhood is perceived as an arbitrary concept. Rather, the achievement of adulthood is based on economic independence, marriage and having children. Without achieving these landmarks, a person may legally be an adult, but will always be seen as somewhat lacking, or incomplete (see also Nsamenang, 1992; Omari and Mbilinyi, 1997). In this way, it is possible for a 14- or 15-year-old adolescent to become an adult by virtue of marriage and parenthood while an unmarried, childless person, 24-years-old or older, remains socially immature and excluded from full adult status as they have not passed the necessary rituals to achieve adult status (Twum-Danso, 2008).

Following on from the notion that childhood is a social and cultural concept, critics of the Convention have argued that the right to development, which is one of the principles on which the Convention is based, is intrinsically linked to a particular type of development. Specifically, it is based on modern theories of childhood development originating from Western Europe, which claim that any child's development follows a universal and unilear progression. In fact, as Stephens (1995) argues, by referring to the rights of the child, rather than the rights of children, the Convention is endorsing a universal child who follows a particular development trajectory and requires particular entitlements. The resulting impact of this is that child development that deviates from this model is seen as abnormal, malformed, faulty and requiring assistance to return to the norm.

However, there is a need to go beyond the arguments put forward by relativists and explore the social and political implications of their stance. Stephens (1995) has asked how far it is wise to travel along the road of relativism while millions of children around the world are being exploited and abused as a result of their very vulnerability and subordination as children. The problem here is that if we accept that childhood is a social construction and thus, relative, does it mean that we cannot criticise or judge violations against children in different parts of the world? Does it mean that we cannot criticise certain phenomena such as early marriage and child labour, which have an impact on children's physical and educational development? These are serious questions that those advocating for childhood as a relative concept or a social construction need to take into consideration in their conceptual arguments.

At the heart of the relativists' argument is the claim that children's rights, and indeed human rights more generally, have their roots in 18th-century Western European philosophical theory and ideologies. These philosophical beliefs inform the human rights tradition, as we understand it, in which the rights of the individual are at its very core. As Leary (1990: 18) asserts, given the primacy of the individual in the modern Western conception of rights, there is little room for a concept of group or communal rights. The very definition of human rights underlines the individuality central to the doctrine and as Donnelly (1990: 39) argues, 'human rights are, by definition, the rights, in the strict and strong sense of entitlements that one has simply because one is a human being'. Without the enjoyment of human rights one is almost certain to be alienated or estranged from one's moral nature.

Critics of the human rights doctrine argue that, in contrast to Western societies, which are 'obsessed' with the dignity of the individual, his worth, personal autonomy and property (Legesse, 1980, quoted in Silk, 1990: 310), other cultures are characterised as communal or group-oriented. In 'traditional' African societies, for example, some argue that the collective is stressed and, as a result, the individual is not allowed to exercise any claims that may override those of the kin group. Any individual rights that are exercised within this tradition are based on group membership and not on the basis of one's humanity, and hence are not universal. This means that while members of the group are able to claim entitlements from society, others are excluded, including slaves, serfs, aliens and, to some extent, women and children (see Ojo, 1990).Thus, in this tradition, it is the collective that is sacralised and individual rights have to be viewed within the context of the community.With regards to children's rights, those claims that children have in international law can be made not only against the state, but also against the society and the group, which undermines the sacralisation of the collective. Herein lies the bone of contention for relativists. In cultures where the focus is on the interests of the group or the extended family, the family's interests and those of the children become inseparable (Bennett, 1999: 96). In fact, children within these contexts have no especially favoured position in relation to their parents and other relatives. A child's claim against the family for food and shelter is of little account because it is taken for granted that all members of a family will be adequately maintained (Bennett, 1999).Therefore, when children are perceived in law to have claims that can be made not only against the state, but also against the society and the group, the collective is undermined and this causes resistance.

This discussion provokes several questions. Can commentators still talk in terms of traditional African society and can policy makers continue to devise laws and policies based on this idea in the 21st century, after centuries of contact with European cultures and decades of colonisation, which was closely followed by the globalisation of culture, economies and development? Howard derides those commentators who talk of traditional African society in the present tense as if it still exists. She argues that 'the present and the past tenses are used interchangeably in the literature; traditional African society is frequently referred to as if it still exists in unaltered form' (Howard, 1990: 163).This leads her to claim that it is, in fact, a version of the 'myth of Merrie Africa' that has been heavily critiqued (see Howard, 1990).Therefore, there is a need to acknowledge the impact of social change on society.

Many have tried to counter the arguments put forward by relativists by focusing attention on the fact that the Convention has been ratified by virtually all countries of the world. However, as Twum-Danso (2008) stresses, one cannot easily conclude that governments' ratification of the Convention signifies universality in attitudes towards children's rights. Indeed, many African governments rushed to ratify the Convention but almost 20 years later the fruits of ratification are yet to yield – even at the legislative and policy levels.This has led Twum-Danso to go further and argue for the need to examine the motivation for ratification. She refers to de Waal (2002) who bluntly argues that some African states are likely to have acceded to the Convention without their leaders genuinely acknowledging the commitments they were making or simply in bad faith, without a real intention to deliver on their commitments. In some cases, presidents may have regarded ratifying the Convention as little more than signing up to the World Declaration and Plan of Action at the September 1990 World Summit on Children, which were, indeed, no more than unenforceable promises (see Twum-Danso, 2008).

An incident that caused controversy in Nigeria highlights this point well. Although the government of Nigeria was one of the first to ratify the Convention in 1991, its domestication met with severe obstacles. In October 2002, the Children's Rights Bill, which aimed to harmonise national legislation with the Convention's standards, was overwhelmingly rejected by the Nigerian federal legislative lower Chamber – the House of Representatives – at Second Reading. (The Bill was later passed by the federal government in 2003 but has still not been passed by all state governments.) The representatives particularly objected to the establishment of 18 as the minimum age for marriage as they felt that it was incompatible with religious and cultural values in various parts of the country, especially the north, where women are often married before the age of 16. According to the then Member of Parliament for Benue (North Central Nigeria), Hon. Ohepo Ejiga, the Bill neglected the dynamism of the Nigerian sociocultural background and he was concerned that it might have a counter effect on cultural values (Twum-Danso, 2008). In contrast, supporters of the Bill argued that the practice of early marriage has resulted in a large number of cases of vesico-vaginal fistula, a condition caused by giving birth when the cervix is not fully developed. Victims of fistula are often ostracised and abandoned as the uncontrollable trickle of urine makes these women unhygienic and physically offensive to their families, who abandon them as a consequence. One of the aims of the establishment of 18 years as a minimum age for marriage in the Act was to reduce this occurrence.

What this example shows us is that although Nigeria became one of the first countries to ratify the Convention in 1991, when the time came to harmonise the Convention's standards into national law 11 years later, politicians reverted to cultural and traditional values to explain their opposition. Hence, this further highlights the argument that the universality of opinion on children's rights cannot be claimed on the basis of state ratification of a treaty alone (Twum-Danso, 2008).

Twum-Danso (2008) goes on to argue that the depth of the consensus underpinning the Convention is further thrown into doubt when the African Charter on the Rights and Welfare of the Child is drawn into the analysis. Despite the fact that the Charter was adopted only a year after the Convention, it took nearly 10 years for the requisite 15 African states to ratify it, even though its provisions are broadly similar to the Convention. It finally came into force on 29 November 1999. As of June 2008, however, only 38 out of the 53 African Union member states have ratified the Charter, although many were quick to ratify the UNCRC in the first few years after its adoption. Even those who did ratify the Charter were hesitant to do so, although, arguably, they could claim greater ownership over it (Twum-Danso, 2008). Ghana, for example, was the first country to ratify the Convention in February 1990, but it did not ratify the Charter until June 2005. Thus, there are questions that need to be asked about the motivation of governments ratifying in conventions and the extent to which they do it as a symbolic act in order to increase their status in the eyes of the international community (see de Waal, 2002).

Conclusion

This chapter has shown that, despite the turning point that many believed the UNCRC represented, its impact on the lived experiences of millions of children around the world has been severely limited. Hence, its vision is far from being realised. These limitations mean that it is important that the Convention cannot, and should not, be seen as an end in itself. It does, indeed, provide fundamental building blocks, but these need to be built on and strengthened through further dialogue within countries (with the public, not just among policy makers), and through revisions, reformulations and action (Twum-Danso, 2008; see also Freeman, 2000). Key to this process is the need to engage in a discussion about how children's rights can be realised in ways that meet international standards, but also appreciate local realities – be they cultural, religious or socioeconomic. Without this broad and open approach the vision to which the Convention aspired will remain a stark contrast to the reality of children's lives around the world.

References

Archard, D. (2004) *Children: Rights and Childhood* (2nd edition), London and New York, NY: Routledge.

Atafori, A. (2006) 'UK pledges £105 million for FCUBE', *New Statesman*, 25 July.

Bennett, T.W. (1999) *Human Rights and African Customary Law under the South African Constitution*, Cape Town: Juta and Co Ltd.

Boyden, J. (1997) 'Childhood and the policy makers: a comparative perspective on the globalization of childhood', in A. James and A. Prout (eds) *Constructing and Reconstructing Childhood: Contemporary Issues in the Sociological Study of Childhood* (2nd edition), London and New York, NY: Routledge Falmer.

Dasberg, L. (1989) 'What is a child and what are its rights', in E. Verhellen and F. Spiesschaert (eds) *Ombudswork for Children: A Way of Improving the Position of Children in Society*, Acco: Leuven/Amersfoort.

de Waal, A. (2002) 'Realising child rights in Africa: children, young people and leadership', in A. de Waal and N. Argenti (eds) *Young Africa: Realising the Rights of Children and Youth*, Trenton, NJ/Asmara: Africa World Press.

Donnelly, J. (1990) 'Human rights, individual rights and collective rights', in P.R. Baehr, J. Berting, J. Herman Burgers, B. De Klerk, C. Flinterman, R. Kroes, C. A. Van Minnen and K. Vanderwal (eds) *Human Rights in a Pluralist World: Individual and Collectivities*, Westport, CT, and London: Meckle.

Freeman, M. (1992) 'The limits of children's rights', in M. Freeman and P. Veerman (eds) *The Ideologies of Children's Rights*, Dordrecht, Boston and London: Martinus Nijhoff Publishers.

Freeman, M. (1996) 'Introduction: children as persons', in M. Freeman (ed) *Children's Rights: A Comparative Perspective*, Aldershot: Dartmouth Publishing.

Freeman, M. (2000) 'The future of children's rights', *Children & Society*, vol 14, no 4, pp 277-93.

Gagnon, L. (2005) *Access to Justice by Children*, Accra: Judicial Service of Ghana, UNICEF-Ghana and CUSO.

Ghana Statistical Service (2003) *Ghana Child Labour Survey*, Accra: Ghana Statistical Service.

Howard, R. (1990) 'Group versus individual identity: the African debate on human rights', in A. A. An-Na'im and F. M. Deng (eds) *Human Rights in Africa: Cross-Cultural Perspectives*, Washington, DC: Brookings Institution.

Leary, V. (1990) 'The effect of Western perspectives on international human rights', in A. A. An-Na'im and F. M. Deng (eds) *Human Rights in Africa: Cross-Cultural Perspectives*, Washington, DC: Brookings Institution.

Mulinge, M. (2002) 'Implementing the 1989 United Nations' Convention on the Rights of the Child in sub-Saharan Africa: the overlooked socioeconomic and political dilemmas', *Child Abuse & Neglect*, vol 26, no 11, pp 1117-30.

Muscroft, S. (1999) *Children's Rights: Reality or Rhetoric: The United Nations Convention on the Rights of the Child: The First 10 Years*, London: International Save the Children Alliance.

Nsamenang, A.B. (1992) *Human Development in a Cultural Context: A Third World Perspective*, Newbury Park, CA: Sage Publications.

Ojo, O. (1990) 'Understanding human rights in Africa', in P. R. Baehr, J. Berting, J. Herman Burgers, B. De Klerk, C. Flinterman, R. Kroes, C. A. Van Minnen and K. Vanderwal (eds) *Human Rights in a Pluralist World: Individual and Collectivities*, Westport, CT, and London: Meckle.

Omari, C. K and Mbilinyi, D. A. S. (1997) *African Values and Child Rights: Some Cases from Tanzania*, Dar es Salaam: Dar es Salaam University Press.

Santos Pais, M. and Bissell, S. (2006) 'Overview and implementation of the UN Convention on the Rights of the Child', *The Lancet*, vol 367, no 9511, p 689.

Sgritta, G. (1997) 'Inconsistencies: childhood on the economic and political agenda', *Childhood*, vol 4, no 4, pp 375-404.

Silk, J. (1990) 'Traditional culture and the prospect for human rights in Africa', in A.A. An-Na'im and F.M. Deng (eds) *Human Rights in Africa: Cross-Cultural Perspectives*, Washington, DC: Brookings Institution.

Stephens, S. (1995) 'Children and the politics of culture in late capitalism', in S. Stephens (ed) *Children and the Politics of Culture*, Princeton, NJ: Princeton University Press.

Temba, K. and de Waal, A. (2002) 'Implementing the Convention on the Rights of the Child', in A. de Waal and N. Argenti (eds) *Young Africa: Realising the Rights of Children and Youth*, Trenton, NJ/Asmara: Africa World Press.

Tengey, W. (1998) *The Convention on the Rights of the Child Impact Study: The Study of Ghana*, Accra: Save the Children UK–Ghana.

Twum-Danso, A. (2003) *Africa's Young Soldiers: The Co-Option of Childhood*, Pretoria: Institute of Security Studies.

Twum-Danso, A. (2008) 'A cultural bridge, not an imposition: legitimising children's rights in the eyes of local communities', *Journal for the History of Childhood and Youth*, vol 1, no 3, pp 391-413.

UN (United Nations) (1989) 'Convention on the Rights of the Child', UN General Assembly, Document A/RES/44/25, available online at www.hrweb.org/legal/child.html (accessed 18/02/05).

UN and Government of Ghana (2004) *Common Country Assessment (CCA) Ghana,* Accra: UN and Government of Ghana.

Veerman, P. (1992) *The Rights of the Child and the Changing Image of Childhood,* Dordrecht: Martinus Nijhoff Publishers.

Verhellen, E. (1996) 'The Convention on the Rights of the Child', in E. Verhellen (ed) *Understanding Children's Rights, Collected Papers Presented at the First Interdisciplinary Course on Children's Rights (July 1996),* Ghent: Children's Rights Centre.

Woll, L. (2000) *The Convention on the Rights of the Child: Impact Study,* Stockholm: Save the Children Sweden.

Eight

Children, young people and the law

Julia Fionda

Introduction: exploring childhood in law

Why does the law need to define what childhood is? Identifying a boundary between childhood and adulthood becomes important in many legal disciplines because a person's legal identity as either a child or an adult may confer a series of legal entitlements, duties, responsibilities and accountability for actions. The child as a legal person both owes duties to society (to bear responsibility for their actions) and, perhaps more importantly, is owed rights and entitlements by their family, the state and society. It is, therefore, important to establish where the child's legal persona transforms into an adult legal persona, when those obligations may come to an end and/or be replaced by an alternative set of duties or entitlements.

Determining where this boundary may lie is difficult and can be achieved in a number of ways. On the one hand, law takes what we may call a *status approach*, which sets strict boundaries based on biological age. For many legal purposes, following the UNCRC (UN, 1989), a child 'comes of age' or crosses the boundary from legal childhood to legal adulthood at the age of 18. Obtaining legal 'majority' at this age signifies the transition to adulthood, a world in which the person may buy alcohol, vote in elections, marry without parental consent, get a tattoo or claim certain welfare benefits in their own right. However, this 'black letter' approach is in itself far from simple. The transition from childhood to adulthood may occur much earlier (or even later) depending on the social context that the law is seeking to regulate. So, surprisingly, a person is permitted to drink alcohol in private at the age of five (even though they cannot buy it until they are 18). They may consent to sexual intercourse (heterosexual or homosexual) at 16 but cannot marry without parental consent until 18. They may be held responsible for a crime at 10, but cannot be responsible for owning a pet until they are 12. They may open a bank account at 14, but cannot seek full-time employment or pay tax until they are 16. This already illustrates the fluidity of the boundary between the two legal identities. There is no coherence or rationality to these boundaries – the assumption is that the child attains adult competence, maturity or capacity for different purposes at different ages.

Hence, taking a strict status approach does not help us in determining what the identity of a child or adult means in legal terms and offers little in the way of a rational understanding of how children are conceptualised in law. Nevertheless, this is often the way in which law is perceived – as setting out rules on what a child is or is not capable of doing, perhaps not unfairly since regulation is a sizeable part of law's raison d'être. Without strict age limits on such activities, regulation would be chaotic. However, the use of this approach in criminal law will be explored in depth below to illustrate how unhelpful it may be in applying the law fairly and rationally in individual cases.

Alternatively, some areas of law are more individualised in their approach and base the boundary on an assessment of competence or capacity – so we might call this the *competence approach*. Under this approach, the boundaries are neither fixed nor clear, but fluid to take into account an individual child's developmental progress, maturity, dependence and mental capacity to take decisions for themselves and accept responsibility for their own lives. In family law, for example, the law recognises that children develop and mature at their own pace and it needs to take a case-by-case approach to determining where on the spectrum between childhood and adulthood the children fall. This enables practitioners to take into account the context in which this judgement is being made – for example, are we allowing a child to make a decision about consenting to medical treatment, to sexual intercourse or to marriage, or are we considering whether the child needs the protection of the state from harm at home, or which parent the child should live with after divorce? In family law, whether on a case-by-case basis or in designing generic legal principles and rules, the boundary has to be constructed based on a judgement of a child's competence, vulnerability, dependence or capacity for responsibility in the context of the law's application to any particular issue.

The question addressed here, in examining the approach in these different legal areas, is whether holistically we can find a defensible rationale for the fluidity of these boundaries, whether they tend to be haphazard or, more particularly, whether they can be empirically justified as opposed to merely politically driven. Law does not exist in a vacuum – it is informed by political policy choices of the government, which passes legislation; contemporary social pressures calling for law to provide solutions; as well as legal traditions such as upholding the rule of law or maintaining the civil liberties of citizens as far as possible without compromising the rights of others. The prominence or otherwise of any of these influences over law will vary across a wide variety of legal disciplines and in the context of family law and criminal law, discussed here, they may help to inform law's conceptualisation of children.

The child in family law

Family law covers issues as various as marriage, ownership of family property and succession, divorce and state and parental rights and responsibilities in relation to children. Defining a child is therefore of central importance in this area of law and it is here, perhaps more than in any other area of law, that most statutory and judicial attention has been focused on what childhood means and when it begins and ends. Much (although not all) of the modern public law relating to children is contained in the 1989 Children Act, which governs the extent of the state's responsibility for children, particularly those in need of support and protection from harm. This is a good place to start in considering the purpose of much of family law and its philosophical approach to defining the limits of childhood. Put simply, childhood ends in this area where the parental role ends and when the state relinquishes the duty to protect the welfare of a child and expects them to take responsibility for their own lives.

The 1989 Children Act sought to secure the welfare of all children in England and Wales and ensure that where they were 'in need' (Section 17) of welfare provision or support then those needs would be alleviated. However, the state, in bestowing this benevolence, was to do so in partnership with the child's parents, to assist them in carrying out the parental role rather than taking it over in an interventionist and opprobrious way. The state was only to intervene minimally, only where absolutely necessary (particularly in relation to care proceedings – Section 31) and where it was in the best interests of the child to intervene rather than not. The Act also encouraged, wherever possible, that the child should participate in the decision-making process and that the child's wishes should be ascertained as appropriate to their age and understanding (Sections 1(3)(a) and 22). This demonstrates the liberal paradigm of family law, which is designed to create a set of children's rights and parental and state responsibilities without stigma or judgement and which is sensitive to a child's needs and capabilities (Freeman, 1992). Most importantly, Section 1 of the Act establishes the principle that the child's welfare is the *paramount* consideration in any decision making under the powers of the Act.

The Act defines a child technically as a person under the age of 18 (Section 105). So status-wise a child remains the responsibility of their parent (and the state in this context) until they reach the traditional age of majority. The Act provides a further duty on the state to advise and assist young people up to the age of 21 (Section 24), where necessary, but relinquishes strict statutory duties to provide welfare benefits and acknowledges the end of parental responsibility (in law at least) at 18. However, family law does not slavishly adhere to this status approach in the way that criminal law tends to and the House of Lords case of *Gillick* (1986) authoritatively confirmed the competence approach now embedded in the Act.

Victoria Gillick was the mother of five daughters all under the age of 16. When the Department of Health and Social Security issued a circular to doctors indicating that in exceptional circumstances they may lawfully offer contraceptive medical treatment to patients under 16 without parental consent she sought a declaration from the courts that the policy was unlawful because, under the 1969 Family Law Reform Act, a minor (under the age of 16) could not consent to medical treatment in their own right – this responsibility was conferred to the parent. The courts therefore had to decide on the limits of parental responsibility and thus the upper parameters of dependent childhood. The House of Lords (per Lord Scarman, *Gillick*: 188) responded by stating as a legal principle that parental rights do not end abruptly at the age of 16 in this context, but applied a transitional analysis and suggested that parental 'rights' (responsibilities is the preferred term in the Children Act) dwindle as the child matures sufficiently to take responsibility for themselves:

> The law relating to parent and child is concerned with the problems of growth and maturity of the human personality. If the law should impose upon the process of 'growing up' fixed limits where nature knows only a continuous process, the price would be artificiality and a lack of realism in an area where the law must be sensitive to human development and change. (*Gillick*: 186)

This judgment not only recognises that in reality there is a transitional phase of adolescence between childhood and adulthood and that the former does not end abruptly as the latter begins, but also suggests that parental rights only extend as far as is necessary in the best interests of the child and must make way for autonomy when the child is ready to embrace it. This is understandable when the principle of paramountcy is held in such high regard; suggesting that parental responsibilities must accede to children's own rights when a child is capable of exercising those rights. When might this be? Lord Scarman (*Gillick*: 184) elucidated thus: 'parental right yields to the child's right to make his [sic] own decisions when he reaches a sufficient understanding and intelligence to be capable of making up his own mind on the matter requiring decision'.

The competence approach adopted in family law therefore rests on an assessment of mental capacity – equated with intelligence, maturity and powers of reasoning. Ironically, the boundary between childhood and adulthood has subsequently been set rather late given the stringent levels of capacity a child has been expected to demonstrate in order to be judged '*Gillick* competent'. In *Re H* (1993), for example, the court had to decide whether a child who was emotionally disturbed, although of above-average intelligence, could instruct a solicitor in their own right at the age of 15. The court held that a child wishing to do so required sufficient 'rationality' and, in this case, that the level of emotional disturbance is such as to remove the necessary degree of rationality that leads to coherent and consistent instruction' (*Re H*: 449). Such rationality would never be required of an adult in this or any other context. Hence, Freeman (2001: 191–3) suggests that, in this and other cases, children have been expected to be more competent than adults in order to pass this 'test'. Nevertheless, the approach is widely adopted in family law across the spectrum of decision making (Bainham, 2004: 345-59). That said, given its individualised nature, it is unlikely to be (and has not been) applied consistently and Fortin (2003: 123) criticises the competence approach for its covert complexity and ambiguity.

This would suggest that family law constructs (or perhaps presumes) a child as dependent and incompetent (Fionda, 2001), which is unsurprising given that its rationale is to support and protect those whose vulnerability threaten their well-being. A child's transition to adulthood can only be established having rigorously assessed and tested the mental capacities of an individual. Rigid, inflexible age limits have little relevance in this assessment except to offer broad guidance and their application would almost inevitably result in an inappropriate, possibly harmful implementation of the law. For example, had such a rigid approach been taken in *Gillick*, children approaching the age of 16 would never have been able to consent in their own right to contraceptive medical treatment, with all the social, physical and emotional problems that could have ensued.

The child in criminal law

Criminal law as a legal discipline seeks to assign blame for actions that are specifically prohibited under criminal (as opposed to civil) law. All behaviour that is considered 'illegal' is prohibited under either criminal law or the much broader spectrum of civil laws. The boundaries between the two are rather flexible and complex, but for our purposes here we can assume that criminal law is the preserve of only the most harmful or immoral conduct and, generally speaking, legislators apply a sense of minimalism in this area of law given that the outcome is punitive. In this context, therefore, criminal law seeks to attribute blame and accountability for the actions of children where their behaviour falls within this realm of heinousness. The function of criminal law is, therefore, rather different to the multifarious areas of civil law and this results in a different approach to conceptualising childhood. In contrast to family law, criminal law is assessing the extent to which children may be held responsible for the consequences of their actions and how far they should submit to the punishment process.

The boundary between childhood and adulthood in criminal law is, in some respects, less complex than in other areas of law, since the law purports to apply a *status* approach rather than a *competence* approach to defining the parameters of childhood. This is an area where, as a result of recent legislation, childhood effectively ends abruptly on attaining the minimum age of criminal responsibility, which is currently 10 in England and Wales. Above the age of 10, an accused person of any age becomes subject to the principles applied in ascribing criminal liability, irrespective of their maturity, vulnerability or competence. It is true to say that *procedurally* children and young people are dealt with differently as defendants in terms of the mode of trial and, on conviction, by the nature and extent of punishments delivered to them, although it is certainly not true to say that the younger the defendant, the more benevolent or lenient the procedural approach (Fionda, 2005). However, as regards *substantive* criminal law, above the minimum age of criminal responsibility no distinction is drawn between a child and an adult defendant when constructing a case against them.

Thus, the strict legal boundary between the child and the adult in criminal law is age 10. Under this age, children are deemed to be *doli incapax*, literally translated as incapable of evil. What does this mean exactly? In order to understand this we need to examine the way in which criminal law constructs liability against an accused person. Any criminal offence comprises two broad concepts: *actus reus* (the actions or conduct that is prohibited) and *mens rea* (a guilty state of mind coinciding with the commission of the actions or conduct). So, for example, in order to construct liability for murder, the prosecution must establish first that the defendant caused the death of another human being (the *actus reus*) and then that, at the time of causing death, the defendant intended to kill or cause serious harm to the victim (the intention being the *mens rea* or guilty state of mind).

When we say that a child is *doli incapax* or incapable of evil we are not saying that the child is incapable of carrying out the *actus reus* of any particular offence. There is no doubt that many very young children are capable of committing acts of violence, of stealing property or lying and acting fraudulently. Rather, we are saying that the child lacks the ability to form criminal intent because they lack the capacity to fully understand the nature and consequences of their actions. Although the notion of *doli incapax* is based on a lack of *competence* in relation to a child's understanding of their behaviour, it is referred to as a *status* approach here because of the strict application of the age limit. Regardless of any particular child's own understanding or powers of reasoning, criminal law states clearly that if the child is aged under 10 there is a complete bar on prosecuting that child for any offence whatsoever. Conversely, if the child is aged over 10 there is no restriction on prosecuting the child for any offence known to criminal law, subject only to the question of proof of the necessary *actus reus* and *mens rea* requirements. As Smith (1994: 427) argues, '[the law] holds that a person is completely irresponsible on the day before his tenth birthday, and fully responsible as soon as the jelly and ice-cream have been cleared away the following day'.

This may be explained by virtue of the very different rationale behind criminal law, compared with family law. Criminal law conceptualises the child as anything but vulnerable and incompetent – but rather seeks to establish a point in a child's life where they may be held accountable for their actions that cause harm to others or society generally. Therefore, the approach here rests more on status than on competence – making greater use of blind age limits on protection from prosecution and making a significant assumption that, beyond a certain age, children can and *should* be held accountable for their behaviour.

Case study: the doctrine of *doli incapax*: conceptualising the child in law

While this *status* approach appears straightforward, the doctrine of *doli incapax* requires further examination given its symbolic value in aiding our understanding of childhood in law. First, the notion of *doli incapax*, and indeed the phrase itself, suggests that to lawyers, the demarcation between childhood and adulthood is about capacity (or competence), as discussed above. However, the preceding discussion illustrates that in fact criminal law takes a rather 'black letter' approach to understanding competence and tends to make broad assumptions about when a child acquires this competence rather than assessing individuals' maturity in the way that family law does. This may seem contradictory. Indeed, the second symbolic function of the doctrine is to demonstrate an inherent tension between the two approaches. This is manifested in a reluctant acknowledgement that a status approach is facile and unhelpful on the one hand, while recognising, on the other, a political agenda in this area of youth justice that is reluctant to adopt a competence approach – carrying with it as it does a sense of understanding of the individual, possibly confused with benevolence and tolerance. This tension emerged from a recent debate over the value of the doctrine in the 21st century and the appropriate positioning of the boundary between childhood and adulthood.

The minimum age of criminal responsibility in England and Wales was subject to much debate throughout the 20th century, having been raised from 8 to 10 by the 1963 Criminal Justice Act. The 1969 Children and Young Persons Act purported to raise it again to 14, but this was never implemented. Since the 1960s there have been a number of discussions about raising the age again (see, for example, Home Office, 1990: para 8.3), all of which failed to produce legislation. More recently, it has been argued that the minimum age is too high, largely as a response to the murder of James Bulger in 1993 by two 10-year-olds who would not have been prosecuted if they had been slightly younger. The minimum age of criminal responsibility in England and Wales is comparatively low. Many Western European countries set this age at 12 or above (for example, Ireland 12, France 13, Germany 14, Norway 15). Indeed, a number of states set it as high as 16 (Poland, Portugal and Spain) and others do not prosecute children at all, having a minimum age of 18 (Belgium and Luxembourg).

This immediately prompts a discussion of what the minimum age signifies and how it is selected as an appropriate boundary between childhood and adulthood for criminal law purposes. Many commentators (for example, Keating, 2007) take the view that these European states assess a generic sense of the age at which children gain a fuller understanding of their actions and an ability to recognise and take responsibility for the consequences of those actions. This may differ between states given the differential developmental experiences and social norms across varying social cultures. However, these social and cultural differences cannot possibly explain why a child in England and Wales matures to the requisite point at age 10 yet a Norwegian child does not attain this maturity until age 14 or a Belgian child until age 18. A preferable view is, therefore, that the minimum age and the doctrine of *doli incapax* is politically motivated and should more realistically be viewed as a policy decision about at what age any state chooses to subject its children to the criminal trial and punishment process (Fionda, 2001: 85–6). This reflects rather more a state's political view of youth crime and rather less any realistic assessment of the age at which children can actually form criminal intent.

Recent developments in this area illustrate further the two points made above; namely that *doli incapax* is an inherently political doctrine and that the status approach is so nonsensical and unhelpful that in practice we inevitably fall back to utilising a competence approach in order to apply criminal law rationally and fairly to children. Prior to 1998, the boundary between childhood and adulthood in criminal law was more fluid than the strict status approach now indicates. While the minimum age has been set at 10 since 1963, there did exist a presumption against the prosecution of children aged between 10 and 13 inclusive on the grounds that they were *presumed* to be *doli incapax*. This presumption (not bar) could be rebutted where the prosecution could establish that the child in any case actually did understand that their actions were seriously wrong as opposed to merely naughty. In some cases this required the use of expert psychological evidence. In practice, however, the prosecution was often able to rebut the presumption with minimal evidence of a child's awareness of the consequences of their actions – for example, a statement to this effect from the child themselves. The seriousness of the offence in question should not, itself, have rebutted the presumption, but in reality this may sometimes have been the case. In the trial of Venables and Thompson for the murder of James Bulger, for example, there was no discussion of the presumption at all – the implicit suggestion being that the nature of the offence itself was evidence enough that the two boys understood that their actions were legally wrong. This constructed a grey, transitional area between childhood and adulthood, which allowed for the prosecution to demonstrate that an individual defendant did in fact have competence and sufficient understanding to be proceeded against, but which protected the majority of children from prosecution as it was felt that children under the age of 14 generally lack such competence.

This presumption of *doli incapax* has unclear origins, but legal historians have estimated that it had existed in English law for at least 800 years – it is referred to in the first edition of *Blackstone's Commentaries on the Laws of England* published in 1769, which claimed that it dated back to the reign of Edward III (1326–77). Notwithstanding this enduring history, in 1993 the Queen's Bench Division of the High Court decided to abolish the presumption in the case of *C v DPP* (1994). In English Law, some rules or principles exist in what we call 'common law'. This is essentially judge-made law, developed through the precedents made in previous cases. Common law, as opposed to statutory law passed in Acts of Parliament, can be unmade by judges in subsequent cases. As this presumption existed in common law and had no statutory authority, the High Court felt able to abolish even such a longstanding legal rule.

C v DPP (1994) involved a 12-year-old boy charged with attempting to steal a motorcycle. The boy was presumed in law to be *doli incapax* but the prosecution used evidence (namely that the boy ran away from the police when approached) to prove that he understood that his acts were legally wrong and was able to proceed to trial. The boy, convicted of the offence, appealed, challenging the probative value of such evidence to rebut the presumption. In the course of considering the appeal, Mr Justice Laws gave a robust critique of the presumption and promptly abolished it. His critique (*C v DPP*, 1994: 196-7) rested on the assertion that to presume incompetence among all children aged 10 to 14 in the late 20th century was 'perverse' and 'contrary to common sense':

> Whatever may have been the position in an earlier age,
> when there was no system of universal compulsory
> education and when, perhaps, children did not grow up
> as quickly as they do nowadays, this presumption at the

> present time is a serious disservice to our law ... the effect
> of the presumption is then that a defendant under 14 is
> assumed to possess a *sub*normal mental capacity, and for that
> reason to be *doli incapax*. There can be no justification for
> such a bizarre state of affairs.

Mr Justice Laws is therefore presuming that children grow up more
quickly now than they might have done 100 years ago and, as they
do so, they develop a greater moral awareness and a greater capacity
to understand the implications of their behaviour. Of course, the
empirical evidence for this rather anecdotal view may be challenged
(after all, we no longer send children out to work in factories or up
chimneys at the age of eight!). More importantly, the implication
of this judgment was that the courts were proposing to abandon a
competence approach in favour of the stricter and less individualised
status approach. The decision was widely criticised by academics (see
Bandalli, 1998; Walker, 1999) for both political reasons (that the status
approach endorsed here by the courts was part of a wider agenda to
'toughen up' our response to youth crime) and for its hasty and ill-
judged abandonment of the competence approach:

> [F]ar from being an outmoded survival from an earlier era,
> the *doli incapax* rule is fully consistent with our increasing
> knowledge of child development and learning which tells
> us that children mature and learn over differing time spans.
> A presumption acknowledges that there are variations in
> the speed of the maturation process. (Cavadino, 1997: 168)

The defendant in *C v DPP* (1994) appealed to the House of Lords,
where the presumption was briefly reinstated, although not out of
any great support for the presumption itself, but because the Lords
expressed concern over the constitutional propriety of the High Court
abolishing a legal rule of such long standing and carrying such political
overtones. They urged Parliament to revisit this issue as a matter of
urgency, but felt that the old common law position should remain
until Parliament had the opportunity to do this in 1995. The final
death knell was sounded by the incoming New Labour government
who, as part of its wide-ranging review of the youth justice system,
contemplated the future of the presumption in its consultation paper
Tackling Youth Crime (Home Office, 1997a). Part of the political
agenda behind these youth justice reforms was to ensure that young
people were forced to 'take responsibility' for their behaviour. The

government concluded that the presumption of *doli incapax* worked against this aim by protecting children from the full force of criminal law and had become a practical inconvenience:

> The Government believes that in presuming that children of this age generally do not know the difference between naughtiness and serious wrongdoing, the notion of *doli incapax* is contrary to common sense. The practical difficulties which the presumption presents for the prosecution can stop some children who should be prosecuted and punished for their offences from being convicted or from even coming to court. This is not in the interests of justice, of victims or of the young people themselves. If children are prosecuted where appropriate, interventions can be made to help prevent any further offending. (Home Office, 1997b: para 4.4)

Consequently, Section 34 of the 1998 Crime and Disorder Act abolished the presumption, taking criminal law to the clear, if unsatisfactory, position described above where the age of 10 became the strict demarcation between childhood and adulthood.

However, having said 'Goodbye, *doli*' with some regret, the courts in subsequent criminal law cases have resurrected the issue. This has stemmed from the unsatisfactory, perhaps illogical, operation of the status approach. The prosecution may now proceed against any child aged over 10, but it must still prove all *actus reus* and *mens rea* requirements attached to the specific offence charged. In practice, proving *mens rea* in relation to a child who lacks competence to understand the ramifications of their actions has been less than straightforward. A brief overview of some of these cases will illustrate how the competence approach may yet survive the political cull of 1998.

Mens rea in criminal law can take one of two main forms: intention or recklessness. Intention can be proved where there is evidence to suggest that the defendant's aim or purpose was to bring about the *actus reus* (for example, to kill in the case of murder). Recklessness is a slightly less stringent form of *mens rea*, which suffices for less serious offences. Recklessness traditionally involves proving that the defendant foresaw the *actus reus* as a risk or consequence of their actions (for example, the defendant foresaw that some bodily harm may result from their hitting the victim over the head with a baseball bat in the case of an assault). Recklessness in this sense is subjective (that is, judged from the defendant's own perception of the risk involved in their actions) and is not proved where the defendant genuinely could not or did not foresee the risk of the *actus reus* occurring, for whatever reason. In *R v Caldwell* (1982) the House of Lords gave recklessness a more objective meaning so that a defendant who failed to foresee the obvious risk involved in their behaviour, where that risk would have been obvious to the ordinary reasonable person in the circumstances, would be deemed to be reckless. This may have worked well to convict those who failed to foresee a risk for reasons that were reprehensible, such as being too drunk (as in Caldwell's case – he got so drunk before he set fire to a hotel that he was incapable of foreseeing the risk to the lives of the hotel residents) or simply not caring enough to think about the risk to others. However, the objective approach encompassed, rather unfairly, those who failed to foresee an obvious risk through no fault of their own, such as being too young or having learning difficulties (*Elliott v C*, 1983).

In *R v G* (2003), when two 11-year-olds were prosecuted for criminal damage, without the prosecution having to establish that they understood the seriousness of their actions, they were initially, although reluctantly, convicted because, regardless of their extreme youth or any mental incapacity, the ordinary reasonable (adult) person would have foreseen the risks involved in their behaviour. On appeal, the House of Lords not only changed the law and reverted back to a subjective test for recklessness, but did so particularly because they were concerned that the objective state of the law on recklessness took no account of the mental incapacities of some very young children and, citing the UNCRC, claimed that this was 'unacceptable in a modern society'. The subtext here suggests that the courts were bemoaning the fact that if no account of incapacity is taken at the stage of deciding to prosecute then it jolly well should be later at trial when applying *mens rea* principles.

Two further cases involve children aged, respectively, 15 and 13, who were prosecuted for offences committed jointly with their father, where they both claimed to be subject to their father's instructions and too afraid to act in disobedience to him. The question in both cases was whether in law they had independent intention to commit the crimes. In *RSPCA v C* (2001), the defendant was prosecuted for an animal cruelty offence because she failed to secure medical treatment for her ailing cat, despite the fact that her father had decided that the treatment was unnecessary, that he would not pay for it and she felt unable to contradict her father's wishes. It was held in this case that the court had to be mindful of the child's age and subservience to her father as head of the household in attributing blame for her failure to take the cat to the vet and she was not convicted. In *R v Wilson* (2007) a 13-year-old boy was charged with murder. He had assisted his father in killing the victim but claimed that throughout he acted on his father's instructions because he was too frightened to disobey him. At trial these circumstances were put forward by the defence but it was held that they amounted to a plea of the defence of duress (where a defendant claims that they were forced to commit an offence under threat of death or serious injury), a defence that is not ordinarily available on a charge of murder (*R v Howe and Bannister*, 1987). Wilson was denied the defence, but in a reluctant application of the law to a child Lord Justice Phillips stated (*R v Wilson*, 2007: paras 420–1) that:

> There may be grounds for criticising a principle of law that does not afford a 13-year-old boy any defence to a charge of murder on the ground that he was complying with his father's instructions, which he was too frightened to refuse to disobey. But our criminal law holds that a 13-year-old boy is responsible for his actions and the rule that duress provides no defence to a charge of murder applies however susceptible that defendant may be to the duress.

These cases suggest that covertly the courts are revisiting the issue of *doli incapax* through the difficulties encountered in applying criminal law principles to young children who lack the mental capacity for the weight of criminal responsibility. Their response has been universally critical even where they appear to have no choice but to convict. The status approach is clearly problematic. A recent report on English criminal procedure conducted by the Commissioner for Human Rights (Gil-Robles, 2005: 6) suggested that the government might have abolished at haste only to repent at leisure in this context:

> I have extreme difficulty in accepting that a child of 12 or 13 can be criminally liable for his actions, in the same sense as an adult. I do not mean to deny that extreme measures may need to be taken, both to punish the act and to attempt to correct whatever it is that has clearly gone so drastically wrong. From this, however, to considering that a child of 12 can measure with the full consciousness of an adult the nature and consequences of their actions is, in my view, an excessive leap.

In *CPS v P* (2007), Lady Justice Smith made an admirable attempt to further undermine the political agenda in this area. She tentatively suggested that the entire doctrine of *doli incapax* may not have been swept away in the tidal wave of Section 34 of the 1998 Crime and Disorder Act and that a *defence* of *doli incapax* may have survived in common law. Citing Walker (1999), she claimed that while the *presumption* has gone, there is nothing to stop a child claiming a lack of mental capacity or understanding as a defence to a criminal charge. The issue was not materially relevant to the determination of the case, so her comments were necessarily of persuasive value only. Unfortunately, she failed to adequately persuade the Court of Appeal in the later case of *R v T* (2008), which definitively stated that there was no such defence in common law and that Section 34 had indeed abolished the doctrine of *doli incapax* in its entirety.

So, while criminal law purports to take a status view of childhood/ adulthood, in reality we cannot escape considerations of competence because criminal law is assigning responsibility for children's actions. Nevertheless, political agendas may cause legislators to persist in taking a status approach because competence issues smack of leniency, benevolence and tolerance of children's behaviour which have no place in contemporary criminal justice discourse. The cases discussed here have reflected the controversy of this approach, with judges consistently criticising the politicisation of the issue of the criminal responsibility of children.

Conclusion

Once we have found a definition of childhood, or at least some sort of parameters of childhood that distinguish them from adults, we can then consider what it means to be a child in law. This question becomes even more complex, since this differs greatly between the multifarious disciplines within law. Once we begin to ask questions like – How does this legal discipline regard children? What rights or entitlements does it confer? What does this legal discipline expect of children in terms of responsibilities or acceptable behaviour? What capacities do we expect children to possess in carrying out those responsibilities? – we enter a confusing realm of perceptions of childhood that vary according to legal context and in many ways make little sense. The conflicting perceptions of childhood impact greatly on the way that children are treated by the law and how it responds to their needs and interests. What emerges from this discussion is a sense of plurality within what might be mistaken for a homogeneous academic discipline. This plurality, it is argued, is 'driven by socio-political agendas underpinning the law, although perhaps this should come as no surprise ... given that the law must engage with complex social realities' (James and James, 2004: 80).

The debate over the doctrine of *doli incapax* discussed here has served to remind us how political this issue has become, particularly in criminal law, but also throughout the legal system where children's rights and responsibilities are at issue. Lawyers are more explicit about the competence approach in family law where it is politically acceptable because there we are considering the vulnerable, dependent child and bestowing rights and welfare privileges. In criminal law, where we do not talk of children's rights but of the unruly child deserving the status of adulthood, we adopt a stricter status view since the badly behaved child loses the 'privilege' and concomitant protections and entitlements of childhood and enters the more intimidating world of the adult. It is notable, for example, that the child's welfare in criminal law decision making is merely *a* consideration (Section 44 of the 1933 Children and Young Persons Act), not *the first* or most important consideration as it is in family law. This leaves us with a rather chaotic sense of what childhood means in law, who is 'entitled' to inhabit that innocent place and what benefits and privations that place may inflict on an individual.

References

Bainham, A. (2004) *Children: The Modern Law* (3rd edition), Bristol: Jordan Publishing.

Bandalli, S. (1998) 'Abolition of the presumption of *doli incapax* and the criminalisation of children', *Howard Journal*, vol 37, no 2, pp 114-23.

Cavadino, P. (1997) 'Goodbye, *doli*, must we leave you?', *Child and Family Law Quarterly*, vol 9, no 2, pp 165-73.

Fionda, J. (2001) 'Youth and justice', in J. Fionda (ed) *Legal Concepts of Childhood*, Oxford: Hart Publishing.

Fionda, J. (2005) *Devils and Angels: Youth Policy and Crime*, Oxford: Hart Publishing.

Fortin, J. (2003) *Children's Rights and the Developing Law* (2nd edition), Cambridge: Cambridge University Press.

Freeman, M. (1992) *Children, their Families and the Law: Working with the Children Act 1989*, Basingstoke: Macmillan.

Freeman, M. (2001) 'The child in family law', in J. Fionda (ed) *Legal Concepts of Childhood*, Oxford: Hart Publishing.

Gil-Robles, A. (2005) *Report by Mr Alvaro Gil-Robles, Commissioner for Human Rights on his Visit to the United Kingdom*, Comm DH, 6, Strasbourg: Council of Europe.

Home Office (1990) *Crime, Justice and Protecting the Public*, Cm 965, London: HMSO.

Home Office (1997a) *Tackling Youth Crime: A Consultation Paper*, London: The Stationery Office.

Home Office (1997b) *No More Excuses: A New Approach to Tackling Youth Crime in England and Wales*, Cm 3809, London: The Stationery Office.

James, A. and James, A. (2004) *Constructing Childhood: Theory, Policy and Social Practice*, Basingstoke: Palgrave Macmillan.

Keating, H. (2007) 'The "responsibility" of children in criminal law', *Child and Family Law Quarterly*, vol 19, no 2, pp 183-203.

Smith, A.T.H. (1994) '*Doli incapax* under threat', *Cambridge Law Journal*, vol 53, no 3, pp 426-8.

UN (United Nations) (1989) 'Convention on the Rights of the Child', UN General Assembly, Document A/RES/44/25, available online at www.hrweb.org/legal/child.html (accessed 18/02/05).

Walker, N. (1999) 'The end of an old song', *New Law Journal*, vol 149, no 6871, pp 64–5.

List of cases

C v DPP [1994] 3 All ER 190

CPS v P [2007] EWHC (admin) 946

Elliott v C [1983] 1 WLR 939

Gillick v West Norfolk and Wisbech Area Health Authority [1986] AC 112

R v Caldwell [1982] AC 341

R v G [2003] 1 AC 1034

R v Howe and Bannister [1987] AC 417

R v T [2008] EWCA Crim 815

R v Wilson [2007] 2 Cr App R 31

Re H [1993] 1 FLR 440

RSPCA v C (2001, unreported)

Nine

Child protection

Judith Masson

Introduction

The term 'child protection' has been used since the 19th century
to describe action to remove children from harm, most frequently
abuse and neglect. It also describes a whole range of actions taken
by parents and carers to keep children safe. Since the 1990s it has
frequently been replaced by 'safeguarding', which covers a wider range
of actions intended to keep children safe, from accidents, bullying and
involvement in antisocial behaviour, to protecting them from abuse
(Ofsted, 2008). *Staying Safe*, HM Government's (2008) plan for this
area of policy, identifies three levels of safeguarding:

- 'universal safeguarding' actions, which are designed to keep all
  children and young people safe and to create safe environments;

- 'targeted safeguarding' work, which focuses on specific groups
  who are more at risk than others;

- 'responsive safeguarding' interventions to deal with those who
  harm children and to support children and young people who
  are harmed (HM Government, 2008: para 1.8).

Responsive safeguarding most closely reflects narrow ideas of child
protection. It is protective action that is taken in response to risk
or harm to particular children but also needs to be seen within the
broader context of children's safety and welfare. Keeping children safe
is no longer seen just as the responsibility of those caring for them but
a key element in children's well-being and something to which a wide
range of professionals, government departments and agencies should
contribute.

Child protection is about the quality of children's lives, not
just about specific injuries. It is not just individual incidents that

damage children's lives: the whole environment in which they are brought up can impact negatively or positively on their welfare. This chapter explores issues relating to child protection within the broader context of safeguarding children's welfare. It uses the terms 'child protection' and 'responsive safeguarding' interchangeably, and the term 'safeguarding' to cover the full range of protective and supportive activity. In doing so, it examines different perspectives on child protection. How is responsibility for safeguarding children shared between parents, families, communities and the state? How do we know what the risks to children are? What risks do they face? What part do children have in decisions to keep them safe? Finally, the chapter reviews some different measures that are used to safeguard children and young people and examines their impact on children and childhood.

Different perspectives on child protection

Those whose work brings them into contact with children and families – children's centre staff, daycare workers, teachers, healthcare professionals, youth workers, the police and many others – may see or hear things that make them concerned about the way a child is being treated. Government guidance, *What to Do if You're Worried a Child is Being Abused* (DfES, 2006) advises professionals how to make child protection referrals, but individuals first need to recognise that the way the child is being treated means that they ought to take some action and should consider making a referral. Different levels of understanding derived from different professional training, experience and expectations result in very different responses to the same situation from different professionals. What is acceptable or normal to one may be regarded as clearly abusive by others. Consequently, some harm may continue without professional recognition or response. Conversely, children's social care departments may receive repeated referrals of cases that they consider do not require any response. Child protection systems in many countries are continually overburdened by referrals (Melton, 2005; Lonne et al, 2008). Defining child abuse, fixing the point at which action should be taken in response to it and deciding what should be done continue to challenge societies and individuals who want children protected.

Although we might think we understand what child abuse and neglect are, and that others will agree with us, discussions quickly reveal substantial disagreement about what is acceptable in bringing up children. Parents have widely different views on matters such as when children can be home or go out alone, smoking, drinking, sex and smacking. Childcare practices are culturally determined and vary substantially in different communities and over time. This is not just about knowing what dangers exist and understanding their potential to harm children; it is also about society's values. Child protection is a political as well as a professional matter (Parton, 1985).

Decisions in individual cases add a further dimension. How are the actions of carers and their consequences for the child understood? The same behaviours may appear very different in different contexts. For example, the fact that there is little food in the home can give rise to different inferences about parenting depending on whether the family lives in an area that is stricken by famine, the child lives in a household dependent on benefits or in a family in work where the parents spend money freely on themselves. Children in each of these families may go hungry but could be safeguarded in different ways. A universal approach distributing food aid to the region could safeguard children in the first group, assistance with budgeting some of those in the second, but children in the third group may need protection from parents who appear to be disregarding their children's needs for nutrition. Motive can also distinguish actions that are abusive from those that are in a child's welfare. At first sight, a baby being dropped from a balcony may appear to be a victim of murderous ill-treatment but if the flat is on fire this may be the only chance of safety. Making a child go to their room or sit on 'the naughty step' can be a proper form of discipline but could be abusive if it was done with the intention of excluding a child from a family activity without any reason for such treatment. Intention can change ordinary discipline into emotional abuse. Professionals with responsibilities for child protection have to identify and interpret mistreatment often with the limited information from the snapshots of behaviour they or others have seen, where some actions can have multiple different interpretations and carers may give misleading accounts of their own and others' actions and motives.

The term 'threshold' is used to identify the circumstances or standards of care that justify state intervention to protect children. Where the threshold is placed depends on a combination of knowledge about child development and children's needs, beliefs about family privacy and autonomy, and trust in the alternative care provided. High thresholds occur where bringing up children is a private matter and the state only intervenes in the most extreme cases and as a last resort. Even where state intervention is accepted, thresholds for compulsory intervention, for removing children or for requiring parents to use services, are higher than less intrusive actions such as offering support or developing a child protection plan. As a consequence, some children may endure long periods of neglect where parents refuse services but children's care is not considered so poor as to justify formal action, such as applying for a court order to remove them from home.

The 1989 Children Act sets the threshold for compulsory intervention where a child is suffering or is likely to suffer significant harm. Harm is widely defined and includes the full range of actions that can damage children – physical, sexual or emotional abuse and neglect. The harm caused to children by seeing or hearing others being harmed, for example where family life is marked by domestic violence, is specifically mentioned. What makes harm 'significant', serious enough to justify intervention, is not specified but where a case relies on health or development, comparisons must be made with 'a similar child'. Harm must be attributable to failings in parental care or the child being beyond parental control (Section 31). The Act has to be applied so as to comply with human rights law. The European Convention on Human Rights guarantees respect for private and family life (Article 8) and requires state action to be proportionate. Consequently, only serious harm where children cannot be protected in other ways should result in orders to remove children.

Decisions to bring care cases are made by social workers and lawyers in children's social care departments, but many other professionals are involved in identifying and referring cases for child protection processes and making recommendations for further intervention, for example at child protection case conferences. Different professions view harm differently and have different ideas about what justifies action (Birchall and Hallett, 1995). This results from their professional training and knowledge about childcare and development, their experience and exposure to cases and their views about the roles of parents and the state. Generally, there is agreement about what amounts to serious physical or sexual abuse (Corby, 2006) but there is less agreement about sexual relations where one party is between 13 and 16 and the other not much older. Neglect, even where it is having a major impact on a child's life and development, often gets little attention. There is a danger that those who work in very deprived areas come to accept low standards of care as the norm (Dingwall et al, 1983). Getting courts to agree that neglect justifies intervention is thought to be difficult so action is taken only after an incident (Dickens, 2007). Although concerns about too much intervention are sometimes expressed in the media, research evidence indicates that thresholds for compulsory intervention remain high and the courts first seek to make sure that it is not possible for children to be cared for adequately by their parents.

In *A Local Authority v K & Ors* (2008), a three-year-old was brought to hospital with life-threatening injuries that had been inflicted in more than one incident. Neither parent gave a credible explanation, proceedings were brought and care orders were obtained for the child and two siblings. Three years later the mother gave birth to her fourth child. The local authority started care proceedings on the basis that the injury to the sibling meant that the risk of harm necessitated close surveillance of this baby's care. Despite the opposition of the local authority and the children's guardian and negative assessments from two psychiatrists, the judge ordered further assessment so that the parents had every chance of caring for their baby. Nine months later, following an incident of domestic violence where the police were called, the parents separated. The court then had to decide whether the mother could safely care for the baby alone. After hearing oral evidence, the judge concluded that the baby could not be left with the mother. The additional assessments had delayed the proceedings for the baby by many months. Recognising this, the judge concluded that it was 'a price worth paying' because the assessment might have allowed the baby to remain in her family.

Protection from harm: the role of parents, carers, the wider community and the state

Parents and carers

'Parents bring up children, not governments' (DCSF, 2007: 3). Exceptions to this fundamental principle have been rare and are now linked to oppressive policies, for example collective care promoted in communist states and the mass removal and institutionalisation of children from aboriginal communities in Australia, Canada and the US (Stanton, 1999; Swain, 2001). Practices that separate children from their parents are now viewed as generally harmful but they are used as a 'last resort' to protect children who are being ill-treated or neglected. Such state intervention must follow set procedures and be based on clear evidence. Where children are removed for their protection, states are expected to make considerable efforts to secure good, alternative care. In the four countries of the UK and in the US, arrangements are most commonly made for substitute family care – by relatives, adoptive parents or foster carers – rather than placement in institutions.

Parents can choose how they bring up their children although successive governments have passed laws to limit parents' freedom so as to protect children and implement social policies, for example laws passed requiring the use of fireguards and child car seats. Those with responsibility for children can be prosecuted for neglecting or ill-treating them. The standards of the criminal law mark what is clearly unacceptable. Although hitting children is widely used as a means of disciplining children, some countries have enacted laws that outlaw such behaviour (UNICEF, 2004: 6). In England and Wales, parents (but not childminders, foster carers or teachers) are allowed to use physical punishment on their children but can no longer claim that this is 'reasonable chastisement' if they leave bruises or cause other injuries (2004 Children Act, Section 58).

Parents are expected to supervise their children and their children's care. Parental responsibility is not limited to the way children are cared for in the home but includes making sure that arrangements for care by others are safe and effective (Utting, 1997). Where children behave in antisocial ways, vandalising property or joyriding cars, they risk injury and criminal penalties, both of which can have negative long-term consequences for them. The courts in England and Wales can impose Parenting Orders, which require parents to attend courses to improve their parenting (Home Office, 2004a).

The wider community

Societies vary in the extent to which bringing up children is viewed as a private or a community activity (see also Chapter Five). Community influence is not necessarily benign. Valuing boys more highly than girls can lead to selective abortion, abuse and neglect of girls. Discrimination against the girl child is a major problem in many parts of the world; its consequences can be seen in the large numbers of girls consigned to orphanages in China and the distorted sex ratios in India. Although the UNCRC (UN, 1989) prohibits traditional practices that harm children's health, female genital mutilation is widespread in parts of Africa and in the Yemen (UNICEF, 2007: 70).

In Western Europe, particularly in Britain, notions of family privacy are deeply entrenched. The view that to question someone else's child about their behaviour is an unacceptable interference is one explanation for the failure of anyone to stop the two 10-year-old boys who dragged toddler, James Bulger, through the streets of Liverpool (Jenks, 2005: 88). However, relatives and neighbours do raise concerns about child protection.

The state

States' actions and inactions impact on their child citizens. Decisions about the economy and about military action affect children (WHO, 2002) as do policies specifically directed at children such as those relating to the family, to education and to public health. States have a wide range of roles in safeguarding the welfare of children. This is well recognised in the monitoring processes of the United Nations Committee on the Rights of the Child, which requires states to report regularly on their progress in implementing the UNCRC (Article 44). Ratification of the UNCRC signals a state's acceptance of the principles in the Convention, notably to protect children from abuse (Article 19) and to make children's welfare a primary consideration (Article 3).

Notions of parental responsibility and family privacy mean that states cannot dictate how parents care for their children but this does not mean that they cannot influence the ways children are brought up. States with more resources and more developed welfare systems have more capacity to shape childhood and may have ambitions that go beyond protecting children in adverse circumstances to ensuring that all children reach their full potential. The *Every Child Matters* outcomes in the UK (HM Treasury, 2003) provide an example of government ambitions being made explicit. In other countries this may be done through a National Child Development Plan. Free education and healthcare protect children and support parents, particularly those with least financial resources.

There are many other areas where the government, state agencies and other organisations seek to protect children through providing advice and information to parents. For example, following research in New Zealand in the 1980s, the 'Back to Sleep' campaign advised parents that babies under the age of one should always be put to sleep on their backs. This reduced deaths from Sudden Infant Death Syndrome by half (McClay and Wallace, 2003: 501). Small-scale attempts have also been made to warn carers about the dangers of shaking young babies (Shepherd and Sampson, 2000).

Children's role in their protection

Children are not merely passive subjects of abuse or protection at the hands of adults, they have 'agency', that is, they have some capacity to influence what happens in their own lives (James et al, 1998). Growing up is about taking increasing responsibility for self, and that includes learning about risks and how to avoid them. Learning to cross the road was a major focus of young children's safety education in the 1950s and 1960s when children often walked to school alone or with friends. Now it is treated as a matter for parents to decide when to let children out alone, which may be as late as when they start secondary school (see www.direct.gov.uk). In contrast, sex education, which is a part of the national curriculum, has moved from basic biology to advising children of the risks of sexually transmitted diseases. Programmes have also been developed to teach children to protect themselves from abuse or abduction and to tell adults so that adults can help them (Kidscape, 2007).

As well as learning to take care of themselves, children may seek support and protection by telling others things that are worrying them. Children who are bullied or abused tell parents and friends, they phone helplines such as ChildLine (Vincent and Daniel, 2004) and even contact the police or children's services departments (Masson et al, 2007) but many do none of these things and only reveal ill-treatment when they are adults (Cawson et al, 2000). Running away is a common response to abuse (Wade et al, 1998) but this can put children at greater risk than they faced at home.

Where children have disclosed abuse, they have not always been taken seriously. Indeed, the perception that children in care could not be trusted contributed to abuse in institutions that went on in many children's homes in the 20th century (Waterhouse, 2000). Far more attention is now given to 'listening to children' but this is no guarantee that they will feel able to tell or will be heard. In England and Wales where proceedings are brought for a child's protection they will be represented by a lawyer and a children's guardian, a specialist social worker. The children's guardian's role is to represent the child's best interests by instructing the lawyer to advocate this position and to ensure that the court knows what the child's wishes and feelings about their future care are. Only if the child is mature enough to give instructions to a lawyer, typically over the age of 12 years, will the lawyer advocate the child's own position. Children report that they like their guardians and trust them but do not feel that they understand the process or are able to influence what happens to them (Masson and Winn Oakley, 1999).

The view that children have a right to have a say in decisions about their future is increasingly recognised in keeping with the UNCRC (Article 12; see also Chapter Three). From this standpoint, failing to allow children to participate in decisions can be seen as a form of secondary abuse, treating them as 'objects of concern' rather than as people who have an interest in what happens to them. Adults often express anxiety about involving children in decision making on the basis that children should be protected from stress and anxiety, particularly where the decisions are about living with one or other parent after their separation. Some are also concerned that children will make bad decisions that compromise their welfare, and assume that adult-made decisions are necessarily better. Protecting children and engaging them in decision making involves helping them to understand what decisions can be made, that they can choose to leave decisions to others and that adults at least share the responsibility for whatever is decided. Seen in this way, the opportunity to have a say necessarily contributes to a child's welfare rather than undermines it.

Responding to risk – providing protection

Identification and surveillance

Protecting any child involves identifying risks, considering what can be done to remove or reduce the risk and deciding what action to take. Associated with identifying risks is the issue of surveillance. What arrangements should be put in place to collect information about what is happening to children? Who should be covered? What information will aid child protection? How should those who have abused children be monitored? These questions are relevant generally and in individual cases. Health visitors' work, which monitors the growth and development of young children, is a form of surveillance. Child protection registers, now replaced with the recording of child protection plans on the Integrated Children's System (HM Government, 2006), were introduced so that professionals could establish whether serious concerns had been expressed previously. Entering a child's name in a child protection register came to be seen as a mark of serious concern but local approaches to registration varied markedly (Creighton and Noyes, 1989) and more than a quarter of those who are removed for their protection have never been registered (Masson et al, 2008).

   The registration of sex offenders and the requirement on them to notify the police of changes in their address has provided the police with information to monitor individuals. Background checks, such as taking up references and establishing whether a person has criminal convictions, are common for many forms of employment. Those working with children (and vulnerable adults) are now subject to a set of rules and procedures designed to ensure that they are not unsuitable to work with children. There is a register of those considered unsuitable who are therefore barred from working with children. Alongside these developments, with the encouragement of the National Society for the Prevention of Cruelty to Children (NSPCC), sports organisations have adopted codes of practice to safeguard children, requiring member organisations to have written policies on child protection and ensure that volunteers have undergone Criminal Records Bureau checks.

The changes to children's services heralded by *Every Child Matters* (HM Treasury, 2003) and introduced by the 2004 Children Act further extend surveillance with the aim of ensuring that children can be protected, those most at risk can be identified and harm to them prevented. A system is being developed to record details of all children so that concerns can be shared between professionals, who might not otherwise be aware that others share them, and action taken. Parton (2006a, 2006b) has argued that these changes effectively establish a mandatory reporting system based on 'cause for concern' and shift the relationship between the state and the family. The 'preventive state' will not merely provide services but also seek to ensure that services are used for the benefit of children and, in consequence, the state will become more involved in family life.

Registers of whatever type have three major limitations as tools of protection. First, they potentially mislead and can induce a false sense of safety. Absence of evidence does not mean evidence of absence. The fact that a person's name does not appear on a list of unsuitable people does not mean that the person is suitable. The low rates of detection and criminal conviction of those who abuse children means that there are large numbers of abusers who have escaped registration. Second, the systems that lead to registration are prone to all sorts of administrative breakdown and human failure as the Bichard Inquiry showed (Home Office, 2004b). Third, they can only inform those who make requests for information, so those who need the information they contain have to recognise their responsibility to make the necessary enquiries.

Responses to risk – advice, education and training

Different risks require different responses but those developing safeguarding and protection only have a limited range of tools they can use. They can use advice, education or training to raise awareness, provide information and improve capacity to manage issues. This may be provided widely to parents and carers, as in the Back to Sleep campaign, or focused more narrowly on professionals, such as the work done by Cafcass (Children and family court advisory and support service) to ensure that its staff recognise the signs of domestic violence and understand its effect on children and carers (Cafcass, 2007). There is growing interest in parenting education, not as a direct means of child protection but to raise the quality of parenting so that mothers are less stressed, experience parenting positively and can respond more effectively to their children.

Children and young people also need access to advice if they are to take more responsibility for their own protection. However, providing services directly to young people is viewed by some as undermining the role of parents. One clear example of this is the attempt to restrict access to advice and services for sexual health to young people, particularly those under the age of consent (16 years). Young people who are sexually active require protection from sexually transmitted infections and from pregnancy, which they are unlikely to obtain unless they can access confidential services. Providing such services cannot protect young people from sexual abuse within the family or from sexual exploitation. Advisers have to consider how they respond when they are alerted to such abuse, particularly where other young people who are not their clients are at serious risk. Agencies that provide advice to young people need to consider how they respond to young people whose need for protection is beyond the remit of the agency or the capacity of those they serve.

Responses to risk – service provision

Beyond advice and education is the development of services. Services such as refuges help women to protect their children by leaving violent men. Parents who get drawn into the child protection system frequently report that they have previously tried to obtain help from children's services but have been refused (Packman et al, 1985). In the case of neglectful families, social workers are often at a loss to identify services that can engage parents and address the often multiple and interrelated issues that undermine their capacity to parent (Stevenson, 1998). Assessment is crucial if services are to be found that can meet needs. Children may be found nursery places or occasionally respite care to provide compensatory experiences and reduce stress on a parent but this may have no effect on underlying problems. In one study, a quarter of the families whose children became subject to care proceedings had been offered no services by children's social care. More than a third of children had been placed in foster care before proceedings were started but this was more usually a preliminary protective intervention than a means to improve parenting (Masson et al, 2008). Resource constraints are leading to questions of establishing the effectiveness of services. Currently, the evidence base in child protection is inadequate.

Responses to risk – more law

Law has been given a major role in safeguarding and protecting children (see Chapter Eight for more on how the law constructs and deals with children). In addition to the powers through which children are removed from their parents or the systems to bar unsuitable people from working with children, discussed earlier, very many laws have been passed in recent years with the aim of safeguarding children. These different provisions indicate the limits of the law. Whereas car manufacturers can be required to include seatbelts they will not improve safety unless they are used. A substantial and repeated media campaign has resulted in high levels of compliance with seatbelt use, which has been a major factor in cutting child deaths (Christie et al, 2004). Where criminal law is used to mark the unacceptability of abusive behaviour there can be very little expectation that it will stop abuse. It may ensure that offenders are punished but this requires effective enforcement. Changing abusers' behaviour is a much bigger challenge for service providers. Legislating against abuse gives the impression that something is being done but changes little. Even if abusers are convicted, real protection will only occur if they cease to offend in future. There are also major problems in protecting children through criminal law because of the nature of criminal procedure and rules of evidence, which mean that offenders who harm the most vulnerable children (those aged under five and those with major learning or communication difficulties) are not likely to be convicted unless there are other witnesses, forensic evidence or they plead guilty.

Effective protection?

Not all risks can be eliminated and some interventions may do more harm than good so how can policy makers decide how safeguarding should be taken forward? The *Every Child Matters* outcomes set goals but priorities still have to be set and costs considered. A thorough assessment of the likely effects of an intervention and its costs can provide a clear basis for decision making but questions about competing aims and values will remain.

Evaluating community interventions to protect children is much more difficult because the problems of seeking to change human behaviour cannot be ignored. In the US, legislation has been enacted in many states to enable parents and others to find out whether there are sex offenders living in their neighbourhood. These are generally referred to as Megan's Law, named after Megan Kanka who was abducted and killed by a convicted abuser who lived opposite her home, but the provisions and administrative systems vary substantially in different states. There is no evidence that this form of community notification is effective in reducing offending or preventing assaults (Fitch, 2006). There has been little research into issues such as compliance, the costs of running schemes, the numbers of further offences by known offenders and the numbers of children who have identified offenders as parents. This type of law may have considerable negative effects, making children more vulnerable not more protected. There is a danger of vigilantism, attacks on identified offenders and anxiety about this may reduce compliance so that there are more identified offenders whose whereabouts are not known. Many sex offenders, for example fathers who have downloaded abusive images from the internet, have children living with them and community notification can mean that children are unable to mix freely with their peers, and make families less willing to report offences. Those who receive no notification may feel their neighbourhood is safe when abusers there have simply not been detected and not taken sensible steps to safeguard their children. Also, focusing on stranger danger is misleading; most child abuse is perpetrated by relatives and their friends. Despite media campaigns, the introduction of similar laws in the UK has been resisted.

Partly because of campaigns for Megan's Law, 'stranger danger' has become a major concern in the UK. The abduction of children by strangers is a very rare offence (Newiss and Fairbrother, 2004) but one that attracts massive attention in the media. Parents' levels of anxiety about abduction are high; in a survey for the NSPCC, as part of its 'Full Stop' campaign, 80% of parents gave 'fear of strangers' as a reason for not allowing their children to play outside (Morris, 2000). The focus on stranger danger, which is not just a recent practice, has been identified by academics as having potentially very negative effects on children and childhood. Parents and children are given a distorted picture of the dangers of sexual abuse (Franklin, 1999; Greer, 2002), which are far more likely to come from those known to children, including other children, than from adult strangers (Cawson et al, 2000).

Case study: intercountry adoption

Intercountry adoption is the practice of bringing children for adoption
from overseas. Since contraception became widely available there
have been few babies available for adoption in developed countries
and this has contributed to an increase in the number of intercountry
adoptions, which now number almost 30,000 per year. The majority of
children come from China, Guatemala and Russia and are adopted by
couples from North America, particularly the US, or Western Europe
(Selman, 2000). In the UK, concerns following the history of child
emigration (Bean and Melville, 1989; Select Committee on Health,
1997) and the impact on children of transracial placement have meant
that adoption agencies have not developed intercountry schemes.
Agencies have focused their resources on finding adoption placements
for children in state care. Those who want to adopt from overseas rely
on informal networks and the internet to find out how to do this. As a
result, there are comparatively few intercountry adoptions in the UK,
only about 350 each year (DCSF, 2008).

Intercountry adoption is highly regulated in the UK in order
to protect children. There have long been formal procedures for
obtaining approval to bring a child to the UK for adoption but, in
the 1990s, about a third of prospective adopters did not follow them.
Among these were individuals whose own circumstances – poor
health, lack of support and lack of income – meant that they would
not have been approved. Also, some independent social workers who
approved adopters overlooked serious problems that suggested that
applicants were not suitable. There were also cases where children were
bought. Nevertheless, adoption orders were granted (see Re C, 1999;
Re M, 2003); judges felt constrained to approve adoptions because by
the time cases came to official attention the children concerned had
developed close relationships with their prospective adopters. Further
regulation was introduced and only local authorities can now make
assessments of prospective adopters' suitability. Bringing a child to the
UK for adoption without following the formal procedures was made
a criminal offence and local authorities were required to notify the
Home Office if they came across such cases.

There were growing concerns about practices particularly in
Cambodia and Guatemala. There was evidence that Cambodian
babies were sold for adoption and of corruption among Cambodian
officials. The British government responded by banning adoptions
from Cambodia; a number of parents who were intending to adopt
from Cambodia challenged this decision; the result of the ban meant

that they could not adopt a brother or sister for a Cambodian child they had already adopted, and would have to go through the time-consuming and costly process to be approved for a child from another country. The ban was upheld but one disabled child who had already been matched with a couple was allowed to come to the UK.

Evidence of corruption in Guatemalan adoptions was even more substantial, with examples of babies being stolen and sold for adoption, women pretending to be the mother consenting to the adoption of stolen babies for a fee and lawyers and government officials extracting substantial fees to facilitate adoption (Latin American Institute for Education and Communication, 2000). Pressure was put on Guatemala to reform its adoption law and practice; a number of countries suspended adoptions from Guatemala but each year more than 4,000 children were adopted in the US. As a result of international pressure, Guatemala acceded to the Hague Convention on Inter-country Adoption in 2003. However, various countries, including the UK, were not satisfied that it had eliminated corrupt practices and continued to ban adoptions from Guatemala.

Does banning intercountry adoption protect children? For some children the alternative to intercountry adoption is extreme poverty, institutionalisation and early death. Children adopted from overseas generally gain loving homes and a good education but they also lose aspects of their identity and may be exposed to racism, and this can impact on their psychological well-being in later life. The money expended on intercountry adoption could vastly improve the conditions of many more children in the child's country of origin (Triseliotis, 2000) but adopters spend their money because they want to become parents and may not be such generous donors. Orphanages do obtain donations from adopters; dependence on adopters' money ties them to adoption even where alternatives would be better for the children concerned.

Is it better to allow intercountry adoption than to prohibit it? There is clear evidence that corrupt practices develop where effective regulation is lacking. Guatemala became known as a country where babies were available to those who were willing to pay. The existence of intercountry adoption also skews the provision of welfare services, making it more difficult to develop in-country programmes. For example, social workers who were trained to develop children's services in Romania found that they could earn far more working for agencies arranging intercountry adoptions. Local programmes found it hard to attract and retain the qualified staff they needed to develop foster care and family support services. This was a factor in the decision of the Romanian government to impose an almost complete ban on intercountry adoptions (Dickens, 2002; Hamilton, 2002).

Views about whether child protection protects or harms children are likely to vary according to the faith placed in the effectiveness of regulation in both sending and receiving countries; the weight given to material improvement against risks to emotional, psychological and cultural factors; and the balance between the impact on individual children and on children populations. If practices continue outside the law, children are likely to be at greater risk, for example if they are taken to a new country but do not acquire a legal relationship with their carers or citizenship.

Conclusion

Lord Laming (2003: para 4.190) commented that child protection required those involved to do 'the basic things well'. Protecting children is not a single practice that is generally accepted but a temporary compromise in debates about the role of the state in family life, children's rights and state regulation. There are competing views that have to be balanced, and both positive and negative consequences of interventions. The many different perspectives lead to different priorities and different approaches.

Some substantial improvements in children's lives have been achieved in the last decade, particularly a reduction in Sudden Infant Death Syndrome, improved road safety (OECD, 2004) and efforts to reduce poverty. The recognition that children have rights and are experts in their own lives has changed the way child protection is thought about and practised. The negative impact of domestic violence has been recognised although this has only gone a little way to reducing the harm it generates. Many children face risks and harms that can be barriers to reaching their potential, and for some children these risks are far more numerous and far higher than for others. More has to be done if these children are to have the opportunities of the most fortunate children. Safeguarding is not merely a way of conceptualising the state's responsibilities for children, it has to lead to changes that improve children's lives.

References

Bean, P. and Melville, J. (1989) *Lost Children of the Empire*, London: Unwin/Hyman.

Birchall, E. and Hallett, C. (1995) *Working Together in Child Protection*, London: HMSO.

Cafcass (2007) 'Domestic violence toolkit', available online at www.cafcass.gov.uk/publications/policies.aspx (accessed 20/01/09).

Cawson, P., Wattham, C., Brooker, S. and Kelly, G. (2000) *Child Maltreatment in the United Kingdom*, London: NSPCC.

Christie, N., Cairns, S., Ward, H. and Towner, E. (2004) *Children's Traffic Safety: International Lessons for the UK*, Road Safety Research Report No 50, London: Department for Transport.

Corby, B. (2006) *Child Abuse: Towards a Knowledge Base* (3rd edition), Maidenhead: Open University Press.

Creighton, S. and Noyes, P. (1989) *Child Abuse Trends in England and Wales 1983–1987*, London: NSPCC.

DCSF (Department for Children, Schools and Families) (2007) *The Children's Plan*, Cm 7280, London: The Stationery Office.

DCSF (2008) 'Applications received by the intercountry adoption case work team January 2002 – December 2007', available online at www.dcsf.gov.uk/intercountryadoption/general.shtml (accessed 20/01/09).

DfES (Department for Education and Skills) (2006) *What to Do if you're Worried a Child is Being Abused*, London: The Stationery Office.

Dickens, J. (2002) 'The paradox of intercountry adoption: analysing Romania's experience as a sending country', *International Journal of Social Welfare*, vol 11, pp 76-83.

Dickens, J. (2007) 'Child neglect and the law: catapults, thresholds and delay', *Child Abuse Review*, vol 16, no 2, pp 77-92.

Dingwall, R., Eekelaar, J. and Murray, T. (1983) *The Protection of Children*, Oxford: Blackwell.

Fitch, K. (2006) *Megan's Law: Does it Protect Children?*, London: NSPCC.

Franklin, B. (1999) *Social Policy, the Media and Misrepresentation*, London: Routledge.

Greer, C. (2002) *Sex, Crime and the Media*, Uffculme: Willan.

Hamilton, C. (2002) 'International adoption', in M. Thorpe and C. Cowton (eds) *Delight or Dole*, Bristol: Jordans.

HM Government (2006) *Working Together to Safeguard Children*, London: The Stationery Office.

HM Government (2008) *Staying Safe Action Plan*, London: Department for Children, Schools and Families.

HM Treasury (2003) *Every Child Matters*, Cm 5860, London: The Stationery Office.

Home Office (2004a) *Parenting Contracts and Orders Guidance*, London: Home Office.

Home Office (2004b) *The Bichard Inquiry Report*, 2004, HC 653, London: The Stationery Office, available online at http://police. homeoffice.gov.uk/publications/operational-policing/bichard-inquiry-report?view=Binary (accessed 20/01/09).

James, A., Jenks, C. and Prout, A. (1998) *Theorising Childhood*, Cambridge: Polity Press.

Jenks, C. (2005) *Childhood* (2nd edition), London: Routledge.

Kidscape (2007) 'Keep them safe', available online at www.kidscape. org.uk/download/index.asp (accessed 20/01/09).

Laming, H. (2003) *The Victoria Climbié Inquiry: Report of an Inquiry by Lord Laming*, Cm 5730, London: The Stationery Office.

Latin American Institute for Education and Communication (2000) *Adoption and the Rights of the Child in Guatemala*, Guatemala: ILPEC/ UNICEF.

Lonne, B., Parton, N., Thomson, J. and Harries, M. (2008) *Reforming Child Protection*, London: Routledge.

McClay, E. and Wallace, H. (2003) *Health and Welfare for Families in the 21st Century*, Sudbury, MA: Jones and Bartlett.

Masson, J. and Winn Oakley, M. (1999) *Out of Hearing*, Chichester: Wiley.

Masson, J., McGovern, D., Pick, K. and Winn Oakley, M. (2007) *Protecting Powers*, Chichester: Wiley.

Masson, J., Pearce, J., Bader, K., Joyner, O., Marsden, J. and Westlake, D. (2008) *Care Profiling Study*, Ministry of Justice Research Report 03/2008, London: Ministry of Justice.

Melton, G. (2005) 'Mandated reporting: a policy without reason', *Child Abuse and Neglect*, vol 25, no 1, pp 9-18.

Morris, J. (2000) *Rethinking Risk and the Precautionary Principle*, London: Butterworths Heinemann.

Newiss, G. and Fairbrother, L. (2004) *Child Abduction: Understanding Police Recorded Crimes Statistics*, Home Office Research Findings 225, London: Home Office.

OECD (Organisation for Economic Co-operation and Development) (2004) *Keeping Children Safe in Traffic*, Paris: OECD.

Ofsted (2008) *Safeguarding Children: The Third Joint Chief Inspectors'
Report on Arrangements to Safeguard Children*, London: Ofsted, available
online at www.safeguardingchildren.org.uk (accessed 20/01/09).

Packman, J., Randall, J. and Jacques, N. (1986) *Who Needs Care?*,
Oxford: Blackwell.

Parton, N. (1985) *The Politics of Child Abuse*, Basingstoke: Macmillan.

Parton, N. (2006a) *Safeguarding Childhood: Early Intervention and
Surveillance in a Late Modern Society*, Basingstoke: Palgrave/Macmillan.

Parton, N. (2006b) '"Every child matters": the shift to prevention
whilst strengthening protection in children's services in England',
Children and Youth Services Review 2006, vol 28, no 2, pp 976-92.

Select Committee on Health (1997) *Report on the Welfare of Former
British Child Migrants*, 1997–98, HC 755, London: The Stationery
Office.

Selman, P. (ed) (2000) *Intercountry Adoption*, London: BAAF.

Shepherd, J. and Sampson, A. (2000) '"Don't shake the baby": towards
a prevention strategy', *British Journal of Social Work*, vol 30, no 6,
pp 721-35.

Stanton, S. (1999) 'Time for truth: speaking the unspeakable –
genocide and apartheid in the Lucky Country', *Australian Humanities
Review*, no 14, pp 1-8.

Stevenson, O. (1998) *Neglected Children: Issues and Dilemmas*, Oxford:
Blackwell.

Swain, S. (2001) 'Child rescue: the emigration of an idea', in
J. Lawrence and P. Starkey (eds) *Child Welfare and Social Action in the
Nineteenth and Twentieth Centuries*, Liverpool: Liverpool University
Press.

Triseliotis, J. (2000) 'Who benefits from intercountry adoption?',
Adoption & Fostering, vol 24, no 2, pp 45-54.

UN (United Nations) (1989) 'Convention on the Rights of the
Child', UN General Assembly, Document A/RES/44/25, available
online at www.hrweb.org/legal/child.html (accessed 18/02/05).

UNICEF (United Nations Children's Fund) (2004) *Summary Report:
Study on the Impact of the Implementation of the Convention on the Rights
of the Child*, Florence: Innocenti Research Centre.

UNICEF (2007) *Law Reform and Implementation of the Convention on
the Rights of the Child*, Florence: Innocenti Research Centre.

Utting, W. (1997) *People Like Us*, London: The Stationery Office.

Vincent, S. and Daniel, B. (2004) 'An analysis of children and young
people's calls to ChildLine about abuse and neglect: a study for the
Scottish Child Protection Review', *Child Abuse Review*, vol 13, no 2,
pp 158-71.

Wade, J., Biehal, N., Clayden, J. and Stein, M. (1998) *Going Missing: Young People Absent from Care*, Chichester: Wiley.

Waterhouse, R. (2000) *Lost in Care*, HC 210, London: The Stationery Office.

WHO (World Health Organization) (2002) *World Report on Violence and Health*, Geneva: WHO.

List of cases

Re C (Adoption: Legality) [1999] 1 FLR 370
Re M (Adoption: International Adoption Trade) [2003] 1 FLR 1111
A Local Authority v K & Ors [2008] EWHC 2051 (Fam)

Ten

Children, young people and poverty

Heather Montgomery

Introduction

In 1999, the UK's New Labour government pledged that it would
halve child poverty by 2010 and eradicate it by 2020. Since it made
this commitment it has implemented many anti-poverty measures and,
rhetorically at least, placed children at the centre of its welfare policies.
As a consequence, the number of children living in poverty in the
UK has reduced from one in three (around 4.2 million children) in
1998/99 to one in five (around 3.8 million) in 2005/06 (see Chapter
One). Yet, significant numbers of children continue to live in poverty
and rates of decline have slowed. This chapter will look at how child
poverty has been defined and understood and suggest reasons why the
problem appears to be so entrenched before turning to children's own
experiences of living in poverty.

Definitions and measurements of poverty

There are many ways of defining poverty, ranging from indicators
of social inequality and deprivation, to more common measures
concerning absolute or relative definitions of poverty. Absolute
poverty is defined by using a fixed measure of income such that the
US, for example, has an official 'poverty line' measured in dollars,
which 'represents the annual income required to allow a family of
a given size to purchase the range of goods and services that are
seen as constituting the minimum acceptable way of life in America'
(UNICEF, 2000: 6). The figure used in this case is calculated as
three times the cost of an adequate diet. The UK, along with other
European countries, prefers to use relative measures of poverty, which
calculate levels of inequality. In 1984, the European Union (EU)
defined people living in poverty as 'those whose incomes fall below

half of the average income (as measured by the median) for the nation in which they live' (quoted in UNICEF, 2000: 6). In the UK, however, poverty is generally defined as those households with incomes of below 60% of the national median.

Behind these apparently simple indicators lie much more complex issues and it is obvious from even the briefest look at how poverty is defined that these will have a significant impact on the numbers of people living in poverty. Such figures are also problematic because they suggest a straightforward link between poverty and deprivation, which researchers have questioned, not least because there are many children who might be materially rich but emotionally or socially deprived. Furthermore, some low-income families appear to have an adequate standard of living while other families can have incomes above the poverty line, but remain deprived (Grødem, 2008). This is illustrated by the case of Sweden, a prosperous, socially liberal country with one of the lowest official child poverty rates in Europe. Income inequalities are relatively low and there is significant social support for children and their families. Yet, in 2001, when researchers looked at deprivation rather than poverty among children aged 10-18, they found much higher levels of deprivation than expected. They looked at five indictors of deprivation: '(1) lacking a cash margin of SEK100 [approximately £8.50], (2) not receiving a weekly/monthly allowance, (3) not working during the summer holiday, (4) lacking material resources (TV, video player, TV games, CD players, mobile phone, PC, pet), (5) money available per month' (Grødem, 2008: 109). By using these the researchers concluded that:

> [R]elatively high proportions of Swedish children and youth were deprived by each of these measures, for instance, 35% doubted they would be able to raise SEK100 in one day, 35% received no allowance and 19% owned only 0-1 of the items that made up the consumption index.
> (Grødem, 2008: 109)

These Swedish children may not have been poor but that did not prevent them from being deprived.

Such conclusions are inevitably controversial and many would argue that not owning a CD player is not a sign of poverty or deprivation. However, if children cannot function as 'normal' members of society because they do not have access to the material goods that others deem necessary, then this indicator of deprivation is a useful one. Poverty, deprivation and social exclusion are all much-used terms in policy and much-contested concepts. There is no neat fit between them and they do not always overlap, thus underlying the point that discussions about child poverty are never neutral or purely economic but much more slippery and difficult to deal with.

The effects of poverty

Although children living in households with less than 60% of the national median are defined as poor, many children live in families that have significantly less than this and one in six children in the UK live in a household that has an income below 50% of the national median average, placing them in deeper and often more persistent poverty. Two thirds of children who live in poverty have done so for three out of the last four years (Hirsch, 2006: 17). In this category of deep poverty, children from certain groups are overrepresented and these children face some of the most acute risks. Over 100,000 children are living in temporary accommodation as a result of being classed homeless and around half a million live in homes unfit for human habitation (Hirsch, 2006: 18). The children of asylum seekers are likely to live in some of the very poorest households, where parents cannot work while their claims are being processed, and who are excluded from several of the anti-poverty measures available to other children in the UK (Hirsch, 2006). Gypsy and Traveller children face particular risks of poverty, deprivation and discrimination, and have some of the lowest educational and health outcomes of any children in the UK. Geography also plays a part, with children in certain areas of London and the North East more likely to be poor than elsewhere, although poverty exists throughout the UK, even in very affluent parts of the country. The South East has twice the number of children living in poverty than the North East. Children of disabled parents are also vulnerable to persistent poverty. Their parents are more likely to be unemployed and even when they do work, they face discrimination and barriers to progress. The children of parents who have mental illnesses have also recently been recognised as being at particular risk and researchers have estimated that around 370,000 children are in poverty as a result of their parents' mental health issues (Gould, 2006).

Large-scale studies and longitudinal projects have been vital in showing the correlations between living in poverty and lower outcomes in the future in terms of well-being, education and social exclusion. Both in the UK and internationally, evidence suggests that poor children suffer disproportionately from ill-health, violent neighbourhoods, environmental pollution and lower life expectancies

(Montgomery, 2003). Increasingly, there is also evidence to suggest that poverty and social inequality have devastating impacts on a psychological level and that the ways in which individuals experience poverty damage their health and their quality of life. Wilkinson (2005) has looked at the impact of low social status on ill-health and early death. He found that difficult early life experiences, social marginalisation, feeling undervalued and being seen as socially inferior inflict psychological damage that is reflected in children's performance at school, the level of violence they suffer in their daily lives and the quality of their home and community life. Like others before him, he sees social inequality rather than poverty as the key social problem in modern Britain (see Chapter One).

One way of understanding how individuals internalise these social inequalities can be best expressed through Bourdieu's (1972: 72) concept of habitus. He defined this as:

> the system of durable, transposable dispositions, structured structures predisposed to function as structuring structures, that is, as principles which generate and organize practices and representations that can be objectively adapted to their outcomes without presupposing a conscious aiming at ends or an express mastery of the operations necessary in order to attain them.

Habitus is not simply concerned with the ways that social structures and organising principles such as race, class or gender are internalised by individuals but rather with an individual's dynamic interactions with the social and material worlds. People classify the world through the processes of socialisation but this relationship is constantly changing and being reimagined through their interactions with the social structure. Reay (1995: 354) summarises this succinctly:

> I envisage habitus as a deep, interior, epicentre containing many matrices. These matrices demarcate the extent of choices available to any one individual. Choices are bounded by the framework of opportunities and constraints the person finds herself in, her external circumstances. However, within Bourdieu's theoretical framework she is also circumscribed by an internalised framework which makes some possibilities inconceivable, others improbable and a limited range acceptable.

For socially marginalised children and young people, poverty is not simply that they lack education, go to poorer schools or do not have the books at home to help them, it is also the internal construction of self that makes certain choices unthinkable. This was clearly shown in Reay's (2001) study of the choices made by working-class, mature students about which university to go to. She found that many students would not consider applying to 'prestigious' universities, arguing that they were 'not for people like me', and would rather go to universities where they felt they would fit in better, whatever the social or educational status of that university.

Reay has applied Bourdieu's work to the primary school and shown how, at a very young age, children know their own social status, and draw on ideas about habitus in their everyday lives. She studied the interactions between pupils and teachers in two schools in which she conducted ethnographic fieldwork in London, the first was a predominantly working-class, multi-ethnic school (Milner) and the second (Oak Park) was three miles away in a largely white, middle-class area. At the end of one lesson, the teacher asked the children to tidy up. In Milner, the children, especially the girls, immediately started to tidy up, put books away and put the lids back on felt-tip pens. In Oak Park, however, there was no such rush and some children flatly refused to do it, claiming 'It's not our job' or 'They employ cleaners to do that' (Reay, 1995: 363). In these interactions, Reay looked at how children were deploying habitus as a way of marking their social differentiation. In Milner, the cleaners were likely to be the mothers of the pupils and, as Reay points out, tidying up and helping out were activities that these children, especially the girls, felt at home with – they were what 'people like us' did. In contrast, the Oak Park pupils saw cleaning work as beneath them, something that 'others' did. They saw themselves as the equal of their teachers and did not expect to have to do menial tasks any more than the teachers. None of these children articulated this but, as an outsider, Reay could analyse their 'dispositions' in Bourdieu's terms and look at what they felt was appropriate behaviour and aspirations.

Using this concept of habitus takes the debate about poverty away from economics and the lack of material possessions and back to issues of deprivation and inequality. Poor children also lack what Bourdieu referred to as cultural and social capital. This includes institutional cultural capital (such as academic qualifications), embodied cultural capital (the ways in which people use language, present themselves, display social competence or confidence and so on) and objectified cultural capital (their ownership or use of material goods such as books or paintings). Social capital comprises two aspects, the first being social networks and connections and the second being how these networks are sustained. As Morrow (2001: 41) argues:

> Bourdieu is primarily concerned with how economic capital underpins these other 'disguised' forms, how these forms of capital interact with wider structures to reproduce social inequalities, and how the day-to-day activities of social actors draw upon and reproduce structural features of wider social systems. For Bourdieu, the *outcomes* of possession of various forms of capital (symbolic, cultural, social) are reducible to the economic: but the *processes* that bring about these alternative forms of capital are not.

Poverty, in Bourdieu's formulation, has an obvious material basis but his analysis goes beyond this and social inequalities are shown not simply in what people have or lack materially but also in the networks they have access to and in their aspirations. For example, children may come from loving families with parents who want the best for them but there are many intangible barriers in their way. Parents may not have access to information about which schools are better, they may not share vocabularies or accents with the gatekeepers of the school systems, they may be unaware about rights of appeal, they may not have the same ability to play the system as other parents who share a social background with teachers or officials. Children in this context may be torn between wanting to do well at school, thereby buying into the dominant ideology and social values of the middle classes, and not wanting to leave their own identities, peer group and background behind. Questions of choice become problematic because children are constrained not only by poverty but also by people's assumptions about what is appropriate for them.

Such theories are useful in providing a context in which to discuss child poverty but (with the exception of Reay's work) they say little about children's own experiences. Many studies that look at child poverty tend to take the family or the household, rather than the child, as the unit of analysis and, as Gregg et al (1999: 2) put it, 'Children have been seen by economists in particular as having an effect on the welfare of households rather than their own welfare being the focus of attention'. Several commentators have pointed out that many policies designed to combat child poverty deal with parents rather than children and reflect adult concerns rather than those of children. Ridge (2003: 5) has argued: 'The dangers of social exclusion and poverty for children during childhood have appeared less often on the policy agenda, and when they have, the focus has invariably been on children as "adults-to-be", as future investments'. Prout (2000: 305) has further commented that by relying on studies that link child poverty to poor adult outcomes, the government has ignored the needs of children in the here and now. He claims that the policies concentrate 'on the better adult lives that will, it is predicted, emerge from reducing child poverty. It is not on the better lives that children will lead as children.'

Case study: a child's eye view of poverty and social difference

These issues have come to the fore in more recent qualitative studies, which have begun to look at children themselves and how they understand and experience poverty. One such study was carried out by researchers from Loughborough University's Centre for Research in Social Policy. This project was based on in-depth qualitative interviews with 42 children aged between 8 and 13 who came from contrasting socioeconomic groups; 19 came from a disadvantaged housing association estate and 23 came from a local fee-paying school (Sutton, 2007: 8-9). The researchers were aware from the outset that poverty 'is an essentially contestable term and that … technical measurements of income and material resources are devices to identify and assess the extent of poverty across the population, but do not necessarily match up with the meaning of poverty' (Sutton et al, 2007: 3). They aimed, therefore, to find out what poverty meant to the children and how they understood and experienced their own material, social and cultural circumstances. Perhaps the most surprising thing about the study was that none of the children regarded themselves as either rich or poor. Instead, all of them identified themselves as average and used the terminology of poverty or wealth to differentiate themselves from disliked 'others'. Poverty was identified only in the case of homeless tramps or starving people in Africa. In their own lives, children were determined to be seen as average. One older girl from the estate said emphatically: 'I'm not rich and I'm not poor. I'm nearly in the middle' (Sutton et al, 2007: 10). In the case of the estate children, this sometimes meant 'talking up' what they had and making comments such as 'I've got all the stuff I want' while the privately educated children were more likely to 'talk down' what they had:

> We live in a nice big house with a drive, but I wouldn't say I was more highly put than anybody else really. We are moving into a big house with a drive, but I wouldn't really be like that to anybody else. There are some children who get like absolutely everything they ask for, but like I don't get everything I ask for. (Sutton et al, 2007: 10)

Children living in poverty have many of the same needs and desires as other children, yet because they have been so heavily targeted by policy initiatives, they have often become pathologised. With every correlation drawn between poverty and low educational achievement, obesity, criminality or social exclusion, the more likely it becomes that the problem is seen as being with the child and not with their circumstances. Poor children become, by definition, the children more likely to grow up fat, criminal underachievers. Ridge (2002: 144) comments: 'the labels that society attaches to poor children will have a profound impact on how children see themselves and on how other children see them'. It is hardly surprising, therefore, that few children wish to identify themselves as poor, or claim membership of such a highly stigmatised group, and strive instead to portray themselves as normal. Indeed, the worst fear that the children seem to express is not that they should be poor but that they should be different.

This is not to claim that children in this study are unaware of, or do not care about, social difference and social inequality. Instead, they relabel it and differentiate between people in particular ways, notably by categorising other children as 'chavs' or 'posh' and identifying themselves in opposition to these labels. The children from the estate called the private school children posh, claiming 'They've got the money but they don't have the fun' or 'They stay in too much doing homework and they don't make hardly any friends. That's why people pick on them' (Sutton et al, 2007: 15). In contrast, the private school children referred to those on the estates as 'chavs' and while there was some condemnation of them and their parents there was also sympathy for them and their perceived lack of opportunities.

> I suppose kids would have it rough because they wouldn't have as much money. But they still might have as much love, like the families might be there because they can't get a good enough job, because their parents haven't had the money to give them an education or they were brought up wrong, they weren't brought up to be bright. (Older private schoolgirl, quoted in Sutton et al, 2007: 13)

What is also interesting about these statements is the implicit calls the children make on notions of social and cultural capital. Even as they acknowledge that they are materially worse off than those children who go to private schools, children from the estates claim higher levels of social capital in the form of friends and the fun and freedom they are allowed. In turn, some private school children identified low social capital among the estate children because of their lack of educational opportunities and poor parenting as well as the material circumstances of their lives, such as not having houses with gardens. The habitus of each group of children is also important here: by identifying what is important to them and staking claims to particular forms of normality and expectations, they are displaying their own dispositions and assumptions about the social order. While obviously aware of differences, few children questioned the status quo and simply reflected the expectations of what was normal for 'children like them'. The comment that some children are not 'brought up to be bright' is also revealing in that it implies that the private school children do not see intelligence as something innate but rather as the product of parental choice.

Other work done on children's perceptions of poverty suggests that children's fear of poverty is not a fear of lacking material possessions but of the sense of difference and separateness that being poor brings with it. Ridge (2003: 7) quotes from several children who highlight this aspect of poverty.

> I would like to do more things with my friends, when they go out down the town and that. But we can't always afford it. So I got to stay in and that, and just in here it's just boring – I can't do anything. (Mike, 12 years)

> If you haven't got the right clothes and all your friends have got all the nice clothes you feel left out like. Cos you think to yourself 'Oh they've got all the good clothes and they've got all the money to buy them' and that, and you feel left out ... I sometimes get really worried if, like, I've got all these old-fashioned clothes and I don't like them and everyone else has fashionable ones. (Sue, 11 years)

In other work, Ridge has shown how much children hate the shame of poverty and how they will actively avoid certain help offered to them if they feel it stigmatises them or marks them out as different in any way. Free school meals, for instance, are an obvious marker of poverty and many children refuse to eat them as a consequence.

> There is … a tension between those needs and concerns identified by children and those identified by adults. We may well not value the things that these children identify as important social needs, issues such as friendship and the maintenance of social relationships. However, these are important and critical areas in children's lives and in their social development. (Ridge, 2002: 10)

What is evident from all these studies is that children are acutely conscious of social inequality and social difference, even though they are not necessarily comfortable with the language of poverty or wealth. It is also evident that children make informed choices within the constraints of their lives and remain active, negotiating, social agents. Several children spoke of shielding their parents from requests for money, for instance for school trips, because they knew that it would increase pressure on already stretched household finances (Ridge, 2006). They also attempt to talk up what they have in terms of other forms of social capital. While this may be positive in some circumstances, such as when children are aware that they may be poor and yet claim to have everything they want, or emphasise the closeness of their friends and families, in other ways it can also cement social difference where children create and maintain social divisions between themselves and those they perceive as socioeconomically 'other' to them.

Ways of tackling poverty

It is evident that poverty has complex impacts on many levels and there is an increasing awareness that deprivation and social inequality have to be tackled alongside material poverty. There is a political will to tackle the problem and while child poverty remains a serious problem in the UK, it has changed over time, and there have been some improvements. When New Labour came to power in 1997, the UK had a particularly poor record and by the mid-1990s it had the highest child poverty rate in the EU (Bradshaw, 2006). Children had been especially badly affected by changes in economic conditions and the free-market policies of the 1980s and early 1990s and by 1998 just over a third of all British children were living in poverty (Ridge, 2003). The government prioritised reducing child poverty and introduced far-reaching reforms of the welfare system, which focused on three main areas: support for parents by increasing their participation in the labour force; making sure that they were better off working than staying on benefits; and supporting children through the education system.

As Machin and McNally (2006: 4) note, 'the key cause of poverty, and the rise in poverty over time in the UK, is worklessness'. A brief overview of the statistics from 1968 to 1995 shows that the proportion of children living in families where no adult worked rose from 2% to 10% in two-parent families and from 30% to 58% in lone-parent families during this period (Gregg et al, 1999). These families accounted for 54% of all poor children by the mid-1990s compared with 31% in the late 1960s. During the same period there was a rise in the numbers of poor children living in lone-parent families from 19% to 43%. Gregg et al (1999: 3) claim that 'One-fifth of the overall increase in child poverty can be attributed specifically to the rise in the proportion of children with lone parents'.

The government has attempted to encourage people back into the workplace in a number of ways, including through New Deal programmes, which help people, particularly lone parents, into work by providing training and subsidised employment. It also enabled benefits to be withheld from those who refused 'reasonable employment'. The target was to get 70% of lone parents into work by 2010 (Ridge, 2007: 399). Such policies, also known as welfare-to-work policies, aimed to cut long-term unemployment and deal with child poverty by increasing parental incomes and expectations. By introducing a minimum wage in 1999 and, in 2003, the Child Tax Credit and Working Tax Credit, the government signalled its determination to 'make work pay' and to ensure that those who did take on low-paid jobs would not lose more in benefit entitlement than they could earn in wages.

The third strand of policy that attempted to reduce child poverty concerned education, which was seen as one of the crucial ways of breaking cycles of poverty within families and across generations. This was supported by evidence that showed that, in the UK, poverty predicted poor educational outcomes more than in any other industrialised country. Research showed that by the age of three, poor children lagged behind their better-off peers by almost nine months in educational terms and by the age of 14 this gap had widened to two years (endchildpoverty.org, 2007). Throughout the education system, from nurseries upwards, the government invested billions of pounds and promoted numerous initiatives designed to bridge the disparity between social groups (see Machin and McNally, 2006). For children in the earliest years of life in England, the government set up and promoted Sure Start programmes, which provide integrated services for families with young children, based on the premise that good early years provision can counter some of the disadvantages of living in poverty. There has also been greater emphasis placed on literacy and numeracy in the curriculum as evidence suggests that this has a significant impact on future employment opportunities (Hirsch, 2006: 33).

The reasons why child poverty is not falling as fast as many would like are complex. Each of the three strands of government policy has had flaws and unforeseen consequences. The welfare-to-work programmes, for instance, have proved successful on some levels and have led to a 25% reduction in the number of workless households (Hirsch, 2006). However, they have been less successful in helping hard-to-reach groups who face greater problems in returning to long-term employment. Half of all children whose parents claim out-of-work benefits are either lone parents or disabled people who face discrimination and may, despite government incentives, struggle to make adequate childcare arrangements (Hirsch, 2006). There has also been resistance to such policies by people who feel forced to take on low-paid jobs at the expense of their caring responsibilities and family life.

Looking at micro-level studies of households where lone parents have gone back to work, Ridge has found a mixed picture as to the impact on children. One of the greatest obstacles to lone parents returning to work is the need for adequate childcare. The government anticipated this problem by expanding after-school clubs for children, or 'wrap-around care'. Yet, the quality of these varies enormously and children sometimes resist the stigma that they feel attendance brings. One child described breakfast clubs as being 'for scabs' (Ridge, 2007: 409). Other children, however, relish the freedom and the opportunity to meet new friends that these give them. Similarly, while many children welcomed their mother's return to work, both in terms of the financial benefits it brought to the household, and in terms of their mother's well-being, this depended very much on the hours their mother had to work and the job security it gave them. For those children whose mothers worked irregular hours, nights, or who were liable to be laid off, welfare-to-work programmes increased their anxiety. As Ridge concludes (2007: 413):

Children's insecurities reflect the labour market their mothers are in. Therefore, the type and quality of work available to mothers, and the stability of the labour markets they are encouraged to enter, must be a key consideration if policies seeking to promote employment for lone mothers are to produce security and long-term wellbeing for their children.

The emphasis on welfare-to-work programmes, and the Child and Working Tax credits, has also led to the development of a two-tier system of support for children depending on whether or not their parents are in work. The government's refusal to lift parental support, especially to those parents on long-term benefits, means that the increased fiscal support to certain families has led to a dilution of help to others, often those in the deepest poverty, or the hardest to reach. Many benefits are index linked to inflation rather than average earnings (although there was a guarantee that Child Tax Credit would rise in relation to average earnings until 2009), which, over time, means that the value of benefits decreases. Sutherland et al (2008) have argued that if the current benefit system stays as it is, it will actually double the rate of child poverty by 2018. In his report on the costs of ending child poverty, Hirsch (2006: 12) argues that the most cost-effective policy to end child poverty would be to raise the Child Tax Credit by 50% in real terms. He further claims that increases in child benefits for larger families and rises in the Working Tax Credit for couples, who are currently less favourably dealt with than lone parents, are also needed. At the very least, the level of the National Minimum Wage must keep in line with average earnings.

Evidence about the government's investment in education has also been patchy, with critics claiming that programmes such as the £3 billion Sure Start programme have had little impact on children's skills before they start primary schools. Another flagship scheme, City Academies (schools set up in conjunction with the private sector), have not, as yet, proved very successful and in 2006 half of all City Academies were classified as being the worst-performing schools in England. Perhaps most importantly of all, however, there has been no engagement with some of the other issues raised in this chapter such as social inequality and social capital. Many in the sociology of education have long argued that the debate over poor children and education has been framed in terms of working-class 'failure' and has further pathologised already socially marginalised children. They have looked at how education has been cast as a way of 'fixing' the working class, who often experience school as being fraught with the possibility of failure. As Reay (2006: 301) has argued:

> [Working-class children], in the context of schooling, inhabit a psychic economy of class defined by fear, anxiety and unease where failure looms large and success is elusive; a place where they are seen and see themselves as literally 'nothing'.

Attempting to end child poverty by pouring money into education in order to 'fix' the problem of working-class failure does not deal with the habitus of these children or the paradigm shifts they would have to make in order to succeed. Bourdieu (quoted in Reay, 2001: 337) expresses the conflict that comes from upward mobility as: 'the feelings of being torn that come from experiencing success as failure, or, better still, as transgression'.

Conclusion

Child poverty is a significant topic much debated by economists, politicians, sociologists and activists and in a chapter this length not all aspects of the subject can be covered. By looking at some of the theoretical debates on the issue, however, and introducing contemporary critical thinking on the subject, it is possible to understand some of the different definitions and discourses and the interplay between the micro and the macro, the material and the psychological. Perhaps the most important theme of all that comes out of recent child poverty studies is the importance of listening to children themselves and the need to make policies based on their own accounts of living in difficult circumstances. As children are increasingly acknowledged as social agents able to articulate their own social needs, it is vital that policy makers ground their interventions in children's experiences and expectations, not their own, and look beyond macro-level studies to how children experience poverty in their daily lives. Childhood needs to be valued as a time in which children have particular needs as children, not as future adults. In the mass of statistics, information, initiatives and recommendations, it remains important not to lose sight of children themselves.

References

Bourdieu, P. (1972) *Outline of a Theory of Practice*, Cambridge: Cambridge University Press.

Bradshaw, J. (2006) *A Review of the Comparative Evidence on Child Poverty in the UK: Background Briefing and Summary*, London: Child Poverty Action Group.

endchildpoverty.org (2007) 'Child poverty and education', available online at www.endchildpoverty.org.uk/files/h3107ChildPovertyandEducationbriefing.pdf (accessed 30/08/08).

Gould, N. (2006) *Mental Health and Child Poverty*, York: Joseph Rowntree Foundation.

Gregg, P., Harkness, S. and Machin, S. (1999) *Child Poverty and its Consequences*, York: Joseph Rowntree Foundation.

Grødem, A. S. (2008) 'Household poverty and deprivation among children: how strong are the links?', *Childhood*, vol 15, no 1, pp 107–25.

Hirsch, D. (2006) *What Will it Take to End Child Poverty?*, York: Joseph Rowntree Foundation.

Machin, S. and McNally, S. (2006) *Education and Child Poverty: A Literature Review*, York: Joseph Rowntree Foundation.

Montgomery, H. (2003) 'Children, poverty and inequality', in H. Montgomery, R. Burr and M. Woodhead (eds) *Changing Childhoods: Global and Local*, Chichester: John Wiley.

Morrow, V. (2001) 'Young people's explanations and experiences of social exclusion: retrieving Bourdieu's concept of social capital', *International Journal of Sociology and Social Policy*, vol 21, no 4-6, pp 37-63.

Prout, A. (2000) 'Children's participation: control and self-realisation in British late modernity', *Children & Society*, vol 14, no 4, pp 304-15.

Reay, D. (1995) '"They employ cleaners to do that": habitus in the primary classroom', *British Journal of Sociology of Education*, vol 16, no 3, pp 353-71.

Reay, D. (2001) 'Finding or losing yourself? Working-class relationships to education', *Journal of Education Policy*, vol 16, no 4, pp 333-46.

Reay, D. (2006) 'The zombie stalking English schools: social class and educational inequality', *British Journal of Educational Studies*, vol 54, no 3, pp 288-307.

Ridge, T. (2002) *Childhood Poverty and Social Exclusion*, Bristol: The Policy Press.

Ridge, T. (2003) 'Listening to children', *Family Matters*, vol 65, Winter, pp 4-9.

Ridge, T. (2006) 'Childhood poverty: a barrier to social participation and inclusion', in J. Davis, K. Tisdall, A. Prout and M. Hill (eds) *Children, Young People and Social Inclusion: Participation for What?*, Bristol: The Policy Press.

Ridge, T. (2007) 'It's a family affair: low-income children's perspectives on maternal work', *Journal of Social Policy*, vol 36, no 3, pp 399-416.

Sutherland, H., Evans, M., Hancock, R., Hills, J. and Zantomio, F. (2008) *The Impact of Benefit and Tax Uprating on Incomes and Poverty*, York: Joseph Rowntree Foundation.

Sutton, L. (2007) 'A child's eye view', *Poverty*, vol 126, Winter, pp 8-11.

Sutton, L., Smith, N., Dearden, C. and Middleton, S. (2007) *A Child's-Eye View of Social Difference*, York: Joseph Rowntree Foundation.

UNICEF (United Nations Children's Fund) (2000) *A League Table of Child Poverty in Rich Nations*, Florence: Innocenti Research Centre.

Wilkinson, R. (2005) *The Impact of Inequality: How to Make Sick Societies Healthier*, London: Routledge.

Eleven

Children and consumer culture

David Buckingham and Sara Bragg

Introduction

It is widely accepted that the category of the 'teenager' was the
socially created product of the expanding consumer economy of the
1940s and 1950s: indeed, the term itself seems to have been coined
by market researchers in the late 1940s (Savage, 2007). Young people's
use of the commodities of consumer culture, such as mobile phones
and iPods, to mediate their lives, is often taken as a defining feature of
'youth' (Osgerby, 2004). By contrast, the role that consumer culture
plays in the lives of younger children has often been marginalised.
Even supposedly definitive overviews of the field make little or no
mention of the issue (for example, Corsaro, 1997; James and Prout,
1997; Adler and Adler, 1998). Sidelining questions about consumption
in this way is normative and prescriptive, suggesting that children are
or should be separate from commerce, and that they live a 'natural'
non-mediated childhood (Livingstone, 1998). The study of children's
consumer culture raises some challenging questions about the nature
of childhood and the changing symbolic values of childhood and
adolescence.

Marketing to children, while not new, has intensified in its scope
and intensity in recent decades. Debate in this area is quite starkly
polarised. On the one hand, children are seen as the exploited victims
of consumer culture, while on the other, they are seen as active and
competent in relation to their consumption – not least, for obvious
reasons, by marketers themselves. Such arguments typically ignore the
ambivalence and complexity of children's (and indeed parents') lived
experience of consumer culture. We use the term 'consumer culture'
here (in preference to more judgemental ones like 'consumerism') to
focus on how children and young people may appropriate and use the
material and symbolic resources or commodities available to them.
Consumption is not only an economic process, but also a cultural one

involving 'social activity, identity work and the negotiation of agency' (Nayak and Kehily, 2008: 128).

We begin this chapter by considering some evidence about the scale and nature of contemporary marketing to children and young people. We then look at the broad debates about children's involvement in consumer culture, both within academic research and in the wider public sphere, among campaigners and marketers themselves. The chapter moves on to discuss alternative ways of exploring and theorising this area, and illustrates this through a specific case study of marketing to 'tween' girls – that is, those aged from 8 to around 12 years old who are seen as 'between' childhood and the teenage years. Finally, we look at the global dimensions of children and young people's consumer culture.

Children, youth, marketing and consumption

Estimates of the size of the children's and youth market are somewhat variable, and occasionally seem hyperbolic. Child marketing guru Lindstrom (2003: 2), for instance, argues that US children aged 8-14 spend around $150 billion annually, 'control' another $150 billion of their parents' money and 'influence spending of up to $600 billion a year' (2003: 23). He suggests that across the globe in 2002, tweens 'spent and influenced' $1.18 trillion. However unreliable some of these statistics might be, this is clearly a very large and expanding market. In terms of the UK, a Halifax survey of children's pocket money in 2007 suggested that children aged 7-16 were receiving an average of £32 per month, making a total of £70 million – a figure that has increased by 600% over the past 20 years (HBOS, 2007). Other figures suggest that British children aged 7-15 spend on average £13 per week; and that the child-oriented market in the UK is worth £30 billion (Mayo, 2005). The cost of bringing up a child from birth to the age of 21 is estimated to be in excess of £180,000, a figure that is rising significantly faster than inflation (Smithers, 2006).

Children's involvement in consumption here is threefold. Young consumers are, first, a means of reaching adults: the influence that children exert on adults' purchases is more economically significant than what they buy themselves, and can include choices of holidays, cars, new technology and other expensive goods. Second, they are an increasingly significant market in their own right, through spending their own disposable income. And third, they constitute a future market – a 'market potential' – with whom companies wish to establish relationships and loyalties that they hope will be carried through into adulthood (McNeal, 1999). In addition, marketers must appeal to parents as consumers on behalf of their children.

Historical studies suggest that children have been a key focus of interest to marketers at least since the inception of modern mass marketing in the early 20th century, or even well before this (for example, Cook, 2004; Cross, 2004; Denisoff, 2008). Nevertheless, this activity is now more widespread and occurring on a different scale, through a wider variety of media. Marketers are increasingly seeking means other than direct advertising to access children and young people, not least due to shifting media landscapes and stricter regulation of advertising. For instance, in the UK, the media regulator Ofcom introduced new restrictions on the television advertising of food and drink products to children in 2007; while television advertising to children under 12 has been banned in Sweden since 1991. Other approaches taken by marketers include product placement; endorsements of products by popular characters or celebrities; and synergistic or integrated marketing – where licensing (for example of popular film or television characters) is used to sell a wide range of products, such as toys, food and drink, computer games, books, cartoons and so on, to diverse audiences. Meanwhile, three quarters of UK children aged 9-19 go online daily or weekly (Livingstone and Bober, 2004), and regulations that apply offline do not yet apply online; this has encouraged marketers to move into new media, using new 'stealth' techniques (Calvert, 2008). Many companies have developed 'pop-up' advertisements or advertisements disguised as instant messages; set up their own websites that entice children by offering games and quizzes to win prizes; made deals with other providers, such as the McDonald's deal in 2006 with MSN Messenger; and are using social networking sites such as Bebo or Facebook, as well as blogs, emails, YouTube and so on. Mobile phones, along with accessories, provide a further point of access to children (Kenway and Bullen, 2001).

A thriving research business has grown up around the children's and youth market, which now seeks to access children's perspectives directly, rather than merely those of their parents. Much information is deemed commercially sensitive and reports cost thousands of pounds to purchase. These 'commercial epistemologies' (Cook, 2000) often draw on the creative and ethnographic tools for accessing children's 'voice' developed within academic disciplines such as ethnography and anthropology. For instance, researchers may visit children repeatedly in their homes, spending extended periods with children in their most private spaces – bedrooms and bathrooms. They film children playing with toys and engaged in other mundane tasks such as eating, using these methods because interviews do not always reveal behaviour that children are reluctant to admit (such as playing with toys they claim to have grown out of). In this way, researchers access new information that can be used commercially: for instance, seeing children playing with empty bubble bath containers inspired the redesign of packaging (Schor, 2004). Young people may also be recruited as 'consultants' to supply their own views on products and advertisements, or employed as 'brand ambassadors' to publicise 'cool' new products to their friends (through peer-to-peer and viral marketing). For example, 'Dubit', a Leeds-based youth research company, has a website aimed at young people that pays them to answer surveys about new advertising campaigns, technologies or products, alongside chat and games.

The imperatives of marketing have also led to the subdivision of the children's market. Dividing children into a series of niche markets means that new products can be sold at different stages, while others are cast off or 'outgrown'. Gender is also a key factor, particularly for younger children, where the market is heavily polarised into 'pink and blue'. There are significant risks for marketers here in trying to cross the line, in order to appeal to both groups. It used to be the received wisdom among marketers that the way to succeed was to appeal to boys first – girls were quite likely to buy into boy culture, although boys were less likely to buy into girl culture (Schneider, 1987). More recent analyses of contemporary toy advertising would suggest that this continues to be the case (Griffiths, 2002) and that some products (and indeed entire television channels) are sometimes developed in distinct 'boy' and 'girl' versions. Nevertheless, there are products that seem to cross this divide – particularly those originating in Japan like Tamagotchis, Pokemon and Yu-Gi-Oh. These commercial definitions of childhood or gendered identities are not necessarily coherent or all-powerful: indeed, the central question here is to do with the 'balance of power' between market forces and children themselves.

Responses to children and consumer culture

The first decade of the 21st century has seen growing anxiety about the potential 'commercialisation' of childhood – reflected in publications such as Quart's *Branded* (2003), Linn's *Consuming Kids* (2004), Schor's *Born to Buy* (2004) and Palmer's *Toxic Childhood* (2006). Marketing to children has become a campaigning issue. In Sweden, a parent initiated a successful campaign to stop a chain store selling a children's jacket with a 'sexualised' slogan (Torell, 2004); while in the UK, in 2007, a centre-left group – Compass – set up an online petition called 'Charter for Childhood' (Compass, nd). In 2008, the British government initiated an independent assessment of 'the impact of the commercial world on children's well-being' (DCSF, 2008).

Campaigners on these issues often link the issue of consumerism with other well-known concerns about media and childhood: as well as turning children into premature consumers, the media are routinely accused of promoting sex and violence, junk food, drugs and alcohol, gender stereotypes and false values, and taking children away from other activities that are deemed to be more worthwhile. Of course, this is a familiar litany, since similar concerns have been expressed historically in relation to each new technology or media form. Such debates tend to conflate very different kinds of effects and influences; and they typically construct the child as innocent, helpless and unable to resist the power of marketing. According to such critics, consumer culture is by definition actively opposed to children's well-being and their best interests.

We can also relate this approach to work in the sociology of consumption, where one dominant perspective has been the 'production of consumption' (Featherstone, 1991), a framework that understands consumption as something that is entirely controlled by the relations of production (Martens et al, 2004). There is a long tradition of such work in Marxist critical theory. One of the most evident problems with this perspective is that it is always other people's consumption that is regarded as problematic: the argument is informed by a kind of elitism, whereby largely white, male, middle-class critics have stigmatised the consumption practices of others – women, the working classes and now children (Seiter, 1993).

Marketing discourse offers a strong contrast to these views of children and young people and instead constructs the child as a kind of authority figure. Again, there is a history of this, reaching back at least to the 1940s when retailers began to orient themselves to children rather than their mothers (Cook, 2004). One contemporary example is Lindstrom's *Brandchild* (2003), a study apparently based on research with 2,000 children worldwide conducted by the advertising agency Millward Brown. *Brandchild* focuses primarily on 'tweens', which it defines as children aged 8-14, arguing that marketers need to recognise and respond to the changing needs of this newly identified 'niche' market. According to Lindstrom, tweens are a digital generation, 'born with a mouse in their hands'; and they speak a new language, called Tweenspeak. Yet, they also have anxieties – the stress of growing up, fear of global conflict and so on – which mean that brands can help them to enjoy life despite their difficulties. Indeed, tweens are seen to have a 'spiritual hunger' that brands and marketers alone can satisfy. The tactics that Lindstrom recommends to reach tweens, such as viral and peer marketing, rely on the active participation of the peer group – and they are precisely those that alarm the critics of consumer culture. For the marketers, however, these practices are all about empowerment, about children registering their needs, finding their voices, building their self-esteem, defining their own values and developing independence and autonomy. Interestingly, despite the polarised gender divisions we can identify in this market, Lindstrom's book fails to discuss gender in any sustained fashion.

The theoretical and methodological basis of this kind of market research deserves critical scrutiny. However, the most striking aspect is the very different construction of the child consumer. The child here is sophisticated, demanding and hard to please – 'they get what they want when they want it'. Tweens, we are told, are not easily manipulated: they are an elusive, even fickle market, sceptical about the claims of advertisers, and discerning when it comes to getting value for money – and they need considerable effort to understand and to capture.

There are many ironies and dilemmas here. The campaigners who purport to be speaking on behalf of children and defending their interests tend to present them as powerless; while the marketers, who might be seen as attempting to manipulate them, present them as powerful. The supposedly 'radical' critics of consumerism fall back on conservative constructions of children as innocent, unformed 'becomings', passively socialised by external forces and lacking the skills or rationality that adults are assumed to possess; while the marketers espouse notions of childhood competence, knowledge and agency.

Of course, marketers are bound to present children in this way, in order to deflect accusations that they are merely exploiting them. Yet, their views nonetheless bring them closer to recent thinking in Childhood Studies, which has also argued for a conception of the child as a 'being' rather than a 'becoming', as a competent social agent (James and James, 2004). The marketers' assertions that advertising has relatively little effect are also backed up to some extent by academic research, which tends to confirm that children are not easily manipulated or exploited, and that they can understand the persuasive intentions of advertising from a young age (for example, Gunter and Furnham, 1998; Hansen et al, 2002) – although there is some evidence that newer, less overt marketing techniques may not be recognised as such by children, or indeed by adults (Seiter, 2004). Critics of marketing fail to acknowledge the difficulty of reaching children – the fact that the market in children's products rises and falls in unpredictable ways, and that the failure rate for new products is much higher in the children's market than in the adult market (McNeal, 1999). For all these reasons, there are good grounds for questioning the idea that children are simply helpless victims of consumer culture – although, as we shall argue, this is not to imply that they are necessarily 'empowered' by it.

Rethinking young people's consumer culture

One recurring problem with this debate is its tendency to displace attention away from other possible causes of the phenomena involved: thus, the apparent rise of 'materialistic' attitudes, problems such as obesity and eating disorders, and the spectre of 'sexualisation', are seen to be an inevitable consequence of children's exposure to commercial influences. Yet, it makes little sense to abstract the question of young people's relationship with consumer culture from the broader social and historical context. The growth of consumer society is a complex, multifaceted, long-term development; and displacing broader and more complex problems onto the issue of marketing inevitably results in neglect of the real difficulties at stake.

It seems to be assumed that there is a 'natural' state of childhood that has been destroyed or corrupted by marketers, or alternatively that children's 'real' innate needs are somehow being acknowledged and addressed, even for the first time. It is believed that there is something particular to the condition of childhood that makes children necessarily more vulnerable – or, indeed, spontaneously more wise and sophisticated, for example in their dealings with technology; and that adults are somehow exempted from these arguments (Buckingham, 2000). By contrast, we would argue that 'commercial epistemologies' are now part of the construction and make-up of childhood (Cook, 2000). Rather than the commercial world being an add-on, or an invasion of childhood, it should be seen as part of it, and we should attend carefully to how it constructs and views children.

In terms of social theory, this can be seen to relate to the relationship between structure and agency. On the one hand, there is a risk of overstating the power of young people's agency, while on the other, there is the risk of attributing too great a power to structure. Children may well be using commodities in very active ways, appropriating them and creating their own meanings from them, but that does not mean that they necessarily have power: choice is not the same thing as agency (Buckingham and Sefton-Green, 2003).

Giddens' (1984) theory of structuration can usefully be linked to debates about identity in 'late modernity'. Briefly, Giddens (1991), like Rose (1999) and others, argues that in 'post-traditional' society, individuals (and they refer to adults, not children) are compelled to make a whole range of choices in order to create their own identities. They are guided on such matters by new experts of various kinds, including those in the popular media (for example in the form of lifestyle news, makeover shows and self-help books). As a result, modern individuals are encouraged to be constantly 'self-reflexive', making decisions about what they should do and who they should be. The self becomes a 'project' that individuals have to work on, creating biographical 'narratives' that will explain themselves to themselves, and hence sustain a coherent and consistent identity. The role that consumption plays here is in part to offer individuals multiple possibilities to construct and fashion their own identities, in increasingly creative and diverse ways. Yet, consumers are not totally free, since they have 'no choice but to consume' (Giddens, 1991); and the identities on offer are sometimes also limited and constrained. Giddens regards this generally as a positive development, part of a broader process of democratisation – a more optimistic account, for example, than Rose (1999), who sees it more in terms of the regulation and government of populations. Nonetheless, these theorists recognise that this new freedom places new burdens and responsibilities on people. Such analyses potentially shed new light on children's consumer culture, even though they do not address it directly (Martens et al, 2004).

Martens et al (2004) identify a number of other frameworks for understanding consumption, which offer some constructive directions for empirical research. First, Bourdieu's (1984) notion of the 'mode of consumption' can be used to explore how consumption produces and sustains hierarchies. This primarily relates to class, but in the case of children, we might ask how they use consumer goods, such as mobile phones, as markers of status and authority in the peer group. For example, some research shows how children's clothing purchases can be a site of anxiety about status and belonging as well as of play and creativity (Boden et al, 2004). To what extent does knowledge of consumer culture function as a kind of cultural (or subcultural) capital for children? How do the hierarchies of taste and 'cool' within the peer group relate to the hierarchies within adult culture? How might such hierarchies work against consumer culture (rendering the 'cool' uncool overnight)? How do we interpret the anti-consumerist rhetoric of some forms of youth culture – and the ways in which it has been appropriated for so-called 'ethical' consumption?

Second, Martens et al (2004) argue that we need to understand consumer culture in relation to other social factors. The market works through and with social relationships, including those of the family, the peer group and – increasingly – the school. We need to address how consumption practices are carried out in these different settings, and how they are implicated in the management of power, time and space, as some anthropological work on consumer culture has begun to do in relation to adults (Miller, 1998). The changing role of parenting, and the social expectations that surround it, are particularly important in this respect. The rise of the children's consumer market can be seen as a symptom of what Zelizer (1985) calls the symbolic 'valorization of childhood', which dates back to the early years of the last century. Cross (2004) has identified the tension here between parents' desire to shelter the child, to use childhood as a place for pedagogic nurturing, and their desire to allow the child a space for expression, to indulge the freedom they themselves have lost. As parents spend less and less time with their children, they may be more inclined to compensate by providing them with consumer goods.

Finally, Martens et al (2004) point out that the study of material culture focuses on the 'second' life of commodities, after purchase, and also raises questions about the experience of young people who are excluded from peer group culture because of their lack of access to consumer goods. Not all consumers are equally able to participate, since participation depends not just on one's creativity but also on one's access to material resources: the market is not a neutral mechanism, and the marketised provision of goods and services (not least in the media and in education) may exacerbate existing inequalities (see Chapter Ten). In this context, it is particularly important to understand the consumption practices of children in disadvantaged communities, for whom 'consumer choice' may be a fraught and complex matter. While many children may be able to access some aspects of the goods that become the lingua franca of children's culture – for instance by being part of the audience for the advertising that surrounds them – their experience of the actual products is likely to vary widely with material purchasing power. Chin's (2001) work on poor African American children usefully challenges the idea that less wealthy children are somehow more at risk from the seductions of consumer culture, exploring how their strikingly altruistic consumption practices – during a shopping trip she arranged as part of the research – are embedded within their social and familial relationships.

Case study: tweens, femininity and consumption

A research project by Russell and Tyler (2002) demonstrates the necessity of a multifaceted approach to consumption and indicates some of the complexities involved. Their study focused on Girl Heaven, a chain of UK shops aimed at 3- to 13-year-old (but especially 'tween') girls, offering inexpensive cosmetics, accessories and 'makeovers'. (Illustrating one of the themes of this chapter – the relative unpredictability of the youth market – this chain has since closed, although other chains targeting similar demographics, such as Claire's Accessories, have survived at the time of writing.)

Their methodology, informed by Cultural Studies, had three major elements, corresponding to the 'circuit of culture' (du Gay, 1997). First, they studied the political economy of Girl Heaven, and the perspectives of its producers, through interviews and encounters with the founding directors. Here they note how commercial marketing rhetoric draws on 'post-feminist' notions of 'girl power', and in some ways has the potential to shift traditional values of girl culture: it cannot be considered a wholly conservative force, as some of its critics assume. Yet, at the same time, if the market reflects and mediates some progressive cultural shifts – as Girl Heaven is the retail materialisation of 'girl power' – it does so in order to realise economic value from them.

Second, the authors conducted a textual analysis of Girl Heaven – where the 'text' included marketing, online and promotional material as well as the shop itself, where layout, lighting, displays and so on combine to convey the 'meaning' of 'girl' and 'heaven'. Their analysis focuses on how the shop conflates leisure and consumption and acts as a site for the celebratory 'performance' of femininity and for the realisation of girls' 'dreams' rather than their exploitation. It is also constructed as somewhere mothers could come with daughters – an approach that distinguishes Girl Heaven from other commercial modes of address to children, which often make claims to be 'on the side of the kids' against, rather than with, their parents. This provides an interesting instance of how generational transitions and relationships (and the anxieties that surround both) may be commodified.

Finally, they studied a group of eight 10- to 11-year-old girls, who were taken on a store visit, given money that they could spend there and interviewed afterwards. The girls were also asked to draw a picture of Girl Heaven, in an attempt to understand the non-rational and non-discursive elements of their response to it. Russell and Tyler's analysis aims to convey a sense of young people as active social agents, while also revealing the social context – or the structural factors – within which they shape their 'becoming'. The process of becoming an adult (woman) is shaped by the existence of commercial opportunities through which it can be expressed. As this implies – and as we have argued earlier – consumption does not stand apart as an 'add-on' to childhood, but is deeply bound up with it; there is a complicated relationship here between consumer culture and 'doing' childhood – which, as they emphasise, also means doing femininity (or masculinity) at different ages. As in James' (1993) account of childhood identities, and Alanen's (2001) notion of 'generationing', the construction of childhood identities is seen here as an ongoing process. What it means to be a child (or a tween) is defined in variable ways in the context of specific institutional practices (school, family, peer group – but also the market): we could say that childhood is performed in different ways in different contexts and for different purposes.

As the market provides potentially multiple definitions or accounts of what it means to be a girl, it can permit elements of self-expression and symbolic creativity. This contrasts with earlier feminist analyses, which have often seen consumption as a site of exploitation and manipulation for adult women (for example, Wolf, 1991). Girl Heaven, by its very emphasis on the 'performance' and artificiality of femininity, might be said to open up a space for playing with the codes of femininity rather than adopting them wholesale. Nonetheless, the authors point to the elements of conformity or constraint involved, and they conclude pessimistically that the 'rigid roles on display' in Girl Heaven should caution against recent feminist thinking that has tried to reclaim the pleasures of feminine identity play. Crucially, however, they also show that young girls themselves were reflexive and aware of their ambivalent relationship with commercial culture – another aspect that critics of consumer culture tend to overlook. These girls were followed up two years later (Russell and Tyler, 2005), and in their subsequent work, the authors draw particular attention to the process of 'bricolage', of 'do-it-yourself' assembly, that is involved in the process of building identities.

Children, youth and globalisation

Both economically and culturally, the artefacts of consumer culture – such as the media – play a profoundly ambiguous role in terms of globalisation. They provide powerful and pleasurable forms of 'children's culture' or 'youth culture' that appeal to children and young people living in very different circumstances around the world; yet they also provide symbolic resources with which children and young people come to define their own identities. Like the trade in material goods, the trade in cultural goods is undoubtedly a key factor in the contemporary reconfiguration of relations between the global and the local.

There is certainly an economic logic to the globalisation of children's and youth culture. As we have noted, the youth market is potentially large, but it is also quite fragmented in terms of age and gender. One way for producers to deal with this – to develop economies of scale – is to build markets globally, to amass 'niche' markets into a larger global market. This tendency is also reinforced by the vertical and horizontal integration of the media and cultural industries. 'Vertical integration' refers to the way in which the market is coming to be dominated by a small number of global players, who integrate hardware, software and means of distribution; and these are largely the same players who dominate the adult market (Westcott, 2002). For example, in the case of specialist children's television channels, the market is dominated by Disney, Nickelodeon (owned by Viacom), Cartoon Network (owned by AOL Time Warner) and Fox Kids (owned by Murdoch). These US-based companies dominate the children's market and run more than 30 branded children's channels across Europe, although none invests to any significant degree in local production. These companies are also increasingly operating across media platforms ('horizontal integration'). Nearly all the major children's 'crazes' of the last 20 years (Ninja Turtles, Power Rangers, Pokemon, Beyblades, Harry Potter, Yu-Gi-Oh) have worked on this principle, and it requires global marketing: it would be much harder to achieve in one country alone.

According to some critics, we are seeing the construction of a homogenised global children's culture, in which cultural differences are being flattened out and erased. For authors such as Kline (1993) and McChesney (2002) this is an inevitable consequence of commercialisation: neoliberal economics are, in their view, inherently incompatible with the 'real' needs and interests of children. Within the media industries, there are also frequent calls for government intervention to support indigenous children's production against the pressure of the global market (von Feilitzen and Carlsson, 2002). However, such arguments often seem to rely on judgements about cultural value that are asserted rather than fully justified (Buckingham, 2000). Furthermore, economic domination does not necessarily translate directly into ideological or cultural domination.

A further aspect to this critique is the claim that parents' attempts to sustain their cultural values are increasingly in vain. The media are seen to have disrupted the process of socialisation, upsetting the smooth transmission of values from one generation to the next. Yoon's (2006) work explores how youth and mobile phone technology was represented in South Korea during the period of its introduction (1997–2002). He shows that while computers were often associated with 'successful' globalisation that would enable economic competitiveness, young mobile phone users came to be associated with the more alarming aspects of the rapid globalisation experienced in Korea at this time. They, along with other less powerful social groups such as housewives, were castigated in the press for their 'excessive' and unnecessary consumption, and the technology itself was seen as individualising and thus harmful to young people's understanding of Korean social and group norms. Advertisements for phones were careful to respond to these criticisms, depicting youth in group contexts and incorporating 'local' elements into their language and images. The study as a whole reveals widespread anxieties about Korea's participation in global material culture, and diverse local responses to it.

On the other hand, it could be argued that the media are responsible for a modernisation of childhood, or at least for the growing dominance of a 'modernist' discourse about childhood. The children's channel Nickelodeon provides a symptomatic instance of the ways in which market values have come to be aligned with liberal political arguments about children's rights. The statements of Nickelodeon executives and the rhetoric of its on-screen publicity proclaim its role as an agent of empowerment – a notion of the channel as a 'kid-only' zone, giving voice to kids, taking the kids' point of view, as the friend of kids; and the interests of 'kids' are frequently defined here as being in opposition to the interests of adults (Hendershot, 2004). This 'modernist' discourse has increasingly been adopted by exponents of more traditional children's media, not least in public service television. This is certainly the case in the UK (Buckingham et al, 1999); but it is also apparent, for example, in the (possibly unlikely) case of the Minimax channel in post-communist Hungary (Lustyik,

2003). It might even be possible to talk here about the emergence of a globalised 'modernist style' in children's culture, which seeks to address children across cultural boundaries – in the same way that critics have talked about 'youth culture' as a global phenomenon. The Japanese business consultant Kenichi Ohmae (1995), for example, asserts that children's exposure to such a global culture means that they now have more in common with their peers in other cultures than they do with their own parents.

The ways in which this global 'balance of power' actually works out in practice are not necessarily predictable or guaranteed. This is particularly apparent as societies themselves become more diverse and multicultural, and as children come into contact with a widening range of cultural forms (de Block and Buckingham, 2007). Studies of the global reception and use of phenomena such as Pokemon (Tobin, 2004) show that the process of media globalisation is often a paradoxical phenomenon. For example, White's (1993) anthropological work on Japanese teenagers, which contrasts their material worlds with those of American youth, suggests that cultural differences in how adolescence is conceptualised account for significant differences in the meaning they attach to their experiences and understanding of growing up – despite similarities in the consumer culture they access. As this implies, children and young people's culture is characterised not so much by a one-way process of domination, but by an unpredictable and contested relationship between the global and the local – often expressed in the notion of 'glocalisation' (Robertson, 1994).

Conclusion

In this chapter, we have attempted to show that children and young people's involvement in consumer culture is a highly ambivalent phenomenon. Of course, there is always an economic 'bottom line': the global youth market is a significant source of commercial profit – although profit is by no means easy or straightforward to secure. On the other hand, the cultural meanings and pleasures that consumer culture affords children and young people – and the roles that it can play in the formation of identity – are significantly more difficult to predict. The market clearly does have a considerable power to determine the meanings and pleasures that are available; but it is ultimately children and young people themselves who create those meanings and pleasures, and they may define and appropriate them in very diverse ways. Despite the often melodramatic claims of campaigners and the generalised optimism of the marketers, the outcomes of children's increasing immersion in consumer culture are by no means the same for all. As we have suggested, the relationship between structure and agency in this respect is complicated: it needs careful theoretical elaboration, but it also needs to be understood in relation to the specific social contexts and circumstances of young people's lives.

References

Adler, P. and Adler, P. (1998) *Peer Power: Preadolescent Culture and Identity*, New Brunswick, NJ: Rutgers University Press.

Alanen, L. (2001) 'Explorations in generational analysis', in L. Alanen and B. Mayall (eds) *Conceptualizing Child–Adult Relations*, London: Routledge Falmer.

Boden, S., Pole, C., Pilcher, J. and Edwards, T. (2004) *New Consumers: The Social and Cultural Significance of Children's Fashion Consumption*, Cultures of Consumption Working Paper No 16, London: Cultures of Consumption.

Bourdieu, P. (1984) *Distinction: A Social Critique of the Judgement of Taste*, trans R. Nice, London: Routledge.

Buckingham, D. (2000) *After the Death of Childhood: Growing Up in the Age of Electronic Media*, Cambridge: Polity Press.

Buckingham, D. and Sefton-Green, J. (2003) 'Gotta catch 'em all: structure, agency and pedagogy in children's media culture', *Media, Culture & Society*, vol 25, no 3, pp 379-99.

Buckingham, D., Davies, H., Jones, K. and Kelley, P. (1999) *Children's Television in Britain*, London: BFI Publishing.

Calvert, S.L. (2008) 'Children as consumers: advertising and marketing', *Future of Children*, vol 18, no 1, pp 205-34.

Chin, E. (2001) *Purchasing Power: Black Kids and American Consumer Culture*, Minnesota, MN: University of Minnesota Press.

Compass (nd) *The Commercialisation of Childhood*, London: Compass, available online at www.compassonline.org.uk/publications/ (accessed 30/05/08).

Cook, D.T. (2000) 'The other "child study": figuring children as consumers in market research, 1910s-1990s', *Sociological Quarterly*, vol 41, no 3, pp 487-507.

Cook, D.T. (2004) *The Commodification of Childhood: The Children's Clothing Industry and the Rise of the Child Consumer*, Durham, NC: Duke University Press.

Corsaro, W. (1997) *The Sociology of Childhood*, Thousand Oaks, CA: Sage Publications.

Cross, G. (2004) *The Cute and the Cool*, New York, NY: Oxford University Press.

DCSF (Department for Children, Schools and Families) (2008) 'Children – Review into the impact of the commercial world', Joint DCMS/ DCSF Press Release, 7 April 2008, available online at http://www.culture.gov.uk/reference_library/media_releases/5067.aspx (accessed 27/01/09).

de Block, L. and Buckingham, D. (2007) *Children, Media and Migration*, Buckingham: Palgrave Macmillan.

Denisoff, C. (ed) (2008) *The Nineteenth-Century Child and Consumer Culture*, Aldershot: Ashgate.

du Gay, P. (ed) (1997) *Production of Culture/Cultures of Production*, London: Sage Publications.

Featherstone, M. (1991) *Consumer Culture and Postmodernism*, London: Sage Publications.

Giddens, A. (1984) *The Constitution of Society*, Cambridge: Polity Press.

Giddens, A. (1991) *Modernity and Self-Identity: Self and Society in the Late Modern Age*, Cambridge: Polity Press.

Griffiths, M. (2002) 'Pink worlds and blue worlds: a portrait of infinite polarity', in D. Buckingham (ed) *Small Screens: Television for Children*, London: Leicester University Press.

Gunter, B. and Furnham, A. (1998) *Children as Consumers*, London: Routledge.

Hansen, F., Rasmussen, J., Martensen, A. and Tufte, B. (eds) (2002) *Children: Consumption, Advertising and Media*, Copenhagen, Denmark: Copenhagen Business School Press.

HBOS (2007) 'Pocket money rises 600% in 20 years', Halifax Press Release, 21 July, available online at www.hbosplc.com/media/pressreleases/articles/halifax/2007-07-21-Pocketmone.asp?section=halifax (accessed 30/05/08).

Hendershot, H. (2004) *Nickelodeon Nation: The History, Politics and Economics of America's Only TV Channel for Kids*, New York, NY: New York University Press.

James, A. (1993) *Childhood Identities*, Edinburgh: Edinburgh University Press.

James, A. and James, A. (2004) *Constructing Childhood: Theory, Policy and Social Practice*, Basingstoke: Palgrave Macmillan.

James, A. and Prout, A. (eds) (1997) *Constructing and Reconstructing Childhood* (2nd edition), London: Falmer Press.

Kenway, J. and Bullen, E. (2001) *Consuming Children: Entertainment, Advertising, Education*, Buckingham: Open University Press.

Kline, S. (1993) *Out of the Garden: Toys and Children's Culture in the Age of TV Marketing*, London: Verso.

Lindstrom, M. (2003) *Brandchild*, London and Sterling, VA: Kogan Page Limited.

Linn, S. (2004) *Consuming Kids: Protecting our Children from the Onslaught of Marketing and Advertising*, New York, NY: Anchor Books.

Livingstone, S. (1998) 'Mediated childhoods: a comparative approach to young people's changing media environment in Europe', *European Journal of Communication*, vol 13, no 4, pp 435-56.

Livingstone, S. and Bober, M. (2004) *UK Children Go Online: Surveying the Experiences of Young People and their Parents*, London: ESRC.

Lustyik, K. (2003) *The Transformation of Children's Television from Communism to Global Capitalism in Hungary*, Boulder, CO: University of Colorado.

McChesney, R. (2002) 'Media globalisation: consequences for the rights of children', in C. von Feilitzen and U. Carlsson (eds) *Children, Young People and Media Globalisation*, Goteborg, Sweden: UNESCO International Clearinghouse on Children, Youth and Media.

McNeal, J. U. (1999) *The Kids' Market: Myths and Realities*, New York, NY: Paramount.

Martens, L., Southerton, D. and Scott, S. (2004) 'Bringing children (and parents) into the sociology of consumption: towards a theoretical and empirical agenda', *Journal of Consumer Culture*, vol 4, no 2, pp 155-82.

Mayo, E. (2005) *Shopping Generation*, London: National Consumer Council.

Miller, D. (1998) *A Theory of Shopping*, Cambridge: Polity Press.

Nayak, A. and Kehily, M.J. (2008) *Gender, Youth and Culture: Young Masculinities and Femininities*, Basingstoke: Palgrave Macmillan.

Ohmae, K. (1995) *The End of the Nation State*, New York: Harper Collins.

Osgerby, B. (2004) *Youth Media*, London: Routledge.

Palmer, S. (2006) *Toxic Childhood: How the Modern World is Damaging our Children and What We Can Do About It*, London: Orion.

Quart, A. (2003) *Branded: The Buying and Selling of Teenagers*, London: Arrow.

Robertson, R. (1994) 'Globalisation or glocalisation?', *Journal of International Communication*, vol 1, no 1, pp 33-52.

Rose, N. (1999) *Governing the Soul: The Shaping of the Private Self* (2nd edition), London and New York, NY: Free Association Books.

Russell, R. and Tyler, M. (2002) 'Thank heaven for little girls: "Girl Heaven" and the commercial context of feminine childhood', *Sociology*, vol 36, no 3, pp 619-37.

Russell, R. and Tyler, M. (2005) 'Branding and bricolage: gender, consumption and transition', *Childhood*, vol 12, no 2, pp 221-37.

Savage, J. (2007) *Teenage: The Creation of Youth 1875–1945*, London: Chatto and Windus.

Schneider, C. (1987) *Children's Television: The Art, the Business and How It Works*, Lincolnwood, IL: NTC Business Books.

Schor, J. (2004) *Born to Buy: The Commercialised Child and the New Consumer Culture*, New York, NY: Scribner.

Seiter, E. (1993) *Sold Separately: Children and Parents in Consumer Culture*, New Brunswick, NJ: Rutgers University Press.

Seiter, E. (2004) 'The internet playground', in J. Goldstein, D. Buckingham and G. Brougere (eds) *Toys, Games and Media*, Mahwah, NJ: Lawrence Erlbaum Associates, Inc.

Smithers, R. (2006) 'Average cost of bringing up a child to 21 reaches £180,000', *The Guardian*, 10 November, available online at www.guardian.co.uk/money/2006/nov/10/childcare.familyandrelationships (accessed 30/05/08).

Tobin, J. (ed) (2004) *Pikachu's Global Adventure: The Rise and Fall of Pokémon*, Durham, NC: Duke University Press.

Torell, V. B. (2004) 'Adults and children debating sexy girls' clothes', in H. Brembeck, B. Johansson and J. Kampmann (eds) *Beyond the Competent Child: Exploring Contemporary Childhoods in the Nordic Welfare Societies*, Fredericksberg, Denmark: Roskilde University Press.

von Feilitzen, C. and Carlsson, U. (eds) (2002) *Children, Young People and Media Globalisation*, Goteborg, Sweden: UNESCO International Clearinghouse on Children, Youth and Media.

Westcott, T. (2002) 'Globalisation of children's TV and the strategies of the "big three"', in C. von Feilitzen and U. Carlsson (eds) *Children, Young People and Media Globalisation*, Goteborg, Sweden: UNESCO International Clearinghouse on Children, Youth and Media.

White, M. (1993) *The Material Child: Coming of Age in Japan and America*, New York, NY: Free Press.

Wolf, N. (1991) *The Beauty Myth*, London: Vintage.

Yoon, K. (2006) 'The making of neo-Confucian cyberkids: representations of young mobile phone users in South Korea', *New Media & Society*, vol 8, no 5, pp 753-71.

Zelizer, V. (1985) *Pricing the Priceless Child*, Princeton, NJ: Princeton University Press.

Twelve

Youth, religion and multiculture

Anoop Nayak

Introduction

Religion can be a sphere for shared rituals and spiritual belonging, as well as a site of social division in young lives. This chapter seeks to unravel the varied deployment of religious identification and how it is manifest in state practices. It begins by briefly outlining the direction of early multiculturalism, before documenting how multicultural policies have recently struggled to engage with questions of religious assertiveness and transnational belonging. The third section reveals how Muslim youth have become a new source of 'moral panic' in the nation state and the way in which recent global events are transfiguring their identities. The fourth section considers the opinions of young Muslims themselves to show how they depart from many of the popular and media representations that construct them as 'fundamentalists' with imagined terrorist leanings. In the fifth section the focus is on religion as a dividing line within youth communities where space can become exclusively colonised as 'territory'. The final section considers the other side of this dichotomy through a case study analysis of the Christian metal scene and Rastafarian reggae. Here religious activities among young people can engender new points of belonging and multicultural mutuality.

Multiculturalism/anti-racism

For children and young people, multiculturalism has been most active at the state level of education. Propelled by a belief that the national curriculum did not reflect the multi-ethnic society and inner-city classrooms of Britain, the 1980s witnessed the rise of state-led initiatives that sought to recognise diversity. For journalists and political commentators on the Right, multiculturalism has been the scourge of the nation and press stories have abounded concerning British (read 'white') children being taught Punjabi, Urdu and Hindi at the 'expense' of basic English and Mathematics. Despite the inaccuracy of these reports and the accompanying tabloid outrage, in practice multiculturalism was never more than a mere sideshow in the debate over a broader national curriculum in which whiteness and Britishness continued to be held up as the social norm.

When it comes to the practice of multiculturalism it often presents as well meaning but tokenistic. Its intention has largely been to challenge 'intolerance' and 'prejudice', based on an egalitarian belief that society should celebrate all 'cultures'. Indeed, the term 'culture' is often used here as a euphemism for race or tied to fixed and immobile notions of ethnicity (see Chapter Six). In practice, schools and local education authorities tend to deploy multiculturalism in a piecemeal and additive fashion, incorporating, for example, 'black history week', the celebration of *Diwali* or a home economics session on Indian cookery. One of the problems of this model is that it reduces culture to the 'exotic', attributing it as a fixed property of particular national and ethnic 'groups'. In *Keywords* Williams (1976) argues that culture is not a static object or 'thing', but a process that is dynamic and open to constant reformation. It is, in Geertz's (1983) words, a system of 'knotted-together signs', from which we derive meaning, through the social act of interpretation. The assemblage of these 'signs' is then precarious, contingent and forever in the making. However, the symbolic repertoire through which much school multiculturalism is conceived has tended to be highly select, celebrating difference through a formulaic pastiche of 'steel bangles, saris and samosas'. Such representations only serve to fetishise difference and ignore the reality that much of what we call culture is actually 'ordinary'.

With its focus on 'prejudice', early state multiculturalism placed the onus on individual actions, failing to address racism as systematically embedded in institutions and social structures. In response, more radical proponents favoured a stronger brand of socialist anti-racism, charged with the direct task of eliminating, or at least ameliorating, racism in schools, youth clubs and the street. Anti-racists sought to assert a more strident form of race equality that went beyond the multicultural approach of, say, including pictures of black characters in primary school storybooks. For these ardent activists the liberal practice of multiculturalism was occasionally deemed an exercise in the expiation of white, middle-class guilt. Much classroom anti-racism tended to operate across a black/white binary of power (see Rattansi, 1993), condensed in a familiar mantra of the time, that 'racism = power + prejudice'. Today, this colour-based statement appears outdated in the light of the multiple racisms, religious difference and a set of new cultural inflections barely containable within this formula. Where immigration had once predominantly followed older colonial routes, the globalisation of migration has seen an increase in the diversity of migrants when it comes to their country of origin. Global conflict and insecurity have also seen new communities seeking asylum and refugee status in Western nation states. There is also a need to pay greater attention to the ways in which the social category of race intersects with religion, ethnicity, age, gender, class or sexuality. For all its shortcomings, the old anti-racist couplet, by including power into the equation, is at least attentive to the historical and material circumstances in which race divisions occur (see also Chapter Six).

In my discussions of anti-racism with white, working-class children and young people, I was interested to learn that they interpreted it as a heavily proscriptive device and potentially an attack on 'white rights' (Nayak, 2003, 2008). They referred to selected items that have been 'banned', symbols you have 'gotta have' and things you are 'not allowed' to say or do. In essence, anti-racism and multiculturalism were reproduced, in their opinion, to form what Ball (1990) calls a 'discourse of derision'. The feeling among these school students is that white ethnicity has to be regulated and that multiculturalism/anti-racism is a somewhat arbitrary mode of 'policing'. The popular myths surrounding these initiatives were generated in media presentation and kept alive through intergenerational discussions, anecdotes, hearsay and outright fabrication. In this way it is the feelings, emotions and affects generated by state-imposed multiculturalism that engendered a 'backlash' that carries into daily activity where some children operate under the misguided belief that anti-racism is 'anti-white'.

Britain at a crossroads: the Parekh Report

Since the 1990s, advocates have responded to such critiques by developing what has become known as 'critical multiculturalism', combining anti-racist politics with a reflexive and reconstructed multiculturalism. This version of multiculturalism draws on critical race theory and anti-racist practice, offering an engagement with whiteness and post-structuralist ideas on subjectivity (see May, 1999). These recent tendencies can be traced in a landmark report published on the cusp of a new millennium, where its author (Parekh, 2000: 14-15) ruminates over the future of multi-ethnic Britain:

> Britain confronts a historic choice as to its future direction. Will it try to turn the clock back, digging in, defending

values and ancient hierarchies, relying on a narrow English-
dominated, backward-looking definition of the nation?
Or will it seize the opportunity to create a more flexible,
inclusive, cosmopolitan image of itself?

The 'Parekh Report', as it was termed, offered a template for an
outward-looking Britain, in tune with the image of 'cool Britannia'
signalled in early New Labour politics. Where Britishness had once
been constructed by the Conservative government through a glorious
celebration of the past – its once imperial might, quintessential English
landscapes, two World War victories and 19th-century literature – a
new political moment to redefine the nation for the future emerged.
The rise of Brit-art, Brit-pop and a cosmopolitan sensibility suggested
that Damien Hirst and Noel Gallagher were the vanguard for this
newly confident sense of national identity, removed from the patriotic
baggage of the past. This reconfiguration of Britishness met with
much controversy in sections of the press, where some political
commentators fretted over a loss of national identity, and viewed the
report as an attack on white British traditions. Although Parekh is
far from dismissive of citizenship, the ire of the right-wing press was
especially inflamed when he questioned the value of nationhood in an
era of globalisation, European integration and devolution. 'Is it possible
to reimagine Britain as a nation – or post-nation – in a multicultural
way?' he pondered (2000: 36). For as the nostalgic portrayal of
Britishness undertaken by the Conservative government alludes, and
the wild and cosmopolitan celebration of all things 'British' envisioned
by early New Labourites intimate, nation states are ultimately, in the
words of Anderson (1991 [1983]), 'imagined communities'.

   Reflecting on what appeared to be the 'dawn of a new era', Parekh's
hope-filled 'post-nation' statement is far removed from subsequent
citizenship tests, enhanced security measures and new legislation on
the detention of terrorist suspects – issues we shall turn to in the next
section in a discussion of Muslim youth. Since the destruction of the
World Trade Center on 11 September 2001 and the London bombings
on 7 July 2005, it appears that an embattled sense of Britishness is once
again resurgent. This blinkered, bunkered-down version of Britishness
suggests an identity that is once again uncomfortable with itself and
'under siege'. Threatened from external forces abroad (the wars in Iraq
and Afghanistan, the European Union, an economic crisis and rising
food and oil prices) and also internally at home (Islamic terrorists,
American-style globalisation, new migrant communities, refugees and

asylum seekers), this is not the post-imperial future some may have prophesied.

While the future of multiculturalism remains opaque, it is clear that religion, and particularly Islam, has emerged as a new faultline across which difference is being constituted. Somewhat unfairly, multiculturalism has been charged with facilitating an assertive Muslim identity through celebrating difference and fostering ethnic pluralism. In these (mis)readings, Islam is cast as an obdurate force that refuses to assimilate into mainstream Western society. Where other 'communities' and faith groups are willing to negotiate multicultural living, Islam is represented as an insular and unyielding ideology associated with religious extremism and 'fundamentalism'. Yet, much is obscured in these polarised representations of East and West. That the London bombers were young men who had grown up in England and spoke with broad Yorkshire accents implies more complex relations and split identifications of race, religion and nationhood that are rarely captured in scathing criticisms of multiculturalism. As we will now discover, it is precisely these ambiguities that Muslim youth must struggle to negotiate as they seek to be recognised as young, Muslim and British.

Muslim youth: a new 'moral panic'

In his famous study *Folk Devils and Moral Panics* (1973 [1972]), Cohen examines representations of youth culture in South East England between 1963 and 1966. His account focuses on how two youth subcultures – 'Mods' and 'Rockers' – were represented within the British popular press, through public letters and parliamentary debate. Throughout the late 1960s, Mods and Rockers became notorious for causing trouble and fights between one another in English coastal resorts including Brighton, Clacton and Margate. Cohen explores how these relatively minor altercations became charged with a powerful rhetoric of youth 'deviancy' that cast Mods, Rockers and young people more generally as lawless, savage and beyond redemption. The press hysteria and ensuing public outrage rapidly led to parliamentary discussion and a national vilification. Cohen (1973 [1972]: 88) memorably cites an apoplectic magistrate who demonises the youth, as 'long-haired, mentally unstable, petty little hoodlums … sawdust Caesars who can only find courage like rats, hunting in packs'. For Cohen, the vitriolic abomination of youth subculture is part of a national 'moral panic' that registers with broader fears concerning social change over the last 20 years and the future of the nation state in the post-war period. Reflecting on previous subcultures, such as Teddy Boys, Hell's Angels, Skinheads and Hippies, he remarks on the function they perform in the national imaginary. Cohen (1973 [1972]: 10) recalls how, 'In the gallery of types that society erects to show its members which roles should be avoided and which should be emulated, these groups have occupied a constant position as folk devils: visible reminders of what we should not be'. The casting of Mods and Rockers as 'folk devils' places them outside the nation state as a source of 'moral panic' that can only be redeemed through concerted state intervention – long-term education, stricter criminal punishment, harder political legislation and so on.

Up until the 1990s, South Asian youth in Britain tended to be largely invisible in government policy and media representations. Indeed, in a national school report on educational performance in the mid-1980s, Asian youth were favourably compared with what was then described as 'West Indian' youth. It is a depiction that gives way to a rather different set of racial stereotypes, in which young Asians are construed as passive and hard working with a strict family upbringing. The report (Swann, 1985: 86) proclaimed that Asian youth:

> are given to 'keeping their heads down' and adopting a 'low profile', thereby making it easier to succeed in a hostile environment. West Indians, by contrast, are given to 'protest' and a 'high profile', with the reverse effect.

The political context within which the Swann Report was published followed British urban uprisings in 1981 and 1985 in which black youth were prominent, so presumably 'given to "protest"'. It is clear in this account that British African Caribbean and South Asian youth are being differently racialised through state processes such as education. Written into this dialectical interplay is an abiding sense of cultural homogeneity. Recently, the vectors of this self-contained representation have been reorientated to locate South Asian – and in particular Muslim youth – as bodies out of place in the British nation state.

This displacement has come about through an amalgam of events happening at local, national and global levels, crystallising on the bodies of young Muslims and South Asians more generally. The aftermath of the publication of Salman Rushdie's *The Satanic Verses*, two Gulf Wars, 9/11, the riots in Bradford, Burnley and Oldham, terrorist attacks in Bali and bombings in London have become transposed into the new coordinates through which Islam is identified.

Each of these events holds specific meaning for Australia, Britain and the US, mirroring back fragmented images of the Other that are cut, pasted and circulated anew within popular local and national discourses (Said, 1995 [1978]). These events – and the surfeit of text and images that come to stand in for these happenings – carry with them an intensity of feeling, emotion and affect about young people, race and religion. In these new configurations, South Asian youth, who it was previously alleged 'kept their heads down', come into being as religious fundamentalists; an enactment that follows the similar racialised stereotypes attributed to black youth above. Muslim youth appear as society's new 'folk devils' and, as Alexander (2000: 15) wryly remarks, have 'become the new "black"', with all the associations of cultural alienation, deprivation and danger that come with this position'. It is worth noting that because the early cultural stereotypes of Asian youth were premised on unstable signifiers, these signs can be displaced, appropriated and reworked in the new post-9/11 landscape, as seen below.

'Asian culture' pre-9/11	'Asian culture' post-9/11
Tight-knit	Secretive
Educated	Calculated
Physically passive	Physically intimidating
Religiously subservient	Religiously fundamentalist
Potentially self-sacrificing	Potentially suicide bombers

In the post-9/11 moment, religion has emerged as a crucial marker of difference, overlaying an older 'race relations' paradigm designed across the colour bar. Where colour was once the arbiter of ethnicity, this has been extended to include bodily inscriptions of Islam. It appears that young people who might wear the *hijab*, carry rucksacks, read the Qur'an or grow beards are coming under heightened scrutiny and state surveillance. Hysterical media reporting, public consensus and new political legislation combine to confirm Muslim youth as a new source of moral panic in the nation state – a silent repository on which our darkest fears and anxieties are projected.

This moral panic can be seen at the level of the nation state where a renewed emphasis on Britishness is found with the introduction of 'citizenship tests' and a search for new symbols of national belonging. At this point it is worth reflecting back on the challenge laid down by the Parekh Report, which speculated on the future of multi-ethnic Britain at the watershed of the new millennium. In particular, there have been new state practices and legislation to counter state terrorism and a stricter attitude to surveillance. For example, in 2008, university lecturers were requested to be alert to student terrorist recruitment and plotting on British campuses. At the same time, new security measures were being discussed to increase the detention of terrorist suspects. Where some politicians deemed this a 'necessary measure', others viewed it as a blatant infringement of human rights where terrorism is held apart from other criminal activity, and argued that those detained should be innocent until proven guilty. An abiding fear also concerns the implementation of such measures. In the aftermath of the London bombings the use of counterterrorism powers meant that young people of 'Asian appearance' were five times more likely to be stopped and searched according to figures compiled by British Transport police. Such manoeuvres are unlikely to be based on intelligence (none of those searched were charged) and the risk of discrimination and institutional racism is glaringly apparent.

In order to interpret the renewed regulatory state activities, we have to begin to understand how the bodies of Muslim youth – which were once defined through ethnicity and nationality – are now brought into being through religious modes of identification. What is the effect of this manoeuvre and how does it work to elicit the feelings of hate and terror that culminate in acute moral panic? It is important to reflect that while moral panics certainly have social effects, crucially they also work with and through emotions, generating their own felt intensities. Ahmed (2004) explores the economy of emotions and the ways in which particular affects and feelings become attached to individuals and social collectives. She explores how fear, hatred and loathing can circulate between signifiers in relationships of difference and displacement.

> In such affective economies, emotions do things, and they align individuals with communities – or bodily space with social space – through the very intensity of their attachments … emotions work by sticking figures together (adherence), a sticking that creates the very effect of a collective (coherence), with reference to the figures of the asylum seeker and the international terrorist. (Ahmed, 2004: 119)

In a climate of fear and uncertainty, emotions become a thoroughly unreliable index for making sense of everyday encounters. It seems that in a world of endless artifice and floating signifiers there is a great deal of potential for misrecognition to preside. Such unspoken fear adheres to particular bodies such as those of Muslim youth as they try to negotiate passport control, the security cameras of department stores, the London transport network, neighbourhood spaces, or police stop and search patrols. Fear can then impede mobility. For Ahmed (2004: 121) these emotions have a 'binding' effect on subjects where 'the accumulation of affective value shapes the surface of bodies and worlds'. It is through a dense accumulation of images, text, events, practices, feelings, affects and emotions that a 'hyper-real' idea of what constitutes Muslim youth is assembled.

Beyond the veil: Muslim youth speak back

Given the intensity of feeling surrounding 9/11 and the London bombings, how might we counter this forceful reservoir of emotions and ensuing moral panic? One way in which we can begin this difficult task is to engage with the experiences of young Muslims themselves. Recent research conducted with Muslim young men and women indicates a much more prosaic picture of everyday life than the religious extremism depicted on radio talk shows, in certain documentaries and in the tabloids. For example, in interviews undertaken in schools in Hertfordshire, Dwyer (1999) explored how young British Muslim women negotiate Western and Islamic fashions. In exploring attitudes to Islamic forms of dress such as the *shalwar kameez* (a loose-fitting tunic and trouser suit) or the *hijab* (a scarf that covers the head), Dwyer discloses how an image of 'appropriate' femininity can be constructed. Her respondents reveal how seemingly conservative young British Muslim women wearing the *hijab* can use this powerful, if ultimately superficial, sign to mask the fact that they may date boys or enjoy nights out on the town. The garment provides the illusion of religious observance when in fact it can be imaginatively appropriated. What is interesting about this strategic manipulation is that it presents an outward image of Muslim femininity that others may treat as an authentic signifier reflective of one's behaviour.

Religious clothing continues to remain a political issue in media debates. In French schools, the wearing of a veil or other religious insignia is not permitted on secular grounds. In the Islamic country of Tunisia, formerly under French colonial authority, the veil is also banned from schools on the basis that it signifies political extremism. In Britain, there are as yet no laws concerning the veil, although the uncertainty associated with it is evident in the case of Shabina Begum.

Begum was a 12-year-old schoolgirl who, in 2005, unsuccessfully tried to sue her Luton school for the right to wear the *jilbab*, a single piece of clothing that acts as a full body veil and only exposes the face and hands. This incident, and the extensive press coverage it received, indicates that the idea of Islamic difference has become a dominant trope through which to interpret whole ways of life. However, Dwyer's account informs us of a need to look beyond the exceptional. The culturally hybrid 'pick-n-mix' approach to fashion that many of her young respondents engage in, parallels the way certain music scenes may operate as zones of interruption when it comes to racial fixing and religious orthodoxy. It would now appear that in the post-colonial context, young women are fashioning a new, ethnically assertive British Muslim femininity that is as traditional as it is modern.

Archer's (2003) study of Muslim masculinities suggests a strategic take-up of new subject positions by young men after 9/11. Here, respondents were keen to vacate older racialised stereotypes of Asian youth as weak and feeble by participating in the fearful and excessive image of Muslim masculinity constructed in popular discourse and circulated through global media representations. Certain boys embraced their newfound notoriety as 'deviant', choosing to invest in racialised forms of 'hard' masculinity that could enhance their status. Like the Skins, Teds, Mods and Rockers before them, it is perhaps convenient to only ever think of these young men through the very category that interpolates them: 'Muslim youth'. But as critiques of subcultural studies have developed, writers have pointed to the problem of viewing young people solely through a subcultural lens without considering the different manifestations of a young person's identity at home, in school, at work or in alternative situations where this affiliation may be more precariously inhabited. What Archer and her colleagues (2003: 53–4) found in their school-based interviews with Muslim boys was that 'The boundaries of Muslim identity were constantly negotiated and contested within the discussion groups and the boys asserted, resisted and justified various positionings of themselves within or outside particular boundaries'. This complex repertoire of identification suggests a need to move beyond popular religious and racialised portrayals of 'Asian gangs' (Alexander, 2000). The complex nature of religious identification is evident in focus group discussions undertaken by Hopkins (2007) with young Muslim men in Scotland. Hopkins suggests that respondents move between different intersecting scales, sometimes asserting their identities as 'local' through neighbourhood relations, as 'nationalists' through strong appeals to being Scottish or as 'global' through a spiritual connection to the *umma*, which suggests that Muslims across the world have a mutual and binding relationship through praying to Allah. Yet, in practice, young Muslim men could equally disavow these attachments, for example by making clear distinctions between themselves and the terrorists who brought down the Twin Towers.

What the firsthand accounts of Muslim young men and women suggest is a wide discrepancy between cultural representations and everyday life. Today, young Muslims must be astute managers of 'risk' in an insecure society that positions them as Other to the West in 'out-of-scale' mediated images. Although assigned a location as society's new 'folk devils', Muslim youth are diverse, creative actors who speak back to these dominant images and may resist, overturn or appropriate these signifiers as they see fit. However, this imaginative interplay is always underscored by the Western hegemonic power of representation and its material effects, symbolic workings and affective resonance in modern society. We will now explore how religion can be deployed as a point of difference in young people's lives, before finally considering how it operates as a register for collective identity.

Religion, space and territory

One of the most powerful ways in which religious identities are expressed is through the transformation of space into territory. Religious divisions enacted through space impinge on the access and mobility of young lives. In a study of young people in Northern Ireland, McGrellis (2005) discovered that some young people were relatively mobile while others remained 'stuck' to sectarian cultural practices. Interviews with Catholic and Protestant young people revealed distinctions between 'pure' and 'bitter' spaces. A 'pure' area is one that is traditionally 100% Catholic or Protestant, striving to protect itself from the 'contamination' of outsiders. However, in their efforts to remain 'pure', these spaces can also engender 'bitterness' where the struggle for religious purity becomes all-consuming. McGrellis's (2005: 520) account draws attention to the ways in which space becomes territorialised through rituals and practices such as the deployment of graffiti, marching bands and flags.

Purity is created at a territorial level – spaces are marked out as belonging to one group or the other, often with the help of flags, emblems, murals and painted kerbstones and boundaries. Through this use of space, 'ethnic' differences, not easily ascribed on the basis of biological, cultural or political differences, are more securely established and maintained.

The religious beliefs of Catholics and Protestants do not neatly map onto political affiliations. Some young people's biographies may be marked with a political intensity while in others it can be muted. Many hold complex and competing attachments to politics, nationalism, ethnicity, religion, sectarianism and territoriality that cannot be easily reduced to 'pure' forms of politico-religious identification. The rituals of marching, flag-waving and graffiti are then performances that streamline and simplify this diversity to provide the semblance of 'purity'. While such spectacular displays may capture the imagination, it is often through more mundane practices that the nation is 'flagged' – the habitual interactions Billig (1995) terms 'banal nationalism'.

One of the pertinent findings in McGrellis's study is how new gender positions become available to young people in peacetime. Since the ceasefire, Northern Ireland, like much of the rest of the UK, witnessed the explosion of dance music and drug culture. Attending these events has enabled some young people to cross into hitherto exclusive spaces, while maintaining a strong sense of space as territorially marked. In particular, young women have been seen to have an enhanced mobility where borders appear more fluid when it comes to transgression and safe passage. In contrast, many young men, especially those from high-profile families, continue to be rooted to the 'local'. Unlike their more cosmopolitan female counterparts, a number of young men appear stuck to the neighbourhood and caught in the fix that 'purity is security' (McGrellis, 2005: 520).

This idea that certain spaces are divided across lines of religion and/or ethnicity has also featured in British government policy on 'neighbourhood cohesion'. These debates emerged out of disturbances that took place involving young people living in multi-ethnic quarters of Bradford, Burnley and Oldham in 2001. While various reports have focused on a perceived religious/'racial' divide existing between white working-class and British Asian Muslim youth, it is important not to condense these relations through simple dualisms such as black/white, Muslim/Christian, Pakistani/English and so forth. However, the Ouseley Report (2001) that followed the disturbances in Bradford focused on the 'virtual apartheid' of secondary schooling and the self-imposed segregation elaborated on by South Asian Muslim and white communities alike. The theme of ethnic and religious 'self-segregation' is taken up in another government report chaired by Ted Cantle for the Community Cohesion Review Team, which identifies the 'parallel lives' occupied by white and South Asian communities in Britain whose schools, jobs, places of worship and community centres may appear demarcated. According to this report, 'These lives do not seem to touch at any point, let alone overlap and promote any meaningful interchanges' (Community Cohesion Panel, 2001: 9). This portrayal runs counter to multiculturalism. Both the Ouseley and Cantle Reports, as they became known, frame the debate in terms of a 'clash of civilizations' (Huntington, 2002) between East and West. This is polarised through depictions of an intransient, homogenous white working-class 'community' and an insular, intractable South Asian Muslim 'community'. But how accurate is this frozen portrait of multi-ethnic Britain?

Clearly, ethnic and religious segregation can become dividing issues for young people in rundown areas such as parts of Bradford. Yet, the tendency to racialise the 2001 riots is apparent, where it is young South Asian Muslims who are seen as a self-segregating unit, an 'alien wedge' that threatens the security and stability of (white) British national identity. Although most of those involved in street violence were young working-class men, issues of class and especially masculinity remain underplayed in media and policy reports. As we saw in the case of Northern Irish youth, gender can be pivotal to neighbourhood dynamics. Moreover, where there is conflict there may also be what Gilroy (1993) terms 'conviviality' – a popular multiculturalism, part and parcel of everyday life. This implies that territorial points of religious and ethnic closure are rarely complete but can allow for new forms of cultural syncretism and transaction to occur (Keith, 1993; Back, 1996; Cohen, 1997).

Although moments of religious and ethnic closure may occur, this is often a response to prevailing social conditions and remains a partial and contingent practice. Close empirical investigations undertaken in Bradford and Leeds found that where 'self-segregation' does occur it is not a matter of choice but of circumstance. Such researchers conclude that for many British South Asian residents the 'Key obstacles to mobility included poverty, institutional exclusion, racist harassment and feeling out of place in certain city spaces' (Phillips et al, 2007: 228). Indeed, British South Asian interviewees stated a preference for inter-mixture but the researchers discovered that many white British families would move out of the neighbourhood if they felt that it contained 'too many' Asians. It is interesting to note that while many suburbs and villages may appear as 'white enclaves', this overbearing whiteness is allowed to pass as humdrum and ordinary yet is the standard against which working-class multi-ethnic areas are gauged. What the examples of young Protestant and Catholic youth in Northern Ireland, and British South Asian Muslim youth in Northern

England, suggest is a complex and changing relationship between religion, space and territory. For young people, religious identification can become a source of conflict or conviviality through which multifaceted identities are mobilised, where space is symbolically imagined as multicultural or materially realised as 'territory'.

Case study: popular music and religion – Christian metal and Rastafarian reggae

An interesting, if ambiguous, example of the interplay between religion, music and youth, can be traced in Jones' (1988) cultural analysis of reggae music during the late 1980s. Here, the author turns his attention to a subculture of young, white Rastafarians living in the multi-ethnic inner-city neighbourhood of Balsall Heath in Birmingham. He discloses how a number of white working-class youth are drawn to the 'protest' dimension of reggae music and use it as a template through which to fashion their sense of ethnic identity. A few committed white reggae enthusiasts adopted the full flush of Rastafarian style including the appropriation of cannabis, dreadlocks, Jamaican patois and a spiritual interest in the Rastafari religion. However, most young people simply 'tried on' selective aspects of black style such as sporting dreadlocks to enliven their white subjectivities, as a passing moment in their transition to adulthood. Just as Buddhists may shave their heads in a spiritual act of renunciation, or Sikhs may be forbidden from cutting their hair, dreadlocks were originally cultivated to offer a religious and political statement of one's being. Mercer (1994: 107) documents the way in which race and religion are semiotically entwined in the wearing of dreadlocks, 'within the strictures of Rastafari as spiritual doctrine'. He draws attention to the manner in which dreadlocks, like the 1960s Afro, were seen as a celebration of 'natural' black aesthetics and appear in stark contrast to the hair-straightening styles said to 'mimic' white fashion. However, he reminds us (1994: 108), 'these hairstyles were never just natural, waiting to be found: they were stylistically cultivated and politically constructed in a particular historical moment as part of a strategic contestation of white dominance and the cultural power of whiteness'.

The act of donning dreadlocks is not unlike the participation in Irish youth marching bands. Each of these performances is engaged in an imagined construction of 'community', rather than any authentic 'recovery' of it. Yet, these encounters must be read as political practices that require a historical revisionist understanding of race, religion and territory in the postcolonial moment. Today, many white youth who sport dreadlocks may have little time for reggae music let alone the religion of Rastafari. In youth contemporary culture, dreadlocks are an open signifier that may be associated with other subcultures such as eco-warriors, crusties, hippies, skaters or hip-hop enthusiasts. This symbolic interaction with global black culture and world religions is widely recognised to be part of 'a phantom history of race relations' (Hebdige, 1987 [1979]: 45), played out on the loaded surfaces of British working-class youth culture throughout the post-war period to the present. These stylistic interactions intimate how black history, beliefs, culture, music and style can be 'emptied out' of meaning and imported into contemporary youth cultures where they are given new signification. The 'hollowing out' of Rastafarian ideology can be seen when any wider spiritual or political meanings are 'flattened' and rendered obsolete through corporate merchandising. The new capitalist commodities may include red, green and gold wristbands, records, clothes and other products torn from their historical and geographical contexts. hooks (1992: 21) argues that this process offers a 'touch of spice' from which to enliven the bland palette of whiteness; an act of consumption she terms 'eating the Other'.

The contemporary heavy metal music scene is often seen as a dark and nihilistic fringe activity. Lyrics, album covers and dress regularly make reference to death, skulls, suicide and even occult or satanic rituals. The 'black metal' scene in particular appears in stark opposition to Christianity and its holy beliefs. Even so, within this subculture other genres have been spawned, including a number of Christian metal bands. Although early metal bands such as Stryper in the US and Jerusalem from Sweden had gained some success peddling a Christian ethos, thrash metal outfits such as Deliverance and Tourniquet, and later death metal acts like Mortification and Deuteronomium, would achieve popular cult followings. Moberg (2008) identifies the significance of place to the early Christian metal scene, which became particularly widespread among young people in Northern Europe – Belgium, Germany and the Netherlands – but especially in Nordic countries such as Finland, Norway and Sweden. He explains that a reason for this place-specific popularity is largely due to the evangelical Protestantism of Christian metal, which is less likely to have appeal in Catholic countries or in spaces without significant Protestant populations. A feature of Christian metal is that it must also elicit an 'uncompromising rhetoric, attitude and lifestyle' (Moberg, 2008: 90) if it is to develop an aesthetic that is meaningful to its fan base. Some Christian metal bands manage to cross over into 'mainstream' metal scenes, while it is also the case that a number of Christian followers will also listen to other metal artists. According to Moberg, famous Christian metal musicians can become known as 'metal missionaries' or 'ministers' imbued with a 'religious capital' of near Messianic proportions.

Recent years have witnessed the remaking of Christian metal youth communities through what Moberg (2008: 81) identifies as a 'transnational Christian metal music "scene"', developed mainly by young fans through the internet. This 'scenic infrastructure' (2008: 92) is almost entirely virtual, operating through web forums, magazines and electronic fanzines, but it can occasionally come 'alive' in the fleshy encounters between fans at actual music festivals. What is interesting about these new virtual communities is the way in which a relatively small number of young fans – supporting a subgenre within a subculture – with limited resources can develop an explicitly religious popular music scene at a transnational scale. Moreover, this 'subcommunity' has also developed in part as a resistance to the dominant versions of Christianity celebrated by elder generations. For Moberg (2008: 89):

> Christian metal scenes function as a means of both constructing and reinforcing an alternative Christian identity and forms of religious expression that is, in many ways, directed against traditional notions about which forms Christian worship and evangelism should take.

This suggests that for at least some young people the heavy metal scene can be a site for new forms of religious identification. The development of a disparate, transnational internet community further suggests the significance of new technologies in the bringing into being of youthful religious identities.

While dreadlocked Rastafarianism may be thought of as an authentic emblem of black culture, and heavy metal music considered the antithesis of Christianity, the case accounts are informative of the complex relations between popular music, religion and ethnicity. Young people are capable of inhabiting subcultures with religious roots such as Rastafarianism and may take on or reject the spiritual components. They may also archive alternative spaces within a seemingly secular scene such as that of heavy metal to perform new modes of religious subjectivity enhanced by electronic media and a series of temporal, virtual assemblages.

Conclusion

Although modern diasporas and migrations have resulted in scattered, transnational belongings across time and space, this has been accompanied by new forms of religious revivalism and ethnic tribalism. As we witnessed in various youth accounts of neighbourhood life, religion can segment local and national space into fixed and demarcated territories, be it in Belfast, Bradford or Beirut. The contemporary geopolitics of the post-9/11 moment have also seen a fusing together of racism with religious intolerance, primarily directed at the bodies of South Asian Muslim youth living in the West. It is argued that vectors of hate are projected onto their identities, which are imbued with a great deal of affect and emotion, culminating in a 'crisis' of Britishness and a 'moral panic' about the place of Islam in young people's lives. In contrast, the testimonies of young Muslims themselves are far more prosaic and thought provoking than the spectacular tropes of 'terrorism', 'fundamentalism' and 'Asian gangs' would intimate. Finally, in exploring the relationship between music and religion through case studies of white Rastafarian reggae aficionados and Christian 'metal heads' we can envision how new faith communities and youth cultures can be produced, consumed, regulated and performed.

References

Ahmed, S. (2004) 'Affective economies', *Social Text*, vol 22, no 2, pp 117-39.

Alexander, C. (2000) *The Asian Gang: Ethnicity, Identity, Masculinity*, Oxford: Berg.

Anderson, B. (1991 [1983]) *Imagined Communities: Reflections on the Origins and Spread of Nationalism*, London: Verso.

Archer, L. (2003) *Race, Masculinity and Schooling: Muslim Boys and Education*, Maidenhead: Open University Press.

Back, L. (1996) *New Ethnicities and Urban Culture: Racisms and Multiculture in Young Lives*, London: UCL Press.

Ball, S. (1990) *Politics and Policy Making in Education*, London: Routledge.

Billig, M. (1995) *Banal Nationalism*, London: Sage Publications.

Cohen, P. (1997) *Rethinking the Youth Question: Education, Labour and Cultural Studies*, Basingstoke: Macmillan.

Cohen, S. (1973 [1972]) *Folk Devils and Moral Panics*, St Albans: Paladin.

Community Cohesion Panel (2001) *Community Cohesion: A Report of the Independent Review Team*, London: Home Office.

Dwyer, C. (1999) 'Negotiations of femininity and identity for young British Muslim women', in N. Laurie, C. Dwyer, S. Holloway and F. Smith (eds) *Geographies of New Femininities*, Harlow: Pearson.

Geertz, C. (1983) *Local Knowledge: Further Essays in Interpretive Anthropology*, New York, NY: Basic Books.

Gilroy, P. (1993) 'The end of antiracism', in J. Donald and A. Rattansi (eds) *'Race', Culture and Difference*, London: Sage Publications/Open University Press.

Hebdige, D. (1987 [1979]) *Subculture: The Meaning of Style*, London: Methuen.

hooks, b. (1992) *Black Looks*, New York, NY: Routledge.

Hopkins, P. (2007) 'Global events, national politics and local lives: young Muslim men in Scotland', *Environment and Planning*, vol 39, no 5, pp 1119-33.

Huntington, S. (2002) *The Clash of Civilizations and the Remaking of World Order*, New York, NY: Free Press.

Jones, S. (1988) *Black Culture, White Youth: The Reggae Tradition from JA to UK*, Basingstoke: Macmillan.

Keith, M. (1993) *Race, Riots and Policing: Lore and Disorder in a Multi-Racist Society*, London: UCL Press.

McGrellis, S. (2005) 'Pure and bitter spaces: gender, identity and territory in Northern Irish youth transitions', *Gender and Education*, vol 17, no 5, pp 515-29.

May, S. (ed) (1999) *Critical Multiculturalism: Rethinking Multicultural and Antiracist Education*, London: Sage Publications.

Mercer, K. (1994) *Welcome to the Jungle: New Positions in Black Cultural Studies*, London: Routledge.

Moberg, M. (2008) 'The internet and the construction of a transnational Christian metal music scene', *Culture and Religion*, vol 9, no 1, pp 81-99.

Nayak, A. (2003) *Race, Place and Globalization: Youth Cultures in a Changing World*, Oxford: Berg.

Nayak, A. (2008) 'Young people's geographies of racism and anti-racism: the case of North East England', in C. Dwyer and C. Bressey (eds) *New Geographies of Race and Racism*, Aldershot: Ashgate.

Ouseley, H. (2001) *Community Pride Not Prejudice: Making Diversity Work in Bradford*, Bradford: Bradford Vision.

Parekh, B. (2000) *The Future of Multi-Ethnic Britain: The Parekh Report*, London: Runnymede Trust.

Phillips, D., Davids, C. and Ratcliffe, P. (2007) 'British Asian narratives of urban space', *Transactions for the Institute of British Geographers*, vol 32, no 2, pp 217-34.

Rattansi, A. (1993) 'Changing the subject: racism, culture and education', in J. Donald and A. Rattansi (eds) *'Race', Culture and Difference*, London: Sage Publications/Open University Press.

Said, E. W. (1995 [1978]) *Orientalism: Western Conceptions of the Orient*, Harmondsworth: Penguin.

Swann, Lord (1985) *Education for All*, London: The Stationery Office.

Williams, R. (1976) *Keywords: A Vocabulary of Culture and Society*, Glasgow: Fontana/Croom Helm.

Thirteen

Children, young people and sexuality

Mary Jane Kehily

Introduction

In Western societies, sexuality remains a site of regulation and
emancipation, much struggled over in contemporary debates on law
and morality. This chapter will explore the domain of the sexual as
it features in the lives of children and young people. Adult ideals of
childhood innocence commonly fuel the idea that children should be
protected from sexual knowledge. In the present climate, such ideals
readily tumble into a general mistrust of adults and fear of that most
vilified of sexual categories, the paedophile. While it is not possible to
cover all aspects of sexuality in relation to children and young people,
the chapter aims to cover some key themes and issues as documented
in research-based accounts. Specifically, the chapter is divided into five
sections, heuristically devised to make sense of the literature: theories
of sexuality; sexual socialisation; school-based sexualities; gay pride and
post-pride; and a case study on teenage pregnancy. First, however, the
chapter looks at the question of what is sexuality.

Weeks (1986: 11) points to some of the difficulties of understanding
sexuality in contemporary culture, suggesting that it has become a
'transmission belt for a wide variety of needs and desire: love and
anger, tenderness and aggression, intimacy and adventure, romance
and predatoriness, pleasure and pain, empathy and power'. For Weeks,
the powerful feelings produced by sexuality indicate that the realm
of the sexual is a vehicle for strong emotions, deeply embedded in
Western culture. The range and scope of these feelings convey notions
that sexuality is a natural force, takes place between members of the
opposite sex and that through sex we are 'expected to find ourselves
and our place in the world' (1986: 12). The cultural assumptions
surrounding sexuality suggest that the term 'sex' can define both an
act and a category of person. The approach to sexuality as natural

and naturalised is one that, according to Weeks, has been endorsed by modern sexologists who have codified and thereby regulated the ways in which sexualities are lived and organised. He postulates that the sexual tradition of the West offers two ways of looking at sex: sex as dangerous and needing to be channelled by society into appropriate forms; and sex as healthy and good but repressed and distorted by society. Weeks (1986: 81) poses an alternative to the binary of regulatory versus the libertarian positions:

> [s]ex only attains meaning in social relations, which implies that we can only make appropriate choices around sexuality by understanding its social and political context. This involves a decisive move away from the morality of 'acts' which has dominated sexual theorising for hundreds of years and in the direction of a new relational perspective which takes into account context and meanings.

In this formulation, Weeks suggests that sexual practices can be understood in relation to, and as part of, wider social relations in an exploration of the contexts in which acts become meaningful.

Theories of sexuality

Giddens (1993: 181) describes sexuality as 'a terrain of fundamental political struggle and also a medium of emancipation'. But how has this status been achieved? In Western culture, psychoanalytic traditions have been central to defining what sex is and how it can be understood. Psychoanalytic approaches to sexuality assume the existence of an active and insistent unconscious in which repressed desires speak through the subject. Freud offers a framework for understanding the interior landscape of the unconscious, providing a perspective on human sexuality that points to the significance of unconscious 'events' and early life experiences in the emergent sexuality of individuals. In *Three Essays on the Theory of Sexuality* (1977 [1905]), Freud refutes the Romantic notion of childhood innocence and proposes that child development is marked by specific psychosexual stages as innately sexual individuals negotiate their way to adulthood, from sexually amorphous baby to gendered adult. Freud's notion of 'polymorphous perversity' emphasises the unboundaried nature of desire and suggests that practices that are usually seen as deviations from the sexual norm can be viewed more precisely as stages in the development of human sexuality. According to Freud, the child's resolution of the psychic dramas with key adults, characterised as the 'Oedipal' and 'castration complexes', has a direct bearing on the shaping of sexual subjectivity. Freud's analysis of child development proposes a gendered model of sexual subjectivity that is biologically marked and psychically significant as it centres on the possession, or lack, of a penis. Boys' resolution of the Oedipal drama involves, Freud suggests, giving up desire for the mother due to fear of castration by the father. In contrast, girls' resolution of the Oedipal drama involves relinquishing desire for the mother and replacing it with desire for the father. Freud's analysis of child development and human sexuality has been both generatively received and heavily critiqued by subsequent theorists. While Kristeva (1982), Lacan (1977) and Mitchell (1974), for example, developed Freud's ideas in different ways, second-wave feminists such as Millett (1970), Firestone (1972) and Friedan (1974) took issue with the inherent biologism of Freudian accounts and the lack of attention to power differentials in gender relations.

Foucault's (1978) *The History of Sexuality*, vol 1, begins with a striking counternarrative to the Freudian-influenced 'repressive hypothesis', which posits that the Victorian era was associated with sexual repression and inhibition. Foucault, by contrast, suggests that there has been a 'discursive explosion' on sexual matters since the 17th century. Foucault proposes that sexuality is a historical construct that is brought into being by and through *discourses* in fields such as medicine, religion, law and education, which were underpinned by a notion that sexuality was a thing to be known and spoken about in the 'public interest'. From this perspective, the sexual conduct of a population becomes an object of classification, administration and regulation and Foucault argues that the deployment of discursive strategies in sexual matters creates the conditions for the production of sexual identities. Discourses evolve patterns, processes and ways of operating or, in Foucaultian terms, 'discursive practices' that can be deployed to observe and define individuals and groups. Foucault cites the categories of the hysterical woman; the homosexual; the masturbating child; and the sex worker as actively generated by discourses of sexuality. Within this framework, psychoanalysis can also be seen as an example of a discursive practice that has emerged within a medical discourse to study and define the psychic lives of individuals.

Discourses also function as 'regimes of truth', a phrase that captures the cumulative power of discursive formations as they acquire normative status within the realm of the social. Foucault (1978: 150) suggests that the aim of the 'discursive explosion' of sexuality is to incorporate the sexual into the field of state rationality wherein power can be exercised to reinforce the state itself. He further notes (1978: 30) that '[t]he sex of children and adolescents has become an important area of contention around which innumerable institutional devices and discursive strategies have been deployed'. The power of the state, exercised through forms of governmentality, should not be seen, however, as simply repressive. Rather, power in Foucaultian terms is productive and relational; it can be administrative and regulatory but, importantly, it can also be generated from below in forms of creative appropriation and resistance. In the modern era, discourses of sexuality offer a complex means of policing the person in which individuals are represented as embodying a sexually constituted internality that can be accessed and monitored.

Sexual socialisation

Parker's (1991) compelling ethnography of sexual culture in contemporary Brazil provides a vivid account of the contextual specificities of sexual socialisation. In colonial Brazilian society, patriarchal authority and control shaped relations between the sexes in familiar ways. While daughters were subject to socialisation processes that located them within the domestic sphere and imposed a rigid set of restrictions, especially during puberty, sons were active in plantation life and commonly initiated into sex through relationships with slaves. In the postcolonial period, sexual socialisation begins in early childhood. Girls are largely shrouded from knowledge of their bodies, especially sexual knowledge associated with menstruation and intimate relationships. Adolescent girls find their movements outside of the domestic sphere further curtailed by the fear of 'dishonour' they could bring upon the family. Boys and young men have a markedly different experience. From around the age of five, they are encouraged, indeed coerced, into spending time with other boys and young men outside the home, where the feminine is viewed as a source of contagion and the fear of being seen as sissy haunts many boyhood experiences. Initiation into the culture of heterosexual masculinity includes sexual learning through pornography and prostitution; many young men report that their fathers bought pornographic magazines for them and took them on their first trip to a brothel.

Within the context of asymmetrical power relations between males and females, ways of thinking about sexuality become symbolically coded and embodied in particular ways. The phallus becomes associated with an aggressive form of patriarchal power central to notions of masculinity. As Parker (1991: 39) argues, a woman and, by implication, feminine sexuality in general is characterised by 'the fissure between her legs – the mysterious entrance that somehow defines her entire being'. The mystery, however, is not necessarily enticing or benign; the vagina is commonly associated with notions of impurity, a site of pollution through urine, menstrual blood and venereal disease. Parker suggests that the female figures of virgin, whore and *sapatão* (big shoes or dyke) function symbolically to define the domain of the feminine, articulating both the positive and negative features of a socially constructed feminine role. Parker's ethnography powerfully demonstrates that sexual culture in Brazilian society reflects its unique postcolonial history, drawing on perspectives from organised religion and modern science/medicine as key features in the organisation of sexual relations.

In looking at contemporary sexualities in the UK, a different, but not so dissimilar, picture emerges. Sexual socialisation in the UK has been framed by the post-war period of intense social change. The loosening up of traditional structures and the emergence of 'permissiveness' and countercultural forms in the 1960s signalled a changing sexual climate (Green, 1999). Philip Larkin is famous for suggesting (in his poem 'Annus Mirabilis'; Larkin, 1974) that sexual intercourse began in 1963. The date may be speculative but Larkin's poem imaginatively, if a little miserably, captures the zeitgeist of the 1960s and 1970s as a period of sexual liberation that changed the lives of young people forever. The period was marked by significant social and scientific advances: the advent of the Pill, gay liberation, second-wave feminism and abortion rights, 'a woman's right to choose' and a proliferation of ways to talk about and practise sex – in Foucaultian terms, an 'incitement to discourse'. By the end of the 1980s, sexual practices were changing further in the light of HIV/AIDS.

Influential studies of young people's sexual relations, conducted at about the same time as Parker's ethnography, also highlight the asymmetrical gender relations that characterise young people's sexual cultures and early sexual experiences. Researchers for the Women, Risk and Aids Project (WRAP) and the Men, Risk and AIDS project interviewed a large sample of young people in London and Manchester, aged between 16 and 21 (Thomson and Scott, 1990; 1991). Focusing on the disjuncture between young people's heterosexual relationships and practices to safeguard sexual health, the studies provide an up-close account of the conservatism inherent in young people's practices of intimacy. These studies suggest that young people's sexual encounters are strongly shaped by normative gender arrangements that define young men as active and young women as passive to the point where masculine dominance exists for young women as 'the male in the head' (Holland et al, 1998). The studies suggest that the public character of intimate encounters placed young men in the impossible position of sexual hero and conqueror while young women remained vulnerable to male advances and a damaged reputation. Importantly for sexual health, young people's sexual practice was shaped by peer group values and normative gender relations rather than sexual safety. Young women, for example, did not like to ask their partners to use condoms as, in keeping with local mores, this indicated that they may be sexually loose and open to the charge of 'slag'. To avert the moral pincer movement of entrapment and censorship, young women tended to characterise all sexual encounters as a pursuit for love, trust and companionship. Some young people in the study did successfully negotiate more equal relationships, usually in contexts where they could establish some privacy and develop a sense of themselves as a couple.

A further portrayal of young people's sexual socialisation in the UK is provided by modern artist Tracey Emin's (2004, 2005) autobiographical accounts of sexual initiation in her home town of Margate. As a working-class girl growing up in a down-at-heel English seaside resort in the 1970s, Emin recalls a local practice where teenage girls were 'broken in' for sex by local boys. First sex for young women in this context could involve the less than romantic experience of penetration, and possibly coercion, in the public pleasure zone of the sea front. Emin herself was 'broken in' at the age of 13. Characteristically, she turns personal experience into art in the feature film *Top Spot* (2004). Emin introduces the film with an establishing narrative:

> *Top Spot* was here. Here somewhere. Giant ballroom with chandeliers and red velvet curtains. We'd snog and kiss, be fingered, titted up. It was a place to experiment. You know what top spot is don't you? Top spot is when a man has sex with a woman or a girl, when the penis hits the neck of the womb. That's when it hits top spot. I mean who would ever call a teenage disco *Top Spot*? (quoted in Hemingway, 2006: 437)

Top Spot creatively reveals the messiness of adolescent girls' life-worlds as they seek pleasure, encounter pain and have fun. Teenage protagonists retell Emin's story and that of her friends as they come of age in the faded splendour of Margate's tourist attractions. Sexual experimentation became part of the girls' repertoire in the real–life seaside postcard of snatched moments and erotic opportunity redolent with comedic potential. Controversially, the film includes Emin's friend Laura's experience of teenage pregnancy and her subsequent suicide. Emin's collected volume, *Strangeland* (2005), further explores the pain of teenage sexual activity in its documentation of incidents of unplanned pregnancy, sexual coercion and sexually transmitted disease. Emin's work, and the WRAP research project and the Men, Risk and AIDS project, serve as a powerful reminder that the sexual liberation heralded by the 1960s and 1970s remains patchy, haphazard and contextually specific. Working-class young women, for example, remain subject to structures of constraint. Amid all the trauma of showing and telling, however, Emin (2004) insists that the overarching message of *Top Spot* is an empowering one:

> When you're growing up things can look really desperate and really totally bleak. And I'm here to tell you it doesn't have to be like that. You can turn every thing around. You can turn your experiences into something positive and that's what I hope the film gives to people, a positive outlook in the end. (quoted in Hemingway, 2006: 437)

School-based sexualities

How do ideas about sexuality relate to young people in school? The concept of the 'hidden curriculum' has been used by educationalists to acknowledge that learning extends the boundaries of the official curriculum and may have inadvertent effects. What is learned by pupils may not fit with the intended aims of teachers and educational policy makers, and pupils learn to conform or resist the official culture of the school (see Hammersley and Woods, 1976, for an early exposition of these themes). The 'hidden curriculum' can also be seen in terms of the regulation of sex–gender categories. Within the context of the school much informal learning takes place concerning issues of gender and sexuality; the homophobia of young men, the sexual reputations of young women, the pervasive presence of heterosexuality as an 'ideal' and a practice mark out the terrain for the production of gendered and sexualised identities. Furthermore, such social learning is commonly overt and explicit rather than hidden.

The Foucaultian perspectives discussed earlier have been influential in many analyses of school-based sexualities (Sears, 1992; Mac an Ghaill, 1994; Britzman, 1995; Epstein and Johnson, 1998; Rasmussen, 2006). Schools can be conceptualised as a discursive field in which a number of discourses offer competing and sometimes contradictory ways of understanding the aims and purposes of education in contemporary society. In the domain of the sexual, for example, the discourse of the official school assumes that students are sexually innocent and in need of protection while the discourse of the informal school assumes an active and knowing sexuality manifest in peer relations and exchanges between pupils and teachers. Discursive practices bring into being 'the pupil'; school children who can be observed, known and categorised according to their orientation to the learning process. In keeping with a Foucaultian framework, the hierarchical power relations of schools are acknowledged in specific ways such as teacher/pupil, adult/child, male/female, headteacher/classroom teacher. Many studies also work with the generative Foucaultian notion of power-as-everywhere, indicating that the realm of the sexual offers scope for the creative reworking of power in moments of activity and agency. Contemporary studies of sexuality and schooling rest on the premise that sexual identities are not biologically given but are created through institutional and lived practices. Moreover, schools can be seen as sites for the *production* of gendered/sexualised identities rather than agencies that passively reflect dominant power relations.

In my own study (Kehily, 2002), I explored the ways in which sexuality weaves into school experience and considered why the sexual arena is so highly charged, contradictory and combustible. Ethnographic observations led me to conclude that in the context of the increased regulation of school life through testing, monitoring and processes of individualisation, school-based sexual cultures become important to young people as autonomous, peer-generated sites of resistance, providing 'adult-free and education-free zones in which students can collectively negotiate what is acceptable, what is desirable and what is "too much"'. Drawing strength from each other, young people in school can use sexuality to challenge teachers, generate humour and define their own rules (Kehily and Nayak, 1997). Creative, multiply invoked expressions of an ever-present sexuality are a recognisable part of life in secondary schools. It is also to be found in primary schools. Despite Romantic imaginings and adult investments in notions of childhood innocence, pre-pubescence is also a period fused with erotic events and desires, sexual learning and experimentation.

In a qualitative study focusing on children's relationships in primary schools, myself and colleagues (Kehily et al, 2002) observed routine events and practices that appeared to counter Freud's claim that middle childhood was a period of sexual latency. Rather, we found that sex talk and sexualised themes informed the everyday conversations of girls aged 9-10. Among the most commonly spoken about subjects were puberty and periods, erotic attachments and imagined romantic encounters. A recurrent theme generating much excitement involved the various declarations of interest in boys in the class. One particular group of girls worked with an economy of desire that placed 'bad boys' at the apex of attraction. These girls were drawn to the good-looking, high-profile boys who, in the Byronic tradition, were compelling, dangerous and treated girls badly. This desire could be expressed as a form of masochistic pleasure in the pursuit of unrequited love:

> Lakbiah: [referring to Sunil] If he killed me I don't care but I still love him.
>
> Selena: [referring to Ben] I love him, I love him, I love him.
>
> Lakbiah: I don't mind 'cos it's me who likes him. I don't care if he doesn't like me, he's still for me.
>
> Sarah: [to Selena of Ben] Do you mind, do you mind if you never see him again in secondary school?
>
> Selena: I don't mind, I still know I love him.

While this approach to boys may not appear to be an endorsement of new femininities or indeed a healthy expression of girlhood desire, we suggested that the 'masochistic' selfless female can be seen as one version of erotic desire that exists alongside other more agentic forms. Holding such discussions within the context of a same-sex friendship group provides the girls with a relatively 'safe' space for fantasy and the articulation of different forms of intimacy and connection.

Gay pride and post-pride

In *Telling Sexual Stories*, Plummer (1995) reminds us that while same-sex attraction may be universal across time and space, the homosexual is a modern Western concept invented by a Belgian doctor, circa 1867. Prior to Stonewall and the gay liberation movement of the mid-20th century, homosexuality was criminalised, forced into clandestine spaces and subterranean existence, so the story goes. A changing social climate, discussed earlier, however, makes the 'coming out' story tellable to an audience that is ready to hear it. In the new sexual climate, homosexual culture can come out of the closet and individuals can tell their personal story of being gay. Coming out heralds the 'end of a long silence' of guilt, shame and resistance and the emergence of a gay identity that can be, for the first time, out and proud. Plummer (1995: 57) writes: 'Coming out was the critical life experience of lesbians and gays during the 1970s and 1980s' and served both as a way of organising politically and a personal narrative of self. Coming-out stories can be viewed as a specific genre of storytelling that obeys certain conventions within a specific temporal sequence. The story begins in childhood. The gay adult recalls that they were different and had trouble fitting in. Childhood was an unhappy time accompanied by feelings of guilt and shame, not to mention the hurt of homophobic abuse and alienation. Later, usually in early adulthood, there is a realisation that other gay people also exist. The 'finding' of a community marks the emergence of a more confident self that prioritises sexual identity. Plummer cites many examples of coming-out stories from a range of sources, marked by familiar leitmotifs of isolation, resolution and beautifully remembered details.

McNair (2002) expands on this observation by adding that, despite the intimate nature of sexuality, these struggles have taken place in public and are, increasingly, part of the public domain. The coming-out story no longer holds the same caché in the media-saturated world of celebrity culture, reality television and soaps where queer is reclaimed and has become commonplace, existing alongside many other forms of sexual expression. McNair's analysis suggests that the post-war period in the West has been characterised by the commodification of desire, witnessed in the increased sexualisation of culture across a range of local and global media. Central to McNair's argument is the role of the media and particularly new media technologies. McNair (2002: 11) suggests that new media technologies have aided the growth of a more commercialised, less regulated and more pluralistic sexual culture, promoting, in his terms 'a democratisation of desire'. For McNair, the 'democratisation of desire' describes the present period in which there is popular and widespread access to diverse forms of sexual expression; the availability of pornography through the internet, for example, and simultaneously there are more ways of being a sexual subject within

Western cultures. If we think about these themes in relation to young people's lives it may be possible to suggest that young people are the newly emergent sexual citizens of a democratised and richly diverse sexual culture. But are they? In the following section I focus on the experience of teenage pregnancy as a case study to indicate that a democracy of desire may not be available to all.

Case study: teenage pregnancy

On the political stage, in the UK and the US, teenage pregnancy is regarded as a social problem. The Social Exclusion Unit's report on teenage pregnancy in England (SEU, 1999) was followed by the setting up of the Teenage Pregnancy Unit, a cross-government initiative to reduce the under-18 conception rate by half by 2010. Among the range of strategies to reduce teenage pregnancy, the Unit was established to provide support for young mothers, as well as offering sex and relationship education, easy access to contraception and life skills designed to delay early sexual activity. These interventions seek to address policy concerns regarding the long-term pattern of 'intergenerational transmission' that sees early motherhood repeated in subsequent generations. However, the 'problem' of teenage pregnancy needs to be placed within the experience of first-time motherhood more generally. The trend in the UK and most Western countries is towards later motherhood for the majority of women and early motherhood for a minority. In 2003, the average age of first-time mothers in the UK was 29.3 – an increase of 2.5 years over a 20-year period. Large-scale surveys in the UK, such as the Millennium Cohort Study (Hawhes et al, 2004), indicate that the age at which women become mothers reflects their socioeconomic status. Typically, women with higher educational qualifications and professional careers delay the birth of their first child until their late thirties or early forties, while for other women, motherhood comes early, in the mid-teenage years before education has been completed or a place in the labour market achieved. Viewed in this context, teenage mothers appear *out of place* and, from certain perspectives, can be viewed as aberrant, deviant and excessive. Skeggs' (2004) analysis of social class and culture in contemporary Britain points to the enduring status of working-class women as embodying an overly abundant and unruly sexuality that places them dangerously close to the reviled figure of the prostitute. In the past, Skeggs suggests, working-class femininity was redeemable through respectability. In the contemporary period, however, young working-class mothers inevitably fall on the other side of the respectability divide and 'are yet again becoming the abject of the nation' (2004: 23). As Walkerdine et al (2001) point out, teenage pregnancy is largely a working-class affair. Of the 20,000 under-18-year-olds who become mothers every year, the majority are working class and disaffected from school. For middle-class girls, however, pregnancy is usually regarded as a disruption to the educative process and a barrier to educational success. Indeed, the goal of a professional career 'acts as a contraceptive for middle-class girls' (Walkerdine et al, 2001: 194).

A recent research project exploring the experiences of first-time mothers in the UK (Thomson and Kehily, 2008) examined the socioeconomic differences by asking whether motherhood was becoming the site of a new social division between women. The study concluded that age was the 'master category' through which normative notions of mothering are constituted. For teenage mothers, pregnancy constructs them simultaneously as childlike and mature. Pregnancy signals entry into adulthood, but for many young mothers, other signifiers of adulthood such as full-time employment, living independently and sexual partnership may not be part of their profile. Additionally, pregnancy was not experienced in terms of 'choice'; rather, it was something that happened to them and now needed to be accommodated. Many young women in the study found themselves at the centre of familial dramas. Their pregnancy produced strong emotions and, occasionally, moments of conflict for family members, prompting the young women protagonists to look to soap operas and celebrity culture to make sense of their situation. In most cases the family rallied round, pooling resources, sharing advice, attending the birth and actively involving themselves in post-natal care and support of mother and baby.

Some young mothers in the study were accessed through the Milton Keynes Christian Foundation. This facility runs programmes to support young women (aged 15-18) who are pregnant or have a young child. The emphasis is on a range of activities and training sessions to support young mothers, such as parenting classes, relaxation classes, literacy and numeracy classes and support with CVs and job applications – providing practical learning and skills development that prepare young people for parenthood in direct ways. Young people attending the course reported feeling supported and safe. The following biographical profile provides a glimpse into the experience of teenage motherhood drawn from the account of one of the respondents.

Biographical case profile: Sophie Bishop, age 17, eight months pregnant with first child

Situation

- Sophie lives alone in a residential care facility for young mothers and mothers-to-be, run by the local council and a housing association in Milton Keynes.

- Pregnancy disrupted her education, family life and relationship. Her parents kicked her out of home and her boyfriend broke up with her. Seven months into the pregnancy she is reconciled with her parents and her boyfriend.

- Abortion was not seen as an option. She had a humanitarian view that the baby did not ask to be put there and was now her responsibility.

- She had a personal resolution to have the baby despite the trauma of early pregnancy and an active reversal of life plans – she now plans to complete her education and build a career when her child is older.

- She is aware of dominant discourses that position her in negative ways.

- Her construction of herself in interview is as a good mother; competent, responsible and keen to parent.

- She sees motherhood as her route into adulthood. She has no regrets, loves being pregnant and 'can't wait' for the baby's birth. She is ready for the life change, happy to give up the pub/club scene.

- She has changed priorities, new friends and is child-focused.

Interviewing Sophie in the mother and baby residential unit leads to the following observations.

> Sophie meets me and takes me to her unit. It is very small
> – a kitchen/lounge and one bedroom with room for a
> single bed, a chest of drawers and nothing else ... I felt that
> the unit was compact and had everything she needed but

that it was also an infantilising space for a young mother-
to-be. The bedroom in particular seemed to emphasise
her youthful status as a child who was expecting a child. It
was a girl's room, there was a cartoon motif on her duvet
– it's not *My Little Pony* but it reminds me of that. A Moses
basket on a stand and a baby relaxer lined the corridor-like
space next to the bed.... She says it's good to know we are
interested in what young women have to say. (fieldnotes,
22/08/05)

Despite my initial feelings that the residential unit appeared to
infantilise her, Sophie spoke of it as a place where she has found
herself and managed to put her life back together again. Overcoming
the trauma of early pregnancy, her parents' hostile reaction and the
break-up with her boyfriend has been possible through the stability
of the residential centre and the Christian Foundation. Through the
Foundation for Parents course, Sophie has found a way to articulate an
identity as a mother-to-be, in which motherhood offers her a unique
opportunity to re-evaluate her life and become an adult. Throughout
the interview Sophie is keen to counter negative stereotypes by
asserting her readiness for parenthood:

It's given me so much more confidence.... You do feel a lot
more grown up – I do anyway, in myself. I feel like I've got
this like thinking cap on where it's made me grown up all
of a sudden. Before I was rubbish with money and now I
have to budget ... I think it does make you rethink about
everything 'cos you can't be selfish knowing you've got
a little baby and its needs are much more important than
your needs are.

Conclusion

This chapter has explored sexuality as it features in the lives of children
and young people. Beginning with a consideration of sexuality itself,
the chapter asked what it is and why it appears to be a vehicle for
such strong emotions, needs and desires. Drawing on the work of
Weeks (1986), a recurrent theme of the chapter suggests that sexuality
acquires significance and is given meaning within social relations.
The chapter also focused on Freud's contribution to understanding
sexuality and, importantly, his recognition of children as sexual subjects
inextricably caught up in psychosocial dramas in the transition from

child to adult. Freudian perspectives were contrasted with the work of Foucault, who influentially proposed that sexuality was brought into being by and through discourses. Foucaultian approaches to sexuality have been influential in school-based studies of sexuality, providing generative ways of understanding the emergent sexual identities of young people. Moving on to empirically based studies, the chapter emphasised the importance of time and place to the shaping of the sexual domain. Here contemporary Brazil and Margate in the UK exist as illustrative examples of sexual cultures that are both nationally specific and locally inflected. Further sections can also be read through the lens of place and context as young people's sexual identities emerge in the institutional sites of school and family. The final section of the chapter focused on teenage pregnancy as a case study that biographically situated the contradictory nature of sexuality as lived by a young woman in the UK.

References

Britzman, D. (1995) 'What is this thing called love?', *Taboo: The Journal of Culture and Education*, vol 1, pp 65-95.

Emin, T. (2004) *Top Spot* (screenplay and direction), London: BBC3.

Emin, T. (2005) *Strangeland*, London: Spectre.

Epstein, D. and Johnson, R. (1998) *Schooling Sexualities*, Buckingham: Open University Press.

Firestone, S. (1972) *The Dialectic of Sex: The Case for Feminist Revolution*, London: Paladin.

Foucault, M. (1978) *The History of Sexuality*, vol 1, trans R. Hurley, Harmondsworth: Penguin.

Freud, S. (1977 [1905]) *Three Essays on the Theory of Sexuality*, Pelican Freud, vol 7, trans J. Strachey, Harmondsworth: Penguin.

Friedan, B. (1974) *The Feminine Mystique*, New York: Dell.

Giddens, A. (1993) *The Transformation of Intimacy, Sexuality, Love and Eroticism in Modern Societies*, Cambridge: Polity Press.

Green, J. (1999) *All Dressed Up: The Sixties and the Countercultural*, London: Pimlico.

Hammersley, M. and Woods, P. (eds) (1976) *The Process of Schooling: A Sociological Reader*, London: Routledge & Kegan Paul.

Hawhes, D., Joshi, H. and Ward, K. (2004) *Unequal Entry to Motherhood and Unequal Start to Life: Evidence From the First Survey of the UK Millennium Cohort*, CLS Cohort Studies Working Paper No 6, London: Centre for Longitudinal Studies, Institute of Education.

Hemingway, J. (2006) 'Sexual learning and the seaside: relocating the "dirty weekend" and teenage girls' sexuality', *Sex Education*, vol 6, no 4, pp 429–43.

Holland, J., Ramazanoglu, C., Sharpe, S. and Thomson, R. (1998) *The Male in the Head: Young People, Heterosexuality and Power*, London: Tufnell Press.

Kehily, M.J. (2002) *Sexuality, Gender and Schooling: Shifting Agendas in Social Learning*, London: Routledge.

Kehily, M.J. and Nayak, A. (1997) 'Lads and laughter: humour and the production of heterosexual hierarchies', *Gender and Education*, vol 9, no 1, pp 69-87.

Kehily, M.J., Mac an Ghaill, M., Epstein, D. and Redman, P. (2002) 'Private girls and public worlds, producing femininities in the primary school', *Discourse: Studies in the Cultural Politics of Education*, vol 23, no 2, pp 167-77.

Kristeva, J. (1982) *Powers of Horror*, trans L. Roudiez, New York: Columbia University Press.

Lacan, J. (1977) *The Four Fundamental Concepts of Psychoanalysis*, trans A. Sheridan, ed J.A. Miller, London: Tavistock.

Larkin, P. (1974) *High Windows*, London: Faber.

Mac an Ghaill, M. (1994) *The Making of Men: Masculinities, Sexualities and Schooling*, Buckingham: Open University Press.

McNair, B. (2002) *Striptease Culture: Sex, Media and the Democracy of Desire*, London: Routledge.

Millett, K. (1970) *Sexual Politics*, New York: Doubleday.

Mitchell, J. (1974) *Psychoanalysis and Feminism*, London: Allen Lane.

Parker, R.G. (1991) *Bodies, Pleasures, Passions: Sexual Culture in Contemporary Brazil*, Boston, MA: Beacon Press.

Plummer, K. (1995) *Telling Sexual Stories: Power, Change and Social Worlds*, London: Routledge.

Rasmussen, M.L. (2006) *Becoming Subjects: Sexualities and Secondary School*, New York: Routledge.

Sears, J. (ed) (1992) *Sexuality and the Curriculum: The Politics and Practices of Sexuality Education*, New York, NY: Teachers' College Press.

SEU (Social Exclusion Unit) (1999) *Teenage Pregnancy*, London: HMSO.

Skeggs, B. (2004) *Class, Self, Culture*, London: Routledge.

Thomson, R. and Kehily, M. J. (2008) *The Making of Modern Motherhood: Memories, Representations, Practices*, Milton Keynes: The Open University.

Thomson, R. and Scott, S. (1990) *Researching Sexuality in the Light of AIDS: Historical and Methodological Issues*, London: Tufnell Press.

Thomson, R. and Scott, S. (1991) *Learning about Sex: Young Women and the Social Construction of Sexual Identity*, London: Tufnell Press.

Walkerdine, V., Lucey, H. and Melody, J. (2001) *Growing Up Girl: Psychosocial Explorations of Gender and Class*, Basingstoke: Palgrave.

Weeks, J. (1986) *Sexuality*, London: Tavistock.

Fourteen

Children and young people's voice

Mary Kellett

Introduction

In this chapter I explore the concept of children's voice, differentiating this at the outset from children's participation – the frequency with which these two concepts are confused or used interchangeably does not always serve children well. Due attention needs to be given to both as they each represent distinct aspects of children's human rights. Voice is the right to express one's views freely – including an entitlement to be listened to. Participation is the right to be actively involved in matters affecting one's own and others' lives – including decision making.

I begin with an exposition of voice as a concept and where this sits within childhood discourses. This is followed by a discussion of discursive spaces, audience and influence as important elements in the voice continuum (Lundy, 2007). I then examine the power relations that are at work in children's voice and discuss the growth of the political dimension. This is followed by a more in-depth look at one typology of child voice – pupil voice. The chapter concludes with a reflection on implementation issues from children's perspectives and a case study that embeds some of the theoretical frameworks that have been explored. Along the way, I pose some fundamental questions: is voice quintessentially about speaking out or about being listened to? Is child voice in the domain of human rights or the domain of the adult gift? Are some children's voices more powerful than others, and if so, why?

The concept of voice

Hart (2002) defines voice as personal perspectives, expressed both internally and interpersonally, that develop the human capacity for existential thought and choice. This is a useful, if somewhat clinical, definition but it fails to take account of social and cultural dimensions. Individual voices are not neutral, they are layered with other people's voices, and the social practices and contexts they invoke (Maybin, 2001). Voice is surely a social construct operating in a cultural context where shared meaning is negotiated. This immediately raises problems for children's voice because in order to have influence, their voice has to transcend the cultural boundaries of childhood and negotiate a shared understanding in the adult world, yet much of children's voice is not expressed in words – least of all adult words – and the rich tapestry of their non-verbal communication frequently goes unheard.

Lundy (2007: 933) takes the concept of children's voice much further than Hart. She conceptualises it as being constituted in four parts, not one:

- Space: Children must be given the opportunity to express a view.

- Voice: Children must be facilitated to express their views.

- Audience: The view must be listened to.

- Influence: The view must be acted upon as appropriate.

This is a very helpful perspective because it depicts an explicit chronology for voice and highlights the inefficacy of voice operating in a vacuum. There have to be the right conditions in place before children can exercise voice and the mechanisms to carry that voice to an audience in a way that can influence society. Creating space for children to express their views is underpinned by the 'assurance' of this cited in Article 12 of the UNCRC (UN, 1989). This means that adults have to be proactive, provide for, and encourage children to express their views in a safe space without fear of reprisal. Equally, children have a right to dissent – not all children want to express a view and some are hostile to the endless round of government consultations that do not lead to any tangible benefits for them.

Spaces to develop voice

Several writers support the notion that children's voice cannot just happen and, as Lundy (2007) demonstrates, there is an important prerequisite to voice in the discursive spaces required to enable children to experiment with and develop voice. This supports Lensmire's (1998) assertion of voice as 'project', as requiring work to be done and accords with the Bahktinian perspective (see Maybin, 2001) of the 'struggle' to make words carry meaning when they are populated with different connotations and associations. Children need to take ownership of discursive spaces in order to have their voice heard. However, such spaces commonly have political structures imposed on them that are more familiar in adult forums. There is a need for child-friendly spaces to be created that reflect local needs, interests and children's preferred ways of engagement so that children's voices do not become a tool for reinforcing adult governance (Wyness, 2006). At the United Nations Special Summit on Children's Rights in 2002, children and young people identified some of these discursive spaces as access to child-friendly information; sufficient time to digest the issues on which they have a view; a child-led infrastructure in which to formulate views and training for adults in how to overcome their resistance to child voice (Bennett Woodhouse, 2003; see also Chapter Three).

Audiences to receive voice

The requirement for audience emerges from another phrase in Article 12, which refers to the right of children for their views to be given 'due weight'. This is, arguably, the most powerful mandate in the Article since it gives to children something to which even adults do not have an automatic right to – the right to have their views given due consideration. This means that adults have to *listen* to children and not just *hear* what they have to say. Of course, many children do not express their views in words and to accord children their full rights adults must learn how to listen effectively and learn how to interpret non-verbal cues where appropriate. Here again the reality belies the rhetoric, for adults still have the power to decide how to listen and they can listen and then choose not to act on anything they hear. Once voiced, children's views do not necessarily progress to a point of influence.

Children's voice as influence

A combination of circumstances is needed for child voice to have influence, not least a predisposition on the part of adults to value what children have to say and to appreciate the uniqueness of their perspective. Better understanding should lead to better provision for children. This is entirely dependent on goodwill and explains why there are so many discrepancies in the way child voice is received globally. What would take us a step nearer to influential children's voice is the introduction of a form of listening accountability. Just as the 2002 United Nations Special Summit required governments to demonstrate *how* they provided opportunities for children to participate in decision making, a similar mandate could require organisations that consult with children to give feedback to the children on what action they have taken and how they have dealt with the child perspectives expressed. While there are some excellent examples of consultation activities and joint research projects where children's voices have influenced outcomes and policy, these are relatively sparse on the overall canvass.

Power issues and fear of children's voice

It is interesting to reflect on some of the groups we readily link to the notion of 'having a voice'– minority ethnic groups, gay people, prisoners, disabled people, Travellers and, in some cultures, women. They are all marginalised, relatively powerless groups fighting to establish their fundamental human rights. Children are added to this list for exactly the same reasons of powerlessness and marginalisation, with the additional handicap of minority legal status. As long ago as 1975, Ardener discussed the concept of 'muted voices' in relation to women. He argued that women were a muted group, not because they did not speak, but because when they did so they were forced to use a hegemonic language controlled by men. His followers applied such reasoning to children, arguing that they, like women, would always be dismissed as incomplete or incompetent as long as they were denied access to power and had to use the language of adult patriarchy. It is important to establish at the outset, therefore, that for children, as with some other marginalised groups, 'voice' is an emancipatory struggle.

The contention that adults have power over children is indisputable and has a significant bearing on the control they exercise over how children's views are accessed. In some quarters, child voice is seen as having the potential to undermine adult authority and, according to Kilbourne (1998), is a key reason why the US did not ratify the UNCRC. Fielding (2004) maintains that voice is historically embedded in power relations and that the identities of speakers and listeners impact considerably on whether or not their views are given due weight. Jans (2004) further asserts that gatekeepers may even promote child listening activities as a way of controlling conflicts of interest. Such wielding of adult power is not about empowering children with a voice but rather a cynical manipulation of processes. This is perhaps most noticeable around the issue of pupil voice and is examined in more detail later in the chapter.

One interpretation of voice implies a passive role for children, a perception of voice as a gift in the power of adults to bestow rather than a fundamental right. Terms such as 'giving children a voice' do little to dispel this (Lodge, 2005), nor do documents such as *Working Together: Giving Children and Young People a Say* (DfES, 2004; emphasis added). Adult control is evident where young people are given a voice through their views being 'allowed' to emerge (Hamill and Boyd, 2002). This suggests that children are dependent on adults to provide opportunities where their voices can be heard. Adult control is further evident in the stated goal of 'bringing children to voice' (Thorne, 2002). Historically, Western children have been silenced through oppressive conventions that prize children being 'seen and not heard', or by their voice being distorted in the mediated accounts created by historians, anthropologists, sociologists and psychologists (Lloyd-Smith and Tarr, 2000) or, as suggested earlier, because their voices are muted by the lack of access to language and power. Hendrick (2000) bemoans the inability of children to challenge such adult accounts because they lack an 'authorial voice', warning that children's perspectives will continue to be 'muffled' if they are heard only through adult conversations and actions. In this context, Thorne (2002: 251) concludes that voice is 'a metaphor for political recognition, self-determination and full presence in knowledge'; it is the right to speak *and* to be listened to.

Silencing children's voice

As alluded to earlier, silencing of children's voices happens at a number of levels in various manifestations of adult–child power relations and in the failure to provide discursive space and audience that would afford due weight to their voice. Less obvious is the silencing of child voice through adult mediation. When adults speak on behalf of children, misunderstanding and misrepresenting of a child's view is common (Fielding, 2001; Grover, 2004). Closer attention to the circumstances in which adults speak on behalf of children reveals that this often happens in adult forums that are impenetrable to children and do not reflect their purpose (Wyness, 2006). 'Only when the mentality of adultism has been overcome will it be possible to hear a more authentic and, probably, unsettling set of voices' (Hendrick, 2000: 55).

There have been some stark examples of wholesale disregard of child voice. In 2002, the Scottish Parliament was considering legislation to prohibit the smacking of children. Research was carried out to determine the views of children and reported that over 90% were in favour of a ban on smacking. At first it appeared that the perspectives of children would be upheld and a smacking ban introduced but the results of an adult survey found a majority in favour of smacking and the proposed ban was promptly dropped from the legislation in 2003. It begs the question: why consult with children in the first place if their views are going to be ignored? A cynical answer points to child voice being proudly showcased when it accords with prevailing adult positions but otherwise kept firmly under wraps. During the Second Gulf War, adults were allowed to exercise their democratic right to protest against the invasion of Iraq and deployment of British troops but children were threatened with school suspension if they took time out of lessons to join protest marches (see also Chapter One). Embracing child voice turns markedly lukewarm if the reality rocks the status quo, challenges dominant adult thinking or costs the state money. Even processes that are set up to privilege child voice are not immune to suppression mechanisms. An example is the increasingly fashionable school council, purportedly a vehicle for student voice but where the locus of control is still firmly in the hands of adults. And then there is a layering of the silences. The further a child's voice strays from the articulate, performative ideal that is prized in adult forums, the fainter it becomes. Thus, children living on the margins of society are those whose cultures and values are most likely to be ignored.

Children's voice as a political tool

Heralded by many as the great emancipation charter for children, the UNCRC rather fudged the issue of children's voice in the chosen terminology of Article 12:

Article 12

Parties shall assure to the child *who is capable of forming his or her own views* the right to express those views freely in all matters affecting the child, the views of the child being given due weight in accordance with the age and maturity of the child. (emphasis added)

No such constraints appear in Article 13:

Article 13

The child shall have the right to freedom of expression; this right shall include freedom to seek, receive and impart information and ideas of all kinds, regardless of frontiers, either orally, in writing or in print, in the form of art, or through any other media of the child's choice.

The mixed messages thus transmitted were a licence for governments to apply liberal interpretations and, in the case of the UK, stall for over a decade on the legislation that was to embed children's voice as a fundamental human right (2004 Children Act). On close inspection the right to voice is implicit in Article 12 in 'shall assure to the child who is capable of forming his or her own views' since this makes no reference to the competence or maturity of those views, just the ability to form a view. One could argue that a baby is capable of forming a view about being hungry by crying, in which case neither age nor competence are pertinent. Nevertheless, an apparent lack of clarity resulted in many governments and organisations interpreting Article 12 as presupposing a degree of competence and/or maturity that excludes a sizeable proportion of children (see also Chapter Eight).

In the last few years, the political pendulum has started to swing towards acknowledging child voice. Coad and Lewis (2004) note that the concern to hear children's voice has grown to the extent that any child-related policies or research in the UK now carry an imperative to consult children. 'Acknowledging' child voice and 'consulting' children are a league away from 'recognising' child voice and 'listening' to children but it does indicate that children's rights are beginning to creep up the policy agenda. Certainly, there appears to be a new respect for the worth of children's views and the value of their knowledge and understanding of their own lived experiences.

There are a few high-profile examples in the UK of initiatives that promote the empowerment of children directly through the propagation of children's own voice in political and research arenas. One such is *Headlines* (formerly *Children's Express*), a youth news agency that operates on a world stage (www.headliners.org). In 2006, for example, it sent two of its young people to Kenya to report on how young people were involved in fighting the HIV/AIDS epidemic in that country. Their report was shown on BBC News 24 and Sky News and they were interviewed on BBC News 24 and ITV News. In the same year they had appeared on BBC Radio 4 and on the BBC's World Service as part of the Generation Next season. They also published articles in *The Guardian* and *New Internationalist* magazine.

The UK Youth Parliament (UKYP) (www.ukyouthparliament. org.uk) is run by young people for young people and encourages them to use their energy and passion to change the world, providing opportunities for 11- to 18-year-olds to use their voice in creative ways to bring about social change. UKYP was launched at the House of Commons in 1999 and held its first sitting in February 2001 in London. There are currently over 500 elected Members of Youth Parliament (MYPs) and Deputy MYPs including young people from a variety of ethnic backgrounds as well as those with physical and learning disabilities. Additionally, we have the Scottish Youth Parliament, Funky Dragon in Wales and the Northern Ireland Youth Forum. Nationally, the views of young people are represented in the UKYP Manifesto, which contains statements on the issues MYPs think are most important.

The Children's Research Centre at The Open University (http:// childrens-research-centre.open.ac.uk) is an organisation that exists solely to train and empower children and young people as researchers and to support them to research issues that concern them (Kellett, 2005). It operates at an international level and seeks opportunities for children and young people to disseminate their research and enable their voice to have influence in society. Groups of UK children and young people have presented their research at Cabinet Office forums, government departments and various conference platforms. Child researchers have broadcast on Radio 4 and have been featured in several national newspapers (see also Chapter Three).

Pupil voice

This section of this chapter is devoted to the specific typology of pupil voice for two reasons. The first is that children spend a large percentage of their time in school, it is an essential element of childhood and therefore an important focus for child voice. Second, the pupil voice typology encapsulates most of the issues, contradictions and tensions of the wider debates outlined earlier and brings these together into one concentrated mix on a small stage where tokenism, power posturing and abnegation of human rights are not as easily concealed. In the UK, the school environment is one of the most governed childhood arenas outside of youth offending institutions and a location where children are least able to assert their human rights. Children are positioned as 'passive receptors' of educational processes (James and James, 2004: 117), subordinate to adults who control their time, space and mode of interaction (Mayall, 2000), and pupils' interests are likely to conflict with those of adults (Alderson, 2000). The status of children as active citizens with rights to participate in decisions that have the potential to affect their lives cannot be respected in schools, despite the rhetoric, when the competing demands of acting in the child's best interests subject them to increasing levels of care and control. Devine (2003) maintains that the rights discourse in this context focuses primarily on a child's right to education rather than on a child's experiences within the system itself. Children do not have the right to be consulted in decisions made about which school they might attend or to participate in tribunals making decisions about possible exclusion. Wyness et al (2004) assert that while children have a right to welfare, and necessarily rely on adults to provide this, they also have a right to self-determination. These rights have the potential to conflict with power gatekeepers, for example, when children choose not to attend school.

Rudduck and Flutter (2004) report that there has been considerable progress in facilitating children's voices in some schools, albeit relatively few. Citing the requirements of Article 12, Leitch and Mitchell (2007) note that encouraging such shifts by law is one thing but changing the culture of schools is another. Pertinent here is the liberal interpretation of Article 12 where adults (in this case teachers) decide if a child is capable of forming their own views and how much weight can be given to those views. All of this results in a system of top-down control (Wyness, 2006) that perpetuates the traditional hierarchical power relationships between adults and children. Despite the requirements of the 2002 Education Act that schools consult with their pupils, or the recent requirement that Ofsted inspectors report on how a school seeks and acts on the views of its pupils (Ofsted, 2005), engaging children's voices in an active and meaningful way in schools remains a challenge (Leitch and Mitchell, 2007). The danger is that lip service will be rendered to pupil voice for reasons of a school's accountability (Robinson and Taylor, 2007) rather than for reasons of a pupil's human rights.

Pupils are well aware of the powerful and dominant discourses that are discernible in schools and of the messages about membership that these imply (Rudduck and Fielding, 2006). They understand which ways of speaking, which meanings and which experiences are most likely to be valued. It is well known that pupil voice is overpopulated by the articulate few, which can perpetuate exclusionary practices (Rudduck and Flutter, 2004). There is an implicit contract pupils must enter into, requiring them to 'speak responsibly, intelligently and usefully' (Bragg, 2001: 73). Lensmire (1998: 270) goes on to assert that while some voices are 'opened up', others are 'shut down' in the face of the perceived inadequacies of their words and in the face of hostile audiences. Student voices are formed within an oppressive society that privileges the meanings, values and stories of some over others. Indeed, voice initiatives in schools can sometimes reinforce existing dividing practices rather than question them (Rudduck and Flutter, 2004). This situation worsens if participating children are viewed as privileged and has the potential to create hierarchical power structures within the pupil body. Far from being emancipatory, voice can then become a source of silence and suppression for some pupils (John, 1996).

What can be done to redress some of the imbalanced power relations of school contexts discussed above? Smyth (2006) proposes a shift of emphasis in pedagogic and leadership approaches away from the focus on standards and accountability towards 'relational reforms' that address the emotional and personal needs of pupils, thus engendering confidence, trust and respect. Such an approach would seem to accord with Hendrick's (2000) view that it is not always necessary for children to speak 'with' the voices of the dominant discourse but might speak 'through' it, especially if the dominant discourses implicate resistance.

In relation to pupil voice, Fielding (2001) observed that teaching and learning were largely forbidden areas of inquiry, with softer, 'comfort issues' constituting inquiry agendas. Although teachers are aware of the shifting nature of children's status in society towards a recognition of them as social agents, this is only welcomed if it does not challenge their own roles and authority (Hamill and Boyd, 2002; Devine, 2003). To some extent, this is now changing, with more and more examples emerging of pupils contributing to – or in some cases researching – teaching and learning issues (Rudduck, 2006). This emanates from the requirements of the 2002 Education Act and the subsequent guidance document, *Working Together: Giving Children and Young People a Say* (DfES, 2004), which lays down a mandate for creating opportunities to seek pupils' views. The growth of school councils and the establishment of School Councils UK as an empowering organisation have done much to raise awareness about the potential for students to play a part in the leadership and management of schools. In a few schools some students now sit on governing bodies and have a limited role in staff appointment processes. However, a note of caution should be flagged since there is an inherent danger that pupil voice could simply be used to improve individual and organisational performance rather than as a means through which the learning and lives of all those in the school might be improved (Robinson and Taylor, 2007) Close inspection of *Working Together: Giving Children and Young People a Say* (DfES, 2004) reveals that while teaching and learning is listed as one of the possible areas of consultation, the relatively innocuous example of school uniform is given as an example of this. Other references to teaching and learning in the document only refer to the pupils' planning and evaluation of their own learning. The rapidity with which initiatives are put into place is also a point of concern. Rudduck (2006: 133) warns that the plethora of guidance publications manifests 'mile-wide promotion with only inch thick understanding' and calls for 'thoughtfully committed action' rather than 'compliance' prompted through a sense of obligation. This is underlined by Bragg's (2001) contention that when rapid results are needed (and performance league tables spring immediately to mind here) it is easier to listen to those voices that accord with the establishment position rather than those that challenge it.

Case study: foster children in Denmark

Warming (2006) carried out an interesting research project on voice issues for foster children in Denmark, which highlights many of the tensions and dilemmas raised in this chapter. She worked with 15 foster children aged 10-13 years. It is a useful case study to consider because foster children fall into a multiply silenced group, being at once children and further categorised as 'vulnerable'. This frequently translates into exclusion from consultation and participation based on adult judgements that, because of their 'vulnerability', this would not be in their best interests. Their perspectives are often represented by adult retrospectives or within adult evaluation studies where the subjects are predetermined by the adult researchers. Voice for foster children is too often linked to their views needing to accord with those of professionals who determine what is in their best interests. One foster child in Warming's (2006: 42) study expressed this in his own words:

> No, I don't think that she [the social worker] would listen. She would tell my foster parents. And they would then be angry and say that I'm the one causing the problems. They always tell me that I counter-act my own interests.

Warming (2006: 30) is very aware of the discrepancy between the theoretical position and what happens in practice. Despite the legal precedent, the reality is that social workers, hampered by cutbacks in the Danish welfare state and the demands of documented accountability, spend more time at their desks than with the foster children. Warming wanted to explore the possibilities of establishing a voice forum for foster children along the lines of a Children's Parliament (*Bornetinget*). She created a four-stage methodological design, which consisted of individual open-ended interviews, group discussions, a web-based foster children's forum and involvement of the foster children in the interpretation and analysis of the data. The realisation from theory into practice threw up some thought-provoking dilemmas.

The group discussions were set up for the purposes of collecting data from foster children about their perspectives. However, the opportunities to discuss issues pertinent to their own foster care experiences, the emotional peer support the forum provided and the social recognition that voicing their views afforded them proved to be so popular with, and beneficial for, the children that they wanted to continue with them beyond the life of the data collection phase. The children had been brought together from scattered locations in Denmark and the financial constraints of the project, plus the difficulties associated with escorting children to the venue, prevented any continuance. This left the researchers feeling rather uncomfortable and ethically challenged, having set something up to unlock foster children's voice only to find themselves complicit in staunching a new voice flow.

There was a similar response to the web-based forum, which ran for 10 weeks but in this instance the researchers were able to arrange for the forum to continue and develop as costs and escort logistics were not such an issue. An interesting development arose as this project unfolded. It had been set up so that adult researchers could collect data from the foster children. What began to happen in practice was that the children's peer-to-peer conversations turned increasingly into a discussion style akin to interviewing each other to the point where they assumed roles as co-researchers rather than participants (Warming, 2006: 40).

They had been granted the status of experts in the open-ended interviews, the group discussions and on the web forum. As a result, they began to act as co-researchers, asking one another questions and suggesting interpretations of one another's stories.

The children's evolving role as co-researchers also influenced the analysis of the data. It had not been planned at the outset of the project that the foster children would be involved in the analysis of the data but it arose quite naturally and through the children's own action. They prompted the adult researchers that the content on the website forum would not necessarily be intelligible to anyone other than foster children – especially not to adults. This was encapsulated in the telling remark of one of the foster children: 'Are you sure you'll be able to understand what the children write on the website – you're not a foster child – how can you?' (Warming, 2006: 39). This led to a reconvening of the focus group in order for the foster children to provide interpretations of the website data. As Warming (2006: 41) argues:

> The children contributed to interpretation and analysis during the entire process of talking and writing with each other. This is a different kind of analysis than that of the researcher attempting to make an overview of all the contributions through theoretically informed interpretation and analysis. The difference between the contributions from the academic researcher and the children themselves is – together with the difference in power – the essential reason for collaboration between the two.

Warming's case study raises several issues about the relationship between theory and practice. Some of these are summarised below and readers are invited to reflect at length on resulting tensions and dilemmas.

- Focusing exclusively on the legal recognition of children's right to voice elides recognition of the emotional and social nature of that voice.

- Some children's voices are harder to hear than others – foster children suffer in this respect by categorisations of vulnerability, of being too vulnerable to be consulted.

- Legitimate children's voice necessitates a degree of interpretation of views and perspectives by children themselves rather than the common practice of adult mediation of their views.

- Empowerment activities aimed at facilitating child voice sometimes awaken expectations that cannot be fulfilled and we have to find ways to deal with the ethical fallout.

References

Alderson, P. (2000) 'School students' views on school councils and daily life at school', *Children & Society*, vol 14, no 2, pp 121-34.

Ardener, E. (1975) 'Belief and the problem of women', in S. Ardener (ed) *Perceiving Women*, London: J.M. Dent.

Bennett Woodhouse, B. (2003) 'Enhancing children's participation in policy formulation', *Arizona Law Review*, vol 45, no 3, pp 750-63.

Bragg, S. (2001) 'Taking a joke: learning from the voices we don't want to hear', *Forum*, vol 43, no 2, pp 70-3.

Coad, J. and Lewis, A. (2004) 'Engaging children and young people in research: literature review for the national evaluation of the Children's Fund (NECF)', available online at www.necf.org/core_files/Elicitingchdrnsviewsjanecoadannlewisoct2004.doc (accessed 25/03/05).

Devine, D. (2003) *Children, Power and Schooling: How Childhood is Structured in the Primary School*, Stoke on Trent: Trentham Books.

DfES (Department for Education and Skills) (2004) *Working Together: Giving Children and Young People a Say*, London: DfES, available online at http://publications.teachernet.gov.uk/eOrderingDownload/DfES%200134%20200MIG1963.doc (accessed 10/01/07).

Fielding, M. (2001) 'Students as radical agents of change', *Journal of Educational Change*, vol 2, no 2, pp 123-41.

Fielding, M. (2004) 'Transformative approaches to student voice: theoretical underpinnings, recalcitrant realities', *British Educational Research Journal*, vol 30, no 2, pp 295-311.

Grover, S. (2004) 'Why won't they listen to us? On giving power and voice to children participating in social research', *Childhood*, vol 11, no 1, pp 81-93.

Hamill, P. and Boyd, B. (2002) 'Equality, fairness and rights – the young person's voice', *British Journal of Special Education*, vol 29, no 3, pp 111-17.

Hart, S. (2002) 'Making sure the child's voice is heard', *International Review of Education*, vol 43, no 3-4, pp 251-58.

Hendrick, H. (2000) 'The child as social actor in historical sources: problems of identification and interpretation', in P. Christensen and A. James (eds) *Research with Children and Young People: Perspectives and Practices*, London: Routledge Falmer.

James, A. and James, A. (2004) *Constructing Childhood: Theory, Policy and Social Practice*, London: Macmillan.

Jans, M. (2004) 'Children as citizens: towards a contemporary notion of child participation', *Childhood*, vol 11, no 1, pp 27-44.

John, M. (1996) 'Voicing: research and practice with the silenced', in M. John (ed) *Children in Charge: The Child's Right to a Fair Hearing*, London: Jessica Kingsley Publishers.

Kellett, M. (2005) 'Children as active researchers: a new research paradigm for the 21st century?', published online by ESRC National Centre for Research Methods, NCRM/003, available at www.ncrm.ac.uk/research/outputs/publications/methodsreview/MethodsReviewPaperNCRM-003.pdf (accessed 16/03/09).

Kilbourne, S. (1998) 'The wayward Americans – why the USA has not ratified the United Nations Convention on the Rights of the Child', *Child and Family Law Quarterly*, vol 10, no 3, pp 243-56.

Leitch, R. and Mitchell, S. (2007) 'Caged birds and cloning machines: how student imagery "speaks" to us about cultures of schooling and student participation', *Improving Schools*, vol 10, no 1, pp 53-71.

Lensmire, T. (1998) 'Rewriting student voice', *Journal of Curriculum Studies*, vol 30, no 3, pp 261-91.

Lloyd-Smith, M. and Tarr, J. (2000) 'Researching children's perspectives: a sociological dimension', in A. Lewis and G. Lindsay (eds) *Researching Children's Perspectives*, Buckingham: Open University Press.

Lodge, C. (2005) 'From hearing voices to engaging in dialogue: problematising student participation in school improvement', *Journal of Educational Change*, vol 6, no 2, pp 125-46.

Lundy, L. (2007) '"Voice" is not enough: conceptualising Article 12 of the United Nations Convention on the Rights of the Child', *British Educational Research Journal*, vol 33, no 6, pp 927-42.

Mayall, B. (2000) 'Conversations with children: working with generational issues', in P. Christensen and A. James (eds) *Research with Children and Young People: Perspectives and Practices*, London: Routledge Falmer.

Maybin, J. (2001) 'Language, struggle and voice: the Bakhtin/Volosinov writings', in M. Wetherell, S. Taylor and S. Yates (eds) *Discourse Theory and Practice*, London: Sage Publications.

Ofsted (2005) 'Guidance for Inspectors of Schools: Conducting the Inspection', available online at www.ofsted.gov.uk/publications/20070007 (accessed 1/06/07).

Robinson, C. and Taylor, C. (2007) 'Theorizing student voice: values and perspectives', *Improving Schools*, vol 10, no 1, pp 5-17.

Rudduck, J. (2006) 'The past, the papers and the project', *Educational Review*, vol 58, no 2, pp 131-43.

Rudduck, J. and Fielding, M. (2006) 'Student voice and the perils of popularity', *Educational Review*, vol 58, no 2, pp 219-31.

Rudduck, J. and Flutter, J. (2004) *How to Improve your School: Giving Pupils a Voice*, London and New York, NY: Continuum.

Smyth, J. (2006) 'When students have power: student engagement, student voice, and the possibilities for school reform around "dropping out" of school', *International Journal of Leadership in Education*, vol 9, no 4, pp 285-98.

Thorne, B. (2002) 'From silence into voice: bringing children more fully into knowledge', *Childhood*, vol 9, no 3, pp 251-54.

UN (United Nations) (1989) 'Convention on the Rights of the Child', UN General Assembly, Document A/RES/44/25, available online at www.hrweb.org/legal/child.html (accessed 18/02/05).

Warming, H. (2006) '"How can you know? You're not a foster child": dilemmas and possibilities of giving voice to children in foster care', *Children, Youth and Environments*, vol 16, no 2, pp 28-50.

Wyness, M. (2006) 'Children, young people and civic participation: regulation and local diversity', *Educational Review*, vol 58, no 2, pp 209-18.

Wyness, M., Harrison, L. and Buchanan, I. (2004) 'Childhood, politics and ambiguity: towards an agenda for children's political inclusion', *Sociology*, vol 38, no 1, pp 81-99.

Index

A

active citizenship 43
actus reus 133, 138
adoption 81
  intercountry 158-60
Afghanistan 26
Africa
  fostering 81-6
  intergenerational conflict 29-30
  missing boys 80-1, 87
  UNCRC 120, 121-3
African Charter on the Rights and
    Welfare of the Child 122
agency 187-8, 195
Ahmed, S. 206, 207
Alanen, L. 191
Alexander, C. 205
Ali, S. 98, 99
Anderson, B. 202
'Annus Mirabilis' (Larkin) 223
anti-racism 199-201
Archer, L. 208
Ardener, E. 240
Arthurworrey, Lisa 85
ASBOs (Antisocial Behaviour Orders)
    8, 16
asylum seekers 167
Australia 51-2, 149
Aynsley-Green, Al 52

B

B-Boyz 101-2
Baby 'P' 2
Back, L. 92, 100-1
Back to Sleep campaign 151, 154
Ball, S. 201
Balsall Heath 212
Bangladesh 112
Barthes, R. 93
Basijis 36, 38
Begum, Shabina 207-8
Belgium 135, 213
Bennett, F. 15-16
Bhabha, H.K. 100
bhangra 102-3
Bichard Inquiry 154
Billig, M. 210
Birmingham 212

blackness 93, 96, 99, 101-2, 103
*Blackstone's Commentaries on the Laws of
    England* 136
Bledsoe, C. 83
Born to Buy (Schor) 184
Bourdieu, P. 168-70, 178, 188
boys
  domestic labour 71
  and marketing 184
  Muslim 208
  Oedipal drama 221
  sexual socialisation 222, 224
  see also young men
Bradford 210, 211
Bradshaw, J. 15-16
Brandchild (Lindstrom) 185-6
Branded (Quart) 184
Brazil 112, 222-3
Britishness 202, 205, 215
Brocklehurst, H. 25, 31, 34
Bulger, James 134, 136, 150
Bundy, C. 30
Burnley 210

C

C v DPP 136-7
Cafcass 155
Cairns, E. 26
Cairns, L. 50
Cambodia 158-9
Cameroon 82-3, 84
Canada 149
Cantle Report 210-11
Carry On Up the Khyber 94
Carsten, J. 79
Cavadino, P. 137
Centre for Crime and Justice Studies
    17
Centre for Research in Social Policy
    171
Charter for Childhood 185
child poverty 165, 178
  child's eye view 171-4
  definitions and measurements 166-7
  effects 167-71
  New Labour policy 13, 15-16, 174-8
child protection 145-6, 160
  advice, education and training 154-5
  children's role 151-3

different perspectives 146-9
evaluation 156-7
identification and surveillance 153-4
intercountry adoption 158-60
law 156
parents and carers 149-50
service provision 155-6
state 151
UNCRC 110
wider community 150
Child Safety Orders 16
Child Tax Credit 175, 177
childhood
in criminal law 132-4
doli incapax 134-41
in family law 129-32
in law 127-9, 141-2
as relative concept 119-20
ChildLine 152
children
access to advice 155
child protection role 151-3
and consumer culture 181-95
contributions to family labour 69-72
definition 3
and families 62, 64-8, 73-4, 77-8
intergenerational conflict 29-32
as moral guardians 35-6
parents and the state 8-13
participation 43-55
policies to improve lives 13-17
political activism 17-20, 23-4, 36-8
and politics 24-6
preoccupation with 7-8
racism 95-9, 105
and sexuality 219-33
in sociology 62-3
state–society conflict and interstate
  conflict 27-9
voice 237-50
see also young people
Children Act 1989 (England and Wales)
  12-13, 47, 129, 148
Children Act 2004 (England and Wales)
  150, 154
Children (Scotland) Act 1995 12
Children and Young Persons Act 1933
  142
Children and Young Persons Act 1969
  134
Children's Act 1998 (Ghana) 115-18
Children's Express 244
Children's Fund 48
Children's Plan 2

*Children's Poll: A South African Child
  Rights Survey* (Save the Children
  Sweden) 49-50
Children's Research Centre 53, 54, 244
children's rights 1-2, 74, 109-10
  state intervention 11, 12-13
  watchdogs 112
  see also participation; United Nations
    Convention on the Rights of the
    Child; voice
Children's Rights Bill (Nigeria) 122
Chin, E. 189
China
  children as moral guardians 35-6
  di-si-ke 104-5
  girls 150
  intercountry adoption 158
  intergenerational conflict 31-2, 37
  state–society conflict 28, 36, 38
Christian metal 213-14, 215
citizenship 43, 52
City Academies 177
Claire's Accessories 190
Clapham, C. 28
Clark, A. 51
Clausewitz, Carl von 25
Climbié, Berthe 85-6
Climbié, Francis 85-6
Climbié, Victoria 2, 84-6
Coad, J. 243
Cohen, S. 203-4
Coles, R. 24
Colombia 29
Colwell, Maria 2
Comaroff, J. 29
Comaroff, J.L. 29
commercial epistemologies 183, 187
Committee on the Rights of the Child
  see United Nations Committee on
  the Rights of the Child
Community Cohesion Review Team
  210-11
Compass 185
competence approach 128, 130-1, 132,
  133, 141, 142
conflict 25-6, 37
  intergenerational 29-32
  state-society and interstate 27-9
Connolly, P. 95
Conservative Party
  Britishness 202
  education 14
consumer culture 181-2, 194-5
  and globalisation 192

reactions 184-7
rethinking 187-90
Consuming Kids (Linn) 184
CPS v P 141
crime 8, 13, 16-17
Crime and Disorder Act 1998 16, 138, 141
Criminal Justice Act 1963 134
criminal law 52, 132-4, 142
  child protection 150, 156
  doli incapax 134-41
critical multiculturalism 201
Cross, G. 189
Cuba 28
cultural capital 169-70, 173
cultural hybridity 99-103
culture
  and globalisation 192-4
  see also consumer culture

D

Davies, L. 43
de Schweinitz, R.L. 27-8
de Waal, A. 112, 114, 119, 121-2
Denmark 247-50
Denzin, N. 8
Department for Education and Skills (DfES) (England) 48
Department of Social Welfare (Ghana) 117-18
dependency assumption 72
deprivation 166
Devine, D. 245
di-si-ke 104-5
Diamant, N.J. 35
Dingwall, R. 9
discourse 18
discursive spaces 238-9
doli incapax 16, 133, 134-41
domestic labour 70-2
Donnelly, J. 120
Donzelot, J. 10
Douglas, G. 61-2
Dudrah, R. 103
Durham, D. 30
Dwyer, C. 207, 208

E

education
  and child poverty 175-6, 177-8
  Ghana 116
  multiculturalism 199-200

New Labour policy 13-15
  pupil protests in Wales 19-20
  school as a site of political mobilisation 33-5, 37
  school-based sexualities 225-7
  state involvement 9, 10
  voice 242, 244-7
Education Act 1961 (Ghana) 116
Education Act 2002 (England and Wales) 245
Eekelaar, J. 9
Egypt 33
Ejiga, Ohepo 122
Elliott v C 139
Emin, Tracey 224-5
Englishness 94-5
Ethiopia 28
ethnicity 91, 94-5, 104-6
European Convention on Human Rights 148
Evans, M. 16
Every Child Matters 2, 47, 48, 151, 154, 156

F

families 73-4, 77-8, 87-8
  African 80-1
  children's contributions to labour 69-72
  children's notions of 64-8
  relatedness 78-80
  West Africa 81-6
  see also parents
family law 128, 129-32, 142
Family Law Reform Act 1969 130
family privacy 150, 151
family sociology 61-4, 72
Fanon, Frantz 99
FARC 29
Farrer, J. 104-5
Farson, Richard 109-10
Fielding, M. 240, 246
Finland 15, 213
Firestone, S. 221
Fitzgerald, R. 51-2
Flutter, J. 245
folk devils 93, 204, 205
Folk Devils and Moral Panics (Cohen) 203-4
Fortin, J. 131
foster children 247-50
fostering 80, 81-4, 87-8
  Victoria Climbié 84-6

Foucault, M. 97, 221-2, 226, 233
Fox Harding, L. 11
France 134, 207
Franklin, B. 44
Free and Compulsory Universal Basic
    Education (FCUBE) policy 116
Freeman, M. 109, 111, 112, 114, 131
FRELIMO 29
Freud, S. 220-1, 232
Friedan, B. 221

G

Garside, R. 17
gay pride 227-9
Geertz, C. 200
gender
    and domestic labour 71
    and marketing 184
    and space 210, 211
Germany 134, 213
Ghana 54, 111, 112, 115-18, 123
Gibbs, S. 47
Giddens, A. 188, 220
Gil-Robles, A. 140
Gillick 130-1, 132
Gilroy, P. 98, 100, 103, 211
Girl Heaven 190-1
girls
    child protection 150
    domestic labour 71
    and marketing 184
    Muslim 207-8
    Oedipal drama 221
    school-based sexualities 227
    sexual socialisation 222, 223, 224-5
    teenage pregnancy 229-32
    tweens 182, 190-1
    see also young women
globalisation 104-5, 192-4
Goldstein, J. 11
Goody, E. 79-80, 81
Graham, A. 51-2
Graham, William 20
Gregg, P. 170
Grødem, A.S. 166
Guardian, The 105
Guatemala 158, 159
gypsy children 167

H

Re H 131
habitus 18, 168-70, 173

Hague Convention on Intercountry
    Adoption 159
Hall, S. 95
Hamilton, Lewis 98
harm 148
Hart, R. 44-5, 47
Hart, S. 237-8
Hatcher, R. 95-6, 99
Headlines 244
Hear by Right 48
heavy metal 213-14, 215
Hendrick, H. 241-2, 246
Hewitt, M. 9
hijab 207
Hill, M. 62
Hirsch, D. 177
History of Sexuality, The (Foucault)
    221-2
HIV/AIDS 114
Hoffman, D. 29
Holt, John 109
Home Office 137, 138
homosexuality 105, 227-9
hooks, b. 213
Hopkins, P. 208-9
horizontal integration 192
Howard, R. 121
human rights 120
    see also children's rights; parents' rights
Hungary 53, 193
hybridity 99-103
Hylton, C. 67

I

India 150
Integrated Children's System 153
intention 138
intercountry adoption 158-60
intergenerational conflict 25, 29-32, 37
international law 25
    see also United Nations Convention
    on the Rights of the Child
interstate conflict 29
Iran
    children as moral guardians 36, 38
    intergenerational conflict 30, 31, 37
    schools as site of political
        mobilisation 34
    state–society conflict 27
Ireland 134
Islam 203, 205, 215
It Ain't Half Hot Mum 94

J

James, Allison 63, 142, 191
James, C.L.R. 92
Jans, M. 240-1
Japan 194
John, M. 45
Jones, S. 212
Joseph Rowntree Foundation 16

K

Kahn, A. 9
Kamerman, S. 9
Kanka, Megan 157
Keddie, N. 30, 31
Kehily, A. 182
Kent, G. 25
Kilbourne, S. 240
King's College London 17
kinship 78-80
Kirby, P. 47
Kline, S. 192
Korea 193
Kouao, Marie Therese 85, 86
Kristeva, J. 221

L

Lacan, J. 221
Laming, Lord 84, 86, 160
Lansdown, G. 51
Larkin, P. 223
Latin America 34
law 127-9, 141-2
   child protection 150, 156
   criminal law 52, 132-41
   family law 129-32
Laws, Mr Justice 136-7
Leary, V. 120
Leeds 211
Leitch, R. 245
Lensmire, T. 239, 246
Lewis, A. 243
Liddle, R. 85
Lindstrom, M. 182, 185-6
Linn, S. 184
A Local Authority v K & Ors 149
London
   child poverty 167
   cultural hybridity 100-1
   missing African boys 80-1
London bombings 202, 203
lone parents 175, 176-7
Loughborough University 171

Lundy, L. 238
Luxembourg 135

M

McChesney, R. 192
McGrellis, S. 209, 210
Machin, S. 175
McNair, B. 228
McNally, S. 175
Mannheim, K. 33
Margate 224-5
marketing 182-4
Martens, L. 188-9
Massey, D. 101
Mauritius 112
Mayall, B. 47
media 25, 94, 185, 192-4
Megan's Law 157
Mel B 98
Men, Risk and AIDS Project 223, 225
Mende 83, 87
mens rea 133, 138-9
Mercer, K. 212
Mexico 18
Middleton, E. 48
migration 97-8, 201
Milkie, M. 62
Millett, K. 221
Milton Keynes Christian Foundation
   230-2
Mind Your Language 94
Ministry of Manpower, Development
   and Employment (Ghana) 117, 118
Ministry of Women and Children's
   Affairs (Ghana) 118
Mitchell, J. 221
Mitchell, S. 245
mixedness 98, 99
Moberg, M. 213-14
moral panic 203-4, 215
morality 35-6
Moses, S. 49-50
Mozambique 29
multiculturalism 199-201
   Parekh Report 201-3
Muscroft, S. 111, 113
music 212-14
Muslim youth 93, 199, 215
   firsthand accounts 207-9
   a new moral panic 203-7
   self-segregation 210-11
muted voices 240

N

National Youth Agency 47
neighbourhood cohesion 210-11
Nepal 112
Netherlands 213
New Labour
  child poverty 15-16, 165, 174-8
  children and consumer culture 185
  children and young people 8, 13, 17
  cool Britannia 202
  crime 16-17
  education 13-15
  safeguarding 145
  youth justice system 137-8
New Zealand 151
Nickleodeon 193
Nigeria 31, 84, 122
Nolte, I. 31
North East England
  B-Boyz 101-2
  child poverty 167
Northern Ireland
  children as political actors 18
  children's participation in political
    violence 26
  education 15
  intergenerational conflict 31
  spaces 209-10
  Youth Forum 244
Norway 134, 213
Notermans, C. 84
NSPCC (National Society for the
    Prevention of Cruelty to Children)
    154, 157

O

Ohmae, Kenichi 194
Oldham 210
Open University 53, 244
Orientalism 94
Ouseley Report 210
Owen, M. 12

P

Pakistani origin 64, 66-7, 68
Palestine 27, 37
  children's engagement 18, 24, 26, 28
Palmer, S. 184
Parekh Report 201-3, 205
parenting education 155
Parenting Orders 150

parents
  child protection 149-50
  employment 175, 176-7
  importance to children 66
  and state 8-13
parents' rights 8-9, 11
  Gillick 130-1
Parker, R.G. 222-3
participation 43, 44, 55-6, 110
  and child protection 152-3
  children at the centre 51-2
  children as researchers 52-4
  deconstructing 50-1
  impact and meaningful outcomes
    49-50
  political frameworks 47-8
  theoretical frameworks 43-7
  and voice 237
  WeCan2 54-5
Participation Works 48
Parton, N. 10, 154
Percy-Smith, B. 51
pets 68, 73
Phillips, Lord Justice 140
Phillips, D. 211
Piaget, Jean 24
Pieterse, J.N. 102
Pieterson, Hector 28
Pinchbeck, I. 9
Plummer, K. 227-8
Poland 135
politics 8
  and children 24-6, 36-8
  children, parents and the state 8-13
  children's political activism 17-19,
    23-4
  policies to improve children's lives
    13-20
  school as a site of political
    mobilisation 32-5
Pontllanfraith Comprehensive 19-20
popular music 212-14
Portugal 135
poverty 165-7
  see also child poverty
power 97, 222, 226
  and voice 240-1
pregnancy 229-32
Prout, Alan 63, 171
Punjabi 102-3
pupil voice 237, 244-7
Pupuvac, V. 25

Q

Quart, A. 184
Qvortrup, J. 63

R

R v Caldwell 139
R v G 139
R v Howe and Bannister 140
R v T 141
R v Wilson 140
race 91-3, 105
    and cultural hybridity 99-103
racism 95-9, 105
    see also anti-racism
Rastafarians 212-13, 214, 215
Reay, D. 168-9, 178
recklessness 138-9
reggae 212-13, 215
relatedness 78-80
relativism 119-21
religion 199, 203, 205, 215
    and popular music 212-14
    space and territory 209-12
responsive safeguarding *see* child
    protection
revolutionary regimes 28-9, 31-2
Ridge, T. 170-1, 172, 173-4, 176-7
rights *see* human rights
Romania 159-60
Rose, N. 188
RSPCA v C 139-40
Rudduck, J. 245, 247
Rushdie, Salman 204
Russell, R. 190-1
Russia 158

S

safeguarding 145, 146, 160
    see also child protection
Said, E. W. 94
Saifullah Khan, V. 67
Save the Children Sweden 49-50
Scarborough, J. 16
Scarman, Lord 131
'Scary Spice' 98
Schneider, D. 78
school *see* education
school councils 242, 247
school-based sexualities 225-7
Schor, J. 184
Scotland
    children's wishes 12

education 15
    Muslim youth 208-9
    smacking 242
    Youth Parliament 244
Scott, S. 223-4
seatbelts 156
sex education 152
sexual socialisation 222-5
sexuality 219-20, 232-3
    gay pride and post-pride 227-9
    school-based 225-7
    teenage pregnancy 229-32
    theories 220-2
Sgritta, G. 112
Sharma, S. 103
Shepler, S. 29
Shier, H. 45-6, 47
siblings 66-7
Sierra Leone 83, 87
Singer, P.W. 28
Skeggs, B. 229-30
smacking 242
Smart, C. 72
Smith, Lady Justice 141
Smith, A.T.H. 133
Smith, Will 98
Smyth, J. 246
social capital 169, 170, 173, 174
Social Exclusion Unit (SEU) 229
social inequality 168, 172
sociology 61-4, 72, 73
Solomon, E. 17
Somalia 111
South Africa
    children's participation 49-50
    education 34
    intergenerational conflict 30-1, 37
    state-society conflict 24, 27, 28, 37,
        38
    women 29
South Asians 204
    bhangra 102-3
    as folk devils 93, 205, 215
    media representations 94
    North East England 102
    self-segregation 210-11
South East England 167
South Korea 193
space
    discursive 238-9
    and religion 199, 209-12
Spain 135
Sri Lanka 29
Stafford, A. 56

Starrett, G. 33
state 8–13, 151
State of the World's Children, The
(UNICEF) 2
state paternalism 11
state–society conflict 27–9
status approach 127–8, 132, 133–4,
136–7, 141, 142
Staying Safe (HM Government) 145
Steedman, C. 10
Stephens, S. 24, 119, 120
Stevens, O. 18
Strangeland (Emin) 225
stranger danger 157
Strathern, M. 79
Structural Adjustment Programmes
(SAPs) 113, 114
structure 187
Sudden Infant Death Syndrome 151,
160
Sunmonu, Yinka 80–1
Sure Start 176, 177
Sutherland, H. 16, 177
Sutton, L. 171–2
Swann Report 204
Sweden
children and consumer culture 183,
184
Christian metal 213
deprivation 166
education 15

T

Tackling Youth Crime (Home Office)
137
Tamil Tigers 29
targeted safeguarding 145
tea 94–5
teenage pregnancy 229–32
teenagers 181
Telling Sexual Stories (Plummer) 227–8
Temba, K. 112, 114
territory 199, 209–12
Thomas, Cane 20
Thomson, R. 223–4
Thorne, B. 241
Three Essays on the Theory of Sexuality
(Freud) 220–1
Tisdall, K. 62
Tomlinson, S. 14
Top Spot 224–5
Toxic Childhood (Palmer) 184
Traveller children 167

Treseder, P. 45
Troyna, B. 95–6, 99
Tunisia 207
tutelary complex 10
tweens 182, 185–6, 190–1
Tyler, M. 190–1

U

Uganda 112
UK Youth Parliament (UKYP) 244
Umkhontowe-Sizwe 29
UNICEF 2
United Nations Convention on the
Rights of the Child (UNCRC) 1,
2, 23, 74, 109–11, 113, 123, 151
Article 3 47, 52, 151
Article 12 12, 55–6, 152, 238, 239,
242–3, 245
Article 13 47, 243
Article 19 151
Article 42 48
child protection 150, 151
citizenship 52
cultural critiques 118–23
Ghana 115–18
legal majority 127
participation 43, 44, 47, 52, 55–6
recognising achievements 110–11
underlying challenges 112–14
US 240
United Nations Special Summit on
Children's Rights 239, 240
universal safeguarding 145
university students 27, 28, 34
US
child protection 157
civil rights movement 23, 27–8, 34
intercountry adoption 158, 159
poverty line 165
state intervention 149
teenage pregnancy 229
UNCRC 111, 240

V

Varzi, R. 31
Veerman, P. 109
veil 207–8
Verhoef, H. 82–3, 84
vertical integration 192
violence 26
voice 237
audiences 239

concept 237-8
foster children in Denmark 247-50
as influence 239-40
as a political tool 242-4
and power 240-1
pupil voice 244-7
silencing 241-2
spaces to develop 238-9
voting age 18-19
Vygotsky, L.S. 45

W

Wales
education 15
Funky Dragon 244
pupil protests 19-20
Walker, N. 141
Walkerdine, V. 230
war 25, 29, 37
see also conflict
Warming, H. 247-50
Watt, P. 101
WeCan2 54-5
Weeks, J. 219-20, 232
welfare-to-work policies 175, 176, 177
What to Do if You're Worried a Child is
Being Abused (DfES) 146
White, M. 194
whiteness 93, 96, 97, 100, 102, 105
Wilkinson, R. 168
Williams, R. 200
Woll, L. 112
women 29
see also young women
Woods, Tiger 98
Working Tax Credit 175, 177
Working Together (DfES) 241, 247
worklessness 175
WRAP (Women, Risk and Aids)
Project 223, 225
Wyness, M. 245

Y

Yemen 150
Yoon, K. 193
Yoruba 84
Young, I.M. 18-19
Young, R. 99
young men 210, 211
see also boys
young people
definition 3

popular music and religion 212-14
race and cultural hybridity 99-103
see also children; Muslim youth
young women 210
see also girls
Youth Justice Board 16
Youth Offending Teams 16

Z

Zelizer, V. 189
zone of personal development (ZPD)
45